PRAISE FOR *THE FORBIDDEN GAME*

"Captivating"   *Houston Chronicle*

"An illuminating portrait of modern China."   *New Statesman*

"Compelling… Washburn uses the sport with surprising effectiveness as a lens into the country's development over the past two decades."
Los Angeles Review of Books

"I know of no narrative that surpasses *The Forbidden Game* [on the subject of corruption in China]… vivid [and] revealing."
Literary Review

"An intriguing study… an absorbing read."   *Golf Digest*

"*The Forbidden Game* offers a thoroughly new window onto the 'Chinese Dream.' As veteran 'China watcher' Dan Washburn engrossingly reveals, it transpires that the game of golf is a barometer for all China's current concerns – economic growth, 'social harmony,' corruption, the growing wealth gap and, most absorbing, the hopes and aspirations of at least one Chinese man who's daring to dream of a better future."
Paul French, bestselling author of *Midnight in Peking*

"*The Forbidden Game* speaks volumes about how much this country has changed. You can learn more from this engaging, well-written book about golf than from weightier tomes that have tried to tackle China's transformation."
Barbara Demick, author of
Nothing to Envy and *Logavina Street*

"It is classic storytelling – underdog tales of struggle, perseverance and overcoming adversity… It's like the quintessential American Dream story, only it's set in China."
Brian Grazer, award-winning producer of television and film,
including Best Picture Oscar winner *A Beautiful Mind*

"An important and fascinating work… Washburn brings to life the contradictions and complications of this unique nation's struggles."
Alan Shipnuck, senior writer at *Sports Illustrated*
and author of *Bud, Sweat and Tees*

"Revealing and witty… This is a tale about golf no more than *Seabiscuit* is a story about horseracing… Vivid, surprising, and human."

Evan Osnos, staff writer for *The New Yorker*
and author of *Age of Ambition*

"The stunning rise of China is usually told through upheaval in the country's politics and economy. Dan Washburn has been smart enough to spot a much underestimated way to tell the tale… The story of golf has it all in China – from the wild west developments of courses to inspiring stories of success to dark politics."

Richard McGregor, author of *The Party* and public policy
fellow at the Wilson Center, Washington DC

"A rich and fascinating drama on its own terms, and a wonderful portrait of China at this stage of its growth and confusion. It even made me care, a little, about golf."

James Fallows, author of *Postcards from
Tomorrow Square* and *China Airborne*

"*The Forbidden Game* is a propulsive chronicle of an old pursuit thrust into a country undergoing colossal change. But more than that, it's a richly drawn, deeply felt portrait of human striving – a great story."

Tom Vanderbilt, bestselling author
of *Traffic* and *Survival City*

"Sometimes the best way into the heart of an enigma is through a backdoor… Dan Washburn has opened just such a portal for anyone finding the People's Republic of China's unexpected progress perplexing to understand, much less to explain. By giving us a grand tour of the surprising boom in the game of golf in China, he not only illuminates a very concrete slice of life, but gives us a graphic and readable sense of both the energy and inertia that lay at the center of the contradictory phenomena that has come to be known as 'China's rise.'"

Orville Schell, director of the Center on
US–China Relations and author of *Wealth and Power*

"Every bit as energetic and ambitious as the burgeoning China it so evocatively portrays, *The Forbidden Game* is a truly memorable feat of reporting and storytelling… Washburn gets to the heart of what makes China's messy rise one of the century's most compelling tales. A book this richly observed and deeply humane is an all-too-rare beast these days; read it, and then cherish it."

Brendan I. Koerner, author of *The Skies Belong to Us*

THE
FORBIDDEN GAME

Golf *and*
the Chinese Dream

Dan Washburn

ONEWORLD

IN MEMORY OF

Zhou Guangxiang
1937–2014

First published by Oneworld Publications, 2014
This revised edition published 2016

Copyright © Dan Washburn 2014

The moral right of Dan Washburn to be identified as the
Author of this work has been asserted by him in accordance
with the Copyright, Designs and Patents Act 1988

ISBN 978-1-78074-739-2
Ebook ISBN 978-1-78607-020-3

Portions of this book previously appeared, in different form, in
FT Weekend Magazine, Golf World, Omega Lifetime and the
South China Morning Post and on Slate and ESPN.com.

The names of some individuals in the book
have been changed at their request.

Frontispiece copyright © Ryan Pyle. All rights reserved.
Typesetting and Ebook by Tetragon, London
Printed and bound in Great Britain by Clays Ltd, St Ives plc

Oneworld Publications Ltd
10 Bloomsbury Street
London WC1B 3SR
England

Stay up to date with the latest books,
special offers, and exclusive content from
Oneworld with our monthly newsletter

Sign up on our website
www.oneworld-publications.com

CONTENTS

For

I.K.W.
B.I.K.
S.J.W.
D.E.W.
D.T.W.
O & T

Workers tend to one of the many new golf courses on China's Hainan island

PROLOGUE

Zhou Xunshu was not yet thirty-two years old, and he had already far surpassed even his wildest dreams as a child growing up in Qixin, a remote mountain village in southwest China's Guizhou province. But just exceeding his childhood dreams was no longer enough. He wanted more.

When he was in his teens, all he had wanted – all he had ever thought might be possible – was to get out of Qixin. Maybe he'd land a job as a public servant in Bijie, the prefecture-level city closest to his village. If he was lucky, he'd get something lined up in Guiyang, the provincial capital. Either of those options would have been "making it" for a poor peasant boy from Qixin. As far as Zhou was concerned, there wasn't a world beyond Guizhou. Not one that had a place for him, at least.

But that was before Zhou found golf.

In his early twenties, Zhou forced his way out of Guizhou and landed a job as a security guard at something he'd never heard of before – a golf course – in Guangzhou, the birthplace of golf in modern China. And after eight years practicing this foreign game in secret, Zhou became good enough to work as a supervisor at a driving range.

He wasn't getting rich working at the range. Far from it. But the work served as a gateway into a new sort of life. Every day, he was mingling with a class of people typically off-limits to someone of his meager origins. Sure, he was technically working for these people, but just being in their company made Zhou think that some aspects of their lives may now be attainable for him.

Maybe some day he'd be able to buy his own house and move his parents out of the village. Maybe now he could finally think about finding a wife and starting a family of his own. Golf, he was convinced, was the ticket to all the good things life had to offer. It was his ticket to the Chinese Dream.

But just what is the Chinese Dream? It's a phrase that gets tossed around a lot these days, ever since President Xi Jinping co-opted it for use as one of his primary political slogans not long after taking control of the Chinese Communist Party in the autumn of 2012. In his first address to the nation as president, Xi referred to the Chinese Dream repeatedly: "We must make persistent efforts, press ahead with indomitable will, continue to push forward the great cause of socialism with Chinese characteristics, and strive to achieve the Chinese dream of great rejuvenation of the Chinese nation." While Xi says his Chinese Dream is the "dream of the people," it's a vision that seems to be primarily about China's global status, clearly based more on collectivism than individualism. Take the question of the Chinese Dream to the Chinese people, however, and you're unlikely to hear much about military strength, international influence or state solidarity. Their hopes and desires are more concrete, more immediate and, to a Westerner, surprisingly familiar.

The real Chinese Dream has much in common with the American Dream, which has long represented the belief that through hard work and determination, every person, regardless of his or her social standing, has the potential to carve out a better life. While many in China still rightfully believe the deck is stacked against them, it's true that more Chinese than ever before are not only able to dream, but are also in a position to expect some of their dreams may come true. For a certain class of people, the dream is to one day be able to purchase a home or car. For others it could be to provide a quality education for their child. Still more dream that one day they can live someplace where the air is clean, where the legal system isn't corrupt, where they don't have to work on a farm. Often it's not complicated – people simply want a better life, for their parents, for themselves and for the generations to come.

Just a couple of generations ago in China, dreaming was something people only did to escape a harsh reality. This is how Zhou's parents lived. There was no link between reverie and real life. Dreams were diversions. Now, the country and its people find themselves hurtling towards a dramatically new future.

Golf, its emergence and growth in China, is a barometer for this change and the country's rapid economic rise, but it is also symbolic of the less glamorous realities of a nation's awkward and arduous evolution from developing to developed: corruption, environmental neglect, disputes over rural land rights, and an ever-widening gap between rich and poor. The game of golf, and the complex world that surrounds it, offers a unique window into today's China, where new golf courses are at once both banned and booming.

I knew little about the sensitivities surrounding golf in China when I first started covering tournaments there in 2005 for ESPN. com. And while my first assignments involved the likes of Tiger Woods, Ernie Els, Luke Donald and Adam Scott, I quickly gravitated toward China's fledgling domestic professional golf tour, the Omega China Tour, which featured names that few would recognize. Names like Zhou Xunshu. Zhou (pronounced "Joe") and his colorful peers belong to China's decidedly blue-collar first generation of pro golfers, a ragtag group of newly minted professional athletes with personal histories unheard of in the Western world of contemporary golf. They are former farmers, sushi chefs, stunt motorcyclists, *kung fu* experts and People's Liberation Army soldiers, who somehow stumbled into a sport that for most of their lives they never knew existed. Now golf is the means by which they can realize their modest slice of the Chinese Dream.

Until fairly recently, this wouldn't have been possible. Golf, one of many things considered too bourgeois by Mao Zedong and the Communists when they came to power in 1949, had long been forbidden in the country, leading some Western journalists to brand it "green opium" – a dangerous import that Chinese leaders reportedly believed to be a gateway to decadence. It wasn't until the early 1980s, as part of Deng Xiaoping's "reform and opening up" program, that golf gained a foothold in China. Then, it was seen largely as a way to attract foreign investment. Yet, golf remained politically taboo, and remains so today. Its enduring reputation as an elitist, land-and-water-hungry, pesticides-and-chemicals-using pursuit runs counter to everything the Chinese government is supposed to stand for. Truly the "rich man's game," it's restrictively expensive to play golf in China, and so, in the minds of many citizens the game is linked to corruption – the common belief is that any public servant who can afford to play must be corrupt – and the Communist Party has been known to send circulars to cadres warning them not to play. Still, a fair number of Chinese government officials enjoy golf – even Xi Jinping is rumored to have been quite fond of the game during his long tenure in Fujian province – but rarely, if ever, will they participate publicly in such a capitalistic activity. To do so would be career suicide. Instead, politicians register at golf courses using fake names.

As I began to learn the history of the game, I realized quickly that the story of golf in China actually had very little to do with golf itself. I had to conduct much of my research surreptitiously. Many of my conversations had to be off the record. Never was this more true than when I was investigating the murky world of Chinese golf course construction – the world in which I met Martin Moore. Martin didn't particularly enjoy the hassles associated with building golf courses in China – contractors were always trying to cheat him, local governments were self-interested and most Chinese laborers had no idea what a golf course was supposed to look like – but he had little choice. For the better part of the past decade, China had been propping up Martin's flagging industry. More courses were being built there than anywhere else in the world. Lately, if you weren't working in China, Martin's colleagues often said, you weren't working at all.

Indeed, in the past decade China has been the only country in the world to experience what might be called a golf course boom. While the struggling global economy had courses shutting down elsewhere, they were opening by the hundreds in China. From 2005 to 2010, the number of Chinese courses tripled to more than six hundred. An impressive feat, especially when you consider that building new courses has been technically illegal in China since at least 2004. In China, however, there is always a way. And no one knows that better than Martin, who has overseen the construction of more golf courses there than anyone else.

Martin may be considered a trailblazer of sorts these days, but back in the '80s when his career was just getting started, China never crossed his mind. He knew nothing about the place. He ended up in China by accident in 1994, and when he decided to focus his business there, everybody thought he was crazy. The market back home in the United States was still going gangbusters, and Communist China was the last place people thought of when the conversation turned to golf. Now, in an industry full of people shopping their resumés, Martin is at the top of nearly everyone's mailing list.

Martin, with his work boots, golf shirt and baseball cap, may not dress like the typical foreign executive in China, but few would be more adept at navigating the country's byzantine business landscape. Working in the legally nebulous world of golf course construction has a way of educating you fast. He knows how to negotiate with the local government officials who are willing to interpret Beijing's rules to get what they want. He knows how to manage the egos of eccentric owners who are more familiar with Beaujolais and Bentleys than building golf courses. He knows how to get his job done while constantly looking over his shoulder for the "Beijing golf police." These are not attributes Martin aimed for when he was growing up in Florida – but then he never knew he'd end up chasing his dreams in China.

Trying to pin down just how many golfers there are in China is nearly impossible. Estimates range from several hundred thousand to several million, with the truth likely lying somewhere in between. No matter the actual number, one thing is clear: statistically, zero percent of the country's population plays golf. There's no doubt, however, that golf is growing in China. Still, it would be wrong to say golf fever is sweeping the country. China is a nation of peasant farmers, some 700 million of them, and nearly a billion people in the country live on less than five dollars a day. Put simply, most Chinese probably have no idea what golf is. They can't afford to.

Interestingly, these are the very people likely to be affected the most by the expansion of golf courses. I should note here that the issue of land development in rural China is much bigger than golf. In fact, golf-related growth accounts for only a tiny portion of the commercial, industrial and residential projects that continue to transform the countryside. But golf grabs the headlines. Since courses are often built in poor, rural areas, luxury homes can sit across a creek from ramshackle shacks. Two very different worlds collide, and golf maintains its reputation as a rich man's activity.

A recent study showed how the number of government-approved land-grabs in rural China has increased markedly since 2005, with nearly half of the country's villages affected in some way. And of the 187,000 mass demonstrations reported in China in 2010, 65 percent were related to disputes over land. An estimated four million rural inhabitants in China have their land taken by the government each year, and the compensation they receive is far below market value. The government pays farmers on average $17,850 per acre, then turns around and sells the same land to developers for $740,000 per acre. That is when tempers rise.

This is where the story touches Wang Libo, a lychee farmer on China's tropical Hainan island. In Wang's ancient village of Meiqiu, most people still live in small single-story homes with dirt floors – and it's been this way for centuries. But, in 2007, their insulated way of life changed forever. A top-secret golf complex, drawn up to be the world's biggest by far, moved in next door, and land long managed by the residents of Meiqiu was included in the plans. Some villagers were happy to cash in, others protested for more money and nearly everyone worried what life would be like for future generations once large chunks of their family land were in other people's hands.

Meiqiu residents, not to mention the village's leadership, had never encountered this much money before, and its introduction tore the village apart. There was backstabbing and infighting, and the stirring up of long-forgotten family rivalries. But Wang, trying hard to rise above the fray, saw an opportunity in all this uncertainty. He had never heard of golf before 2007, but now his family's future depends inextricably on the massive golf club next door.

This book is about three men – two born in China, and one who never thought he'd end up there – who find themselves, either by accident or fate, caught up in golf's shift to the East. Wang had little choice but to accept the golf developers in his back yard; Martin is just trying to take advantage of the boom as long as he can. And, at the heart of it all, there's Zhou, whose rise from peasant farmer to security guard to pro golfer is the stuff of movies.

Zhou entered my life in the summer of 2006, when he was among a handful of Chinese golfers I interviewed during the Shanghai leg of the Omega China Tour. His powerful story, and the energy with which he told it, stuck with me, and that winter I asked if he'd mind me following him for an entire season. Soon, I found myself sharing cheap hotel rooms with him in rural towns close to golf courses across the country. Before they got to know me, many of the other golfers on the China Tour assumed I was Zhou's coach, despite the fact that no golfer on tour, and certainly not one from Zhou's low-born pedigree, could afford one. Early on, when queried about my role, Zhou added to the mystery, introducing me only as, "My American friend."

And, really, that's what I became. Admittedly, I broke the cardinal rule of reporting – I started to care about who wins and who loses. The more I got to know him, the harder it was not to root for Zhou. And so I followed him long after that first season. I even performed a stumbling toast in broken Mandarin at his wedding.

Zhou is a relatable everyman. He drinks. He curses. He has his demons. But he's also a hard worker, and as honest as they come. Like modern China, Zhou is full of contradictions. He is driven yet jovial, private yet outspoken, confident yet humble. Too proud to ask for money, and too straightforward to schmooze for sponsors, Zhou pays his own way on the China Tour. Does he win a tournament? Maybe. Or maybe it doesn't matter. To me, either way, he is the true embodiment of the Chinese Dream.

THE
FORBIDDEN GAME

1

FOUNDATIONS

Zhou Xunshu never believed in the stone man, though it looked down on him every day from across the valley. Thousands of years ago, according to village legend, there were two stone men, but one of them had been struck by lightning while bathing in a pond at the foot of the cliff. All that was left of him was a large rock, shaped vaguely like a human head. The stone visage of the survivor protruded from the top of a tall white cliff face, and in 1984, twelve-year-old Zhou was trying hard to ignore its presence while he grazed his family's oxen in a clearing on the opposite side of the gorge.

Some villagers feared the stone man. They told with sincerity a more recent tale that centered on a tree that once sat on top of the stone man's head, protecting him like a large umbrella. One day, a family was carrying their daughter to another family's home to give her away for marriage. No one knows why, but on their walk back they decided to chop the tree down with an ax. Not long after, the entire family died.

Some villagers prayed to the stone man, believing he had the ability to protect them and improve their lives. Zhou didn't see any use in praying. He was convinced nothing was powerful enough to make life better in his miserable village. Not even a man made of stone.

By the time Zhou was twelve, he had already been working in the fields for more than two years. He'd take to the grassland with his sickle and harvest fodder for his family's livestock. He'd set out for a clearing with their oxen and wait there as they grazed. Many other village boys would do the same. There was a game the young cowhands would play as their cattle nibbled on the grass. The boys would dig a hole in the earth, about twenty inches in diameter, and using bamboo sticks and their harvesting sickles, take turns hitting a stone or a wad of paper. Whoever hit the "ball" into the hole in the fewest "strokes" would win an item of food from the other players. The boys didn't have a name for this activity. It was just a folk game that had evolved over time, one of the many pastimes the village children invented to stave off boredom. They certainly didn't call it "golf." Nobody in the village of Qixin – and very few people in China – had ever heard of that game. The country hadn't been home to a golf course in nearly four decades.

But that had changed earlier in 1984. Henry Fok, a billionaire tycoon from Hong Kong, had recently opened an eighteen-hole layout designed by the golf legend Arnold Palmer, near Zhongshan, a city in southern China's Guangdong province most famous for being the birthplace of Sun Yat-sen, known by many as the "Father of Modern China." Zhongshan Hot Spring Golf Club may have been the first golf course in Communist China, but China had been home to several courses during the first half of the twentieth century. Most were in the foreign-occupied, self-governing zones of Shanghai, where a group of British executives had opened the city's first golf course in 1896. Its nine holes occupied part of the downtown expanse now known as People's Square. The Shanghai Golf Club sat alongside the Shanghai Racecourse, a wildly popular horse track, the former clubhouse for which – still famous for its grand clock tower – today houses the Shanghai Art Museum.

By the 1930s, the city was home to a handful of courses that catered to its predominantly foreign elite. In 1935, a *Fortune* magazine piece profiled a day in the life of a typical Shanghai-based expatriate, or "Shanghailander": "At noon you make your way to a club for a leisurely lunch and two cocktails… You return to your office. But at four-thirty you knock off again for a game of golf at the Shanghai Golf Club or the Hung-Jao Golf Club, both resembling the Westchester County variety except for the attendants in white nightgowns." Golf's persisting image as a frivolous amusement for the privileged classes is precisely why Mao Zedong denounced it as a "sport for millionaires" when the Communists seized control of China in 1949. Existing courses were plowed under or repurposed – for example, Hung-Jao Golf Club (or "Hongqiao," as it's spelled nowadays) is now the site of the Shanghai Zoo.

But now Mao was dead, and Deng Xiaoping's free-market reforms were in full swing. The Chinese government remained suspicious of golf, that symbol of Western decadence, but it was also pragmatic. Golf could be a magnet for overseas business and tourism, and Zhongshan was just across the border from Macau, a popular destination for Japanese travelers. Government officials were also none too pleased that China was unable to field a team when golf was introduced as a sport in the 1982 Asian Games. "The Red Chinese are convinced that golf is one way they can get elite people to visit there and spend money," Palmer said before his initial China site visit in 1981. Palmer saw opportunities, too: "There are 800 million people. Imagine if just a fraction of them played golf," he noted. Alastair Johnston, then vice president of Arnold Palmer Enterprises, was equally bullish, saying China "could be Japan 100 times over."

When, after a year-and-a-half of negotiations, Palmer's team broke ground at Zhongshan Hot Spring in 1982, it became clear that any golf history or knowledge the country once enjoyed was a distant memory. "The Chinese know nothing about golf. Absolutely nothing," said Palmer, who would later write about his China adventure in his memoirs.

When he arrived for his first site inspection after construction began, Palmer couldn't believe his eyes. All he saw were thatched huts; a pop-up village housing more than a thousand laborers tasked with molding the challenging terrain – nestled between mountains and rice paddies – into the course Palmer had designed. They were doing this all by hand – they had no bulldozers, no tractors and no trucks. Nearly half a million yards of dirt were being moved by industrious men and women using little more than shovels and burlap sacks. "The rocks too big to fit in their sacks were carried on their heads," Palmer wrote. "Boulders were ground to gravel by sledgehammers, with workers lined at the ready to remove the rocks when they were small enough to be carried away. It was an unbelievable sight." He recounted an interaction he had with one of the workmen:

> [I] gave this man a golf ball I had in my pocket. He stared at it for a few moments, then tried to take a bite out of the cover. "No," I said. "You don't eat it." That's when it dawned on me that the men engaged in the grueling labor of building our course had no idea what golf was. When I explained through an interpreter that this ball would be used to play the course our new friend was building, his eyes lit up and he took the ball from me as if I'd just presented him with the crown jewels of China.

Word of the historic course in Zhongshan never made it to Zhou's tiny village nine hundred miles to the northwest, nor word of any of the dozen or so golf courses built in China over the next decade. It'd be another twelve years before Zhou heard the word "golf" or saw a real golf ball. But when he did, it would change his life, far more than the stone man ever did.

Wang Libo didn't think it was possible for his skin to get any darker. He had been laying bricks, one after the other, for five years under Hainan's scorching sun. It was 2004. He was thirty-one years old and, like many Chinese, he dreamed of a better life.

The work was hard and monotonous, and it would often keep him away from home for months at a time. He'd chase jobs all over China's island province, sometimes working with modern rectangular bricks, sometimes lugging the large lava rocks he grew up with. He built houses. He built roads. All for little more than a thousand yuan a month – about $125. But his growing family – he had a wife and three young children back in the village – needed every yuan. The fruit trees his family had relied on for generations were no longer enough. Times were changing, even in remote Hainan.

But Wang's wife was beginning to complain that life was boring with him on the road. She needed his help around the house, and the children needed their father. So Wang vowed to make a change.

Life was simple in tiny Meiqiu village, about fifteen miles south of Haikou, the capital city. Even with his family's small monthly income, Wang had managed to squirrel away a fair bit of cash. So, in the spring of 2005 he decided to invest in his family's future. For twelve thousand yuan, he bought a *san lun che*, or three-wheeled car, which, based on his morning conversations with other drivers at the teahouse, would be his ticket to a better work–life balance. He'd be able to stay close to home, while helping the rural population meet a very basic need: Getting themselves, and their stuff, from one place to another. This part of Hainan, like most of the province, was extremely poor, and very few people could afford vehicles of their own. These three-wheelers had only been around for the past five years or so, and the only vehicles Wang remembered from his youth were dump trucks that transported loads of lava rocks toward the sea.

In years past, most people would simply stay close to home. The villages were largely self-sustaining. But the island economy was changing. *People needed to go places.* They needed to buy, to sell, to figure out new ways to put food on the table. People were adapting. Wang was, too.

The *san lun che*, a common sight on urban and rural streets throughout China, is basically a motorized, modernized rickshaw. They come in a variety of shapes and sizes. Wang's was utilitarian blue, and large enough to carry people and cargo. The front looked kind of like a motorcycle, with a box-like metal carriage affixed just behind the driver's seat. Around eight people could sit, somewhat uncomfortably, facing each other with their backs against the outside walls. Best of all for the passengers, and Wang's precious skin, everything, including Wang's cockpit, was enclosed and shielded from the sizzling sun. This armor, and the unusually loud growl of the engine, gave the vehicle a tank-like appearance, although if you were ever to ride in one you'd know they often feel as though one small pothole could make the whole thing fall apart.

Wang bought the truck on April 13, 2005, but according to the Chinese lunar calendar, that was not a good day to launch a business. So Wang waited a couple of weeks for a day that seemed appropriately auspicious for his initial ride. With nervous excitement, Wang rumbled off, ready to play the role of taxi or delivery truck, hoping his twelve-thousand-yuan gamble would pay off. His family was counting on him.

Wang drove from Yongxing, the closest town to his village, toward Xiuying, an area on the outskirts of Haikou, home to a variety of popular markets. It wasn't long before people were waving him down and paying him the two-yuan fare. He fell into a rhythm. Back and forth. Back and forth. The same road, all day long.

But Wang enjoyed his new job. The route may not have changed, but the passengers did. From morning until night he could meet new people, make new friends and share ideas – that is, when the engine was quiet enough to talk over. He enjoyed the camaraderie with the other drivers, as well. They'd take breaks together at local restaurants and outdoor teahouses. They'd play the local lottery together – everyone, it seems, played the lottery in Hainan – studying confusing sheets of numbers with elaborate care.

Most days, the hours were long, 7 a.m. to 8 p.m., and Wang didn't take weekends off. But the money was good. He could make around a hundred yuan (about $12.50) a day, and up to two or three hundred yuan on really busy days, more than tripling the monthly salary he earned working construction. And the best part of it all? At the end of the day he got to go home to his wife and children.

"It was so much better than laying bricks," Wang said.

When Wang bought his *san lun che*, he was told its expected lifespan was around eight to ten years. And he didn't see any reason why he wouldn't continue working as a driver well into his forties. Maybe it'd be what he did for the rest of his life. This was still Hainan, after all. Change may happen, but it happens slowly. Or at least that's the way it had always been before.

★

When Zhongshan Hot Spring Golf Club opened in 1984, Hainan was not yet a full-fledged province, and most mainland Chinese still observed the island with equal parts curiosity and fear. Despite its close proximity to the mainland – just eighteen miles from the southern tip of Guangdong province – for centuries Hainan was seen as a far-off and dangerous land, home to an unhealthy climate, impenetrable jungles and an unpredictable and treacherous sea. Some wrote it off as nothing more than a typhoon-plagued atoll inhabited by a motley collection of mysterious natives, ruthless pirates, banished criminals and exiled officials. Indeed, in the days before his expulsion to Hainan, disgraced Tang Dynasty chief minister Li Deyu complained he was being sent to the "gate of hell." Several of these perceptions persisted well into the twentieth century. One Hainan local recalled how, when he arrived on the mainland for university in the 1980s, his fellow students were surprised he didn't have a tail.

But it was also during this decade of reform and opening up that top-ranking officials began referring to Hainan as China's "treasure island," both for its rich natural resources and its sun-blessed, palm-tree-lined beaches. The island, although poor and backward, had potential, though at first no one could quite agree what for. Some felt the island should focus on agriculture, others emphasized industry, and there were those who favored the establishment of a free trade zone. Nothing much seemed to happen.

Thus, for Wang Libo, growing up in his tiny Hainan village meant a simple life, with very little interference from the Chinese authorities, let alone the wider world. His hometown, Meiqiu, appeared to be frozen in time. Like many villages on the island's northeast coast, it was laid out in maze-like fashion with narrow stone paths weaving between small, single-story stone homes assembled from irregularly shaped lava rock and sporting tile roofs. Some of the structures were hundreds of years old. Everything was a shade of gray.

As a young child in the early 1980s, Wang attended classes in the village's old stone schoolhouse. There was one teacher for both first and second grades, and there were only two classes: Chinese and math. When first grade was being taught, second grade would take a test, and vice versa. Their work was lit by traditional handheld oil lamps, and Wang recalls each pencil being a precious possession. If Wang lost one – just one – his parents would get very angry.

Outside school, free time was abundant, but Wang and his classmates had to be creative in how they spent it. There were no video games, no televisions and very few toys. He and his friends would play hide-and-seek, marbles and Chinese chess. There were ball games, too. One, played on a patch of dirt in front of the primary school, involved pushing a ball into holes dug in the ground.

But Wang's favorite ways to kill time required cunning and dexterity. He especially liked to catch lizards and birds. The local lizards, about twice the size of a gecko, spent most of their time hidden from view, but when they'd emerge onto rocks hoping to soak up some sun, Wang was ready to pounce. He'd move slowly at first, and then distract the creature by placing a stick or a hand in front of its face. With his free hand he'd snatch the lizard by its belly. Then it was time for the pointed stick – this was no catch-and-release exercise – and an open fire. Meat was still largely a delicacy at the time, reserved for only the most important of holidays, and roasted lizard was a treat for the children of Meiqiu. Their diets at the time consisted primarily of cassava, jicama and other fruits and vegetables. While people had enough to eat, which wasn't the case in prior decades, a lizard here and there provided a pleasant dose of protein. Wang would tuck the cooked lizard inside an edible leaf, sprinkle it with oil and salt, and dig in. "It tasted good," Wang recalled. "So natural."

Almost everyone in Meiqiu could climb trees, quickly. Even the tallest ones. They'd take off their shoes and race up a trunk as if it was a short flight of stairs. "If we can't climb trees, who can harvest the fruits?" Wang asked. And it was deep inside the web of branches created by the village's lychee trees that Wang and his friends took part in another popular pastime: raiding bird's nests. If they found eggs inside, they'd cook them and eat them. If they found infant birds, they'd snatch those up, too, and attempt to raise them as pets. The hatchlings often died.

In 1985, when Wang was twelve, something happened that would change the way the island's youth spent their free time forever: television arrived. The first set in Meiqiu was a black-and-white model with a seventeen-inch-wide screen. It resided in the family room of one of the village's richest men, a public servant in charge of managing the area's roads. Though he lived in a small, single-story lava-rock home like everyone else in Meiqiu, he was more than happy to share this technological wealth. Every night at around seven o'clock, the official and his wife would set out benches for a crowd. Wang recalled that more than twenty people, from young children to grandparents, showed up daily. It was the biggest thing to hit the village since, well... Wang couldn't think of anything else from his childhood days that came close to it. The room was often so mobbed, he'd have to sit outside and peer in through the front door.

The TV received three channels – China Central Television (CCTV), Hainan TV and a local Haikou station – and the villagers would regularly stay and watch whatever was on until midnight. Wang's favorites were *Zaixiang Hushan Xing*, a martial arts drama, and *Dream of the Red Chamber*, a series based on the classic Qing Dynasty novel. "TV dramas were such a precious thing for us," Wang recalled. "Everybody would finish watching them before going to sleep." Of course, there were days when the TV was unavailable, and he was forced to go back to his normal evening routine of doing homework or sitting under the village phoenix tree listening as the adults swapped folk stories. This pause in programming was not because the official and his wife got tired of hosting the community viewing parties. Quite the contrary. They loved the attention and status. Instead, the issue was infrastructure. Electricity was highly unreliable in Meiqiu, and the supply would cut off for days at a time. So it could be TV one day, oil lamps the next.

The village's second TV arrived the following year. "It was color," Wang said.

Martin Moore was never supposed to end up in China. That wasn't the plan – if there was a plan at all. He knew nothing about the place. He could name Beijing, maybe Shanghai, but that was it. He'd never traveled west of the Mississippi River, and he was fine with that, so long as there were golf courses to build and cold beers to drink.

By his own admission, he was "single, crazy, stupid and wild." Here he was in sunny Florida during the boom-boom mid-'80s, five years out of high school and spending all his time thinking about greens and fairways, bunkers and rough. He had landed a job with PGA Tour pro and golf architect Mark McCumber, helping to build courses throughout the South, and it seemed they couldn't build them fast enough. The job suited Martin well. He loved the outdoors, hated working in an office, and golf was pretty much the only thing he knew – even as a kid, his summer jobs had always been at courses in his hometown, Fort Myers. He had worked his way up with McCumber, and now he was driving tractors and bulldozers, becoming trusted enough to put the finishing touches on some holes. He had worked in course maintenance before, but he "fell in love with" the construction side of things. It was partly the machismo required – all the big machines, the moving of earth – but he was also drawn to the artistic side of the job. The open acreage of a course was the ultimate blank canvas, and the before-and-after, the molding of the landscape to match the architect's drawings, lit a fire inside Martin. True, he also liked living out of a suitcase, traveling from project to project. The pay was good, too, especially for someone in his early twenties, and so was the partying. As good as any trader up on Wall Street, Martin and his colleagues worked hard and played harder. The cliché nearly killed him.

He was on the waiting list to be enrolled at Lake City Community College in northern Florida, near the Georgia border. The school was known as "the Harvard of the golf industry" for its ability to churn out top-notch golf course superintendents. Martin, in fact, had been on the waiting list for more than three years, a detail he had nearly forgotten by the time the school called him in early 1986 to tell him he'd been accepted into their Golf Course Operations and Landscape Technology program, and that he could start study-ing in the autumn. His father, aware his son could be heading down a dangerous path, pressured him to go. But by that point, Martin wasn't sure what good it would do him. He already had several years of real-world experience in an industry he knew he loved, and he was enjoying himself, perhaps too much. "I was in another world, and didn't have any intention of going to school," Martin said. "But my father was getting all over my shit."

Martin was working a job in Green Cove Springs, Florida, south of Jacksonville, when he heard from Lake City. He blew off the school. He blew off his father. He focused on the job. "In the con-struction industry, we work all day busting our butts," Martin said. "And after work, someone would buy a case of beer." It was at one of those after-work happy hours that Martin had more beers than he should have. And then he went to a bar and had a few more. This wouldn't have been too big an issue – it wasn't the first time Martin had too much to drink – but Martin was driving that night. He drove a brown 1982 Dodge Ram van with a carpeted interior. His father had bought it for him two months earlier, partly to congratulate him for getting into Lake City, and partly to convince him to go.

Martin was living at a golf course in Middleburg, about fifteen miles away from Green Cove Springs along a narrow two-lane country road. It was pitch black, but that's no excuse. Truth is, Martin was unfit to drive in any conditions. The story he'd tell the police later that night was a little different, but if we're being honest Martin simply drove off the side of the road. He caught himself drifting right, and then overcorrected with a hard left turn and dropped hard, nose first, into a ditch on the side of the road. Martin had a fifty-pound metal Craftsman toolbox in the back, and at the point of impact it buzzed past his right ear and went straight out the windshield. "It's pretty amazing that I didn't get killed," said Martin. "I think that was the wake-up call. I was lucky to be alive."

Lucky indeed. Martin was not wearing his seatbelt, and the van was considered totaled, but he was able to open the driver's side door and walk away from the accident. Other than a bloody forehead from where his head smacked the steering wheel, he was okay. He went to work the following morning – although he had to find a ride, of course.

He felt he had to prove something to his father, who, before the accident, had always been willing to pay Martin's way through school – but no longer. So Martin enrolled at Lake City, taking classes Monday through Thursday and then working thirty-five to forty hours from Friday through Sunday building courses for Mark McCumber to pay his tuition bill. "It was tough," Martin said, "but I got straight As in college. Everybody copied my shit. I'd already lived my stupid, crazy life. I was more responsible and disciplined."

Martin continued working for McCumber, now as a project manager, after graduating from Lake City in 1988. And he was happy. He liked the work, and the industry was booming. In 1989, 267 new golf courses opened in the United States, by far the highest number since the National Golf Federation started keeping track in 1985, and the graph would continue to trend sharply upwards for the next decade. "There was no indication I would ever see anywhere other than America at that stage," Martin said. But in 1989 a conversation with an old friend got Martin an interview with one of the biggest names in the industry: Nicklaus Design, founded by Jack Nicklaus. Martin felt he already had his "dream job" with McCumber, but thought he should at least hear what Nicklaus had to say. He was a sports legend, and had been a prolific course designer since he began mapping out holes in the late 1960s. "I had no intention of working there," Martin said. "But why not take a free flight and go down there and talk?" "Down there" was North Palm Beach, Florida, home of the recently completed Golden Bear Plaza, a multi-million-dollar office complex that bore Nicklaus' nickname and housed his business empire. Of course, Martin was impressed.

He was also somewhat taken aback by their offer. They wanted him to manage one of their golf course construction projects – in Thailand.

"It was pretty good money," Martin said. "And I was single, twenty-seven years old, so it sure made me think. I flew back the next day and went back to my other job, but the offer had my mind going a mile a minute."

A week after his interview, he called the Nicklaus offices and accepted the job.

It was early 1990, and about as far from a direct flight as you can get. Martin was clutching his first ever passport as he boarded the Delta plane in Fort Myers, Florida. Next stop, Atlanta. Then Portland. Then Seoul. And then finally, Bangkok. With each new city, Martin saw more and more Asian faces on his flights, and the reality of his big move began to set in.

He landed at one in the morning, yet the Bangkok airport was packed. He was told someone would pick him up at the airport, but he didn't see his name written on any of the signs being held up by the crowd in the arrivals area. He was tired, confused and intimidated. He couldn't understand what people were saying to him. They couldn't understand what he said in return. "I didn't know what was going on," Martin said. "I was freaking out." Two anxious hours later, his driver arrived.

He was taken to a hotel in the heart of Bangkok and told to await further instructions. By then, it was close to four in the morning, but he couldn't sleep. He lay on his plank-hard mattress, trying to relax, wondering what he'd got himself into.

At 7:30 a.m., there was a knock on Martin's door. When Martin answered, a young man smiled and said, "Khun Suraphan would like to see you in his office now."

He didn't stay long at the office, which was very close to the hotel, in an old building behind the Golden Buddha Temple. Soon he was escorted to an old but well-maintained Jaguar, and driven north, beyond the city limits. And the driver kept driving and driving. Martin's palms began to sweat. *Where were they going?*

"I know someone told me the job was north of Bangkok, but I never thought I'd be so far out in the sticks," Martin said. "I didn't have any idea. I thought Thailand was Bangkok, and Bangkok was Thailand.

"I was wrong."

Martin was crying again. This had become a regular occurrence during his first month in Thailand. He'd sit alone in his room at night and, with nothing else to occupy his attention, he'd just cry. He was convinced he'd made the biggest mistake of his life. He had left a great job in Florida, doing what he loved, working for people who cared for him, living in places that felt familiar. And he abandoned it all – for what? Living by himself in an office on a construction site four hours north of the only Thai city he'd ever heard of (and that was only because of that song by Murray Head). There was a tiny village nearby, but it was unlike any place Martin had ever seen before, and when he went into town, the locals stared at him like he was an alien. And, in many ways, he was.

Martin had never felt so isolated. No one in the village spoke English. Neither did anyone at the job site. The translator he was promised was nowhere to be found. Martin worked long days, but never felt he was making progress. Outside Japan, Nicklaus hadn't designed much for Asia, and Mission Hills Khao Yai – the project Martin had been put on – was among the first batch of bids they had won in Thailand. Many of Martin's workers had never built a golf course. Some had never even heard of the game. He would try to give directions through a combination of charades and doodles. It felt impossible.

Often, the only friend Martin thought he could turn to was the telephone. In those early weeks, he'd make frantic, expensive calls back to the Nicklaus Design reps in Florida. "I can't do this," Martin would say like a junkie during his first week of rehab. "I gotta come home. I can't handle this."

At night, after all the workers made their way home, the hours got longer for Martin. He was having trouble sleeping due to a combination of culture shock and jet lag. So he'd sit there, alone with his thoughts – and the shadow that lurked outside his window. It was a security guard making his rounds, and every fifteen minutes or so the silhouette of the guard and his machine gun would appear on Martin's bedroom curtain. The sight filled him with unease. He wasn't sure what frightened him more: the thought of a man holding a machine gun outside his window, or whatever it was the man with the machine gun was supposed to be protecting him from.

On his irregular visits to the construction site, Mission Hills Khao Yai's owner could sense something was amiss with his project manager. Martin had heard a lot about Suraphan Ngamjitsuksri in the past weeks. An ethnically Chinese man in his late fifties, he was said to be the biggest steel importer in Thailand. He also had his hands in the country's lucrative road construction business, but Martin suspected there was more to the story. He couldn't shake it: Suraphan was like a character out of a mob movie. He was tall among Thai men, an inch or two shy of six feet, and he was bone thin, with sunken cheeks and a poof of wispy dyed black hair on the top of his head. It made him look like a walking skeleton, and many of the workers seemed to be scared to death of him. Despite the large gold Buddha medallions that dangled from his neck, he was an intense man, whose moods changed quickly. He chain-smoked. He yelled a lot, in multiple languages. Martin was happy he appeared to have done something to get on Suraphan's good side. "I think he liked me because I worked seven days a week," Martin said.

Suraphan made it his business to find the cure for what was ailing Martin. "I think you need to go to Bangkok," Suraphan told Martin on his third Saturday in Thailand. "My driver will take you. I've got everything arranged."

Martin wasn't sure what that meant, but he was eager for a change of scenery, and when Suraphan's Jaguar – he had a collection of more than a dozen cars – showed up at around 11 p.m., Martin was ready. The driver did not waste any time, hitting 120 miles per hour as soon as they reached the virtually empty highway, driving like a man who had no fear he'd ever be pulled over. The car had a clunky car phone embedded in the front seat armrest – a luxury rarely seen in north Florida, let alone Thailand – and the chauffeur received several calls during the drive. Martin could hear Suraphan barking orders on the other end of the line. What was normally a four-hour trip was cut nearly in half. Martin had no idea what was in store for him, and was already playing out numerous hair-raising scenarios in his head.

Once in Bangkok, the driver made a quick turn down a narrow, one-lane alleyway off Sukhumvit Road and came to an abrupt stop. A large neon sign on the building flashed, "Darling Turkish Bath."

"I was already freaking out," Martin said. "I was thinking, 'What is this place? Are they going to kill me inside?'"

Far from it. Suraphan owned Darling, and he had clearly sent the message that Martin was to be given VIP treatment. He was greeted with deferential bows and then ushered quickly into a large dark room with one wall made almost entirely of glass. There were women on the other side of the fishbowl, thirty of them, each one more beautiful than the last – an aquarium swarming with supermodels. The women were dressed alluringly; numbers were printed on slips of paper and pinned near their left shoulders. "I didn't know what to think," Martin said. "I was still in culture shock, but I was a single male in my twenties. This was starting to look appealing."

"Choose one!" the manager, a pleasant-looking, middle-aged woman, ordered.

Martin was dumbfounded. He didn't say a word. The host pointed to a couple of the women and provided an overview of the services offered. She also drew Martin's attention to the women who spoke English.

"So, who do you like?" she pressed.

"I guess No. 63 looks nice," Martin mumbled.

"63!" the host yelled, and the woman came out from behind the glass.

"Pick another one!" cried the host.

Another one? Martin thought.

"I think this one is fine," Martin said politely.

"No! Khun Suraphan said you must have two."

"Um, I don't know."

The manager, growing frustrated with Martin's indecisiveness, chose a second attendant for him. Martin and the two masseuses were escorted to a room.

Inside the room, the women started drawing a bath for Martin. Then there was a knock at the door. It was the manager.

"Khun Suraphan said you must have a third one!"

A third masseuse entered the room, and Martin tried hard to relax.

Back at the work site, things started to get better for Martin. A translator eventually arrived, and Martin began to occupy his empty nights by studying the Thai language. He'd force himself to learn ten words each evening before he went to bed, and he'd carry his vocabulary list around with him the following day and practice speaking with anyone who'd listen. Usually it ended up being the local girls who worked in the office. After six months, Martin could have basic conversations in Thai, and started to make friends. Suraphan still insisted he take monthly breaks in Bangkok, but Martin was beginning to grow accustomed to life in the countryside. He was never much of a big city kind of guy anyway.

Still, the job wasn't without its frustrations. Several white-knuckle moments made Martin wonder why he'd ever left Florida. Many of them involved Suraphan, who was proving to be a hair-trigger personality in more ways than one.

Sometimes when Martin was in Bangkok, Suraphan would invite him over to his office. Initially, it didn't appear to be the kind of office one would expect of a man who owned a Jaguar, a Mercedes and a Porsche. Tucked in that old building behind the Golden Buddha Temple, where Suraphan often prayed, the room was dingy and dark, with water-stained walls. It had once been the office of Suraphan's father, and had the feel of an antique shop. The furniture – including Suraphan's unusually large desk – was in the classic Thai style, dark wood with intricately carved detail. Gold, jade and ivory statues, many of them Buddhas, adorned nearly every flat surface in the room, and the walls were covered with portraits of the Thai kings. Suraphan, like many of his country-men, seemed especially fond of King Rama V.

In the morning, Martin would watch as women brought in suitcases full of money, the takings from the previous day's customers at Darling Turkish Bath. This was before Thailand introduced the one-thousand-baht note – up until the mid-1990s, five hundred baht (roughly twenty US dollars) was as big as bills got – so Suraphan's piles of cash grew to be cartoonishly tall. Suraphan would open up some sliding doors on the wall of cabinets behind his desk and place his bounty of baht alongside even more cash, in every currency Martin could imagine. It wasn't all banknotes, either. He thought he saw several bars of solid gold.

Every couple of weeks, Suraphan would fill up a few suitcases with cash and head out to the work site at Mission Hills Khao Yai. He'd ask Martin to be present when he doled out payments to subcontractors. In theory, Martin was there to confirm that the agreed work had been done to his satisfaction. But it was clear only one opinion mattered during these proceedings, and that was the opinion of the man with the loaded gun.

Subcontractors would queue up outside Suraphan's office at the course, waiting to be paid in wads of cash. He'd make them wait for hours, and when they did make it to his desk, Suraphan would never pay them what they thought they were owed. For 100,000 baht's worth of work, he'd pay 80,000 and say, "That's enough." Few subcontractors complained. With all the cash lying around, Suraphan had two armed guards at the door and a nine-millimeter pistol on his desk; it could be intimidating. "It's not a negotiation," Martin said. "If he says you didn't do something, you're not getting fucking paid."

One instance in particular stuck with Martin. It was late, close to 10 p.m., and the subcontractor responsible for building the cart paths on the course had been waiting to be paid since sundown. When the man finally got his turn, he presented Suraphan with a bill for five holes' worth of cart path, calculated by the square meter.

"Square meter?" Suraphan scoffed. "I pay you by linear meter."

The man looked heartbroken. This meant he'd get paid a third of what he was owed. He tried to argue, all the while eyeing the gun on the table. He didn't get very far.

"It's linear meter, right?" Suraphan yelled to his staff, who were not inclined to disagree with him.

"You're right," they said. "Linear meter."

The subcontractor began to cry.

"You're getting paid per linear meter," Suraphan said brusquely. "Here's your money. Now get the hell out of here."

"That guy lost his ass, probably totally went broke," Martin recalled. "I never saw that cart path contractor again."

Six months into the job, Martin learned that Suraphan's gun wasn't just for show. Several families of wild dogs lived near the golf course, and they'd dig holes in fairways and greens. Martin saw them as merely a nuisance, but Suraphan absolutely hated the dogs, and he told his staff to do whatever it took to get rid of the pests. They were costing him money.

Then, during one of his weekend visits to the job site, Martin took Suraphan on a drive around the course so he could update him on progress. Sure enough, there was a wild dog in the middle of one of the finished greens.

"Martin, I told you to fucking kill those dogs!" Suraphan said.

Martin chuckled, thinking Suraphan was just joking.

"Stop! Stop the truck!" Suraphan yelled.

Martin obliged, and in one motion Suraphan hopped out, reached into the waistband at the back of his blue jeans, pulled out his nine-millimeter and shot the dog dead. He got back in the truck, turned to Martin and said, "I don't want to see any more dogs out here."

Martin liked dogs. He had them as pets. And when, a couple of holes later, he spotted another dog, he started shaking his head. He knew what was coming – or at least he thought he did.

"Stop!" Suraphan screamed.

Martin stopped the truck and waited for Suraphan to hop out and shoot the dog. But this time Suraphan handed the pistol to Martin.

"You take care of this one," Suraphan said.

Martin's face went flush, and all the hairs on his body stood at attention. He didn't have much experience with guns, and he had no desire to shoot anything. But he felt he couldn't say no. Nobody could say no to Suraphan.

Martin took the gun and reluctantly left the driver's seat. He could feel the sweat building up on his forehead. He slowly raised his right hand, hoping that, if he delayed long enough, the dog would run away.

"Shoot!" Suraphan screamed. "Shoot him!"

The shots burst out of the gun in such quick succession, Martin wasn't sure how many there were. Five? Six? One thing was obvious: none of the shots came anywhere close to the dog, which had scampered off to safety with the first bang.

Martin was part emasculated, part relieved. Suraphan was laughing hysterically, uncontrollably, like it was the funniest thing he'd ever seen.

"It was all a joke to him," Martin said.

Suraphan killed three dogs that day. And it only took him four shots to do it. Martin hoped he'd never see the nine-millimeter again.

He wouldn't be so lucky. Half a year later, Martin and Suraphan were in a luxury van – yet another member of Suraphan's fleet – returning to Khao Yai after a weekend trip to another Mission Hills project in Kanchanaburi in southwest Thailand, not far from the border with Burma. They were only four miles from the course in Khao Yai, but construction had traffic at a standstill. The road only had two lanes, but that didn't stop some vehicles from trying to create their own, forcing themselves between and around stopped cars, making traffic move even slower. Martin had his attention focused on a ten-wheel dump truck on his side of the van trying to squeeze by them on the shoulder. Suraphan saw it, too.

"What is that asshole doing?" Suraphan roared.

The truck kept inching closer, and Suraphan kept shouting. The van couldn't move, and the truck driver obviously didn't know who he was messing with. He crept closer and closer, until he clipped the sideview mirror on the van and ripped it off. Suraphan was enraged.

"That fucker!" Suraphan screamed.

He reached under his seat, pulled out the pistol and leaned across Martin to slide open the van door. Then, with his arm extended in front of Martin's frozen face, Suraphan aimed at the truck's tires and squeezed the trigger four times. Problem solved,

Suraphan closed the door and put the gun back under his seat. Martin was in shock, his face speckled with gunshot residue, his ears deafened.

"The truck driver didn't do anything in response," said Martin, whose hearing didn't come back for over three hours. "He probably assumed it was a super VIP."

And the driver would have been right. Suraphan was well connected, at the highest levels of the Thai government. Martin saw this influence firsthand. He knew the course at Khao Yai butted up against national park land – he'd seen herds of wild elephants on local roads – but he wasn't aware that the course actually straddled the park. In fact, to get from hole No. 1 to No. 2, and then from hole No. 6 to No. 7, you had to traverse a small mountain that was protected land. Suraphan insisted a path traverse the mountain and connect the holes, and he instructed his workers to begin chiseling and dynamiting away. This effort was soon shut down by park police, and for about six months Suraphan's team wasn't allowed near the mountain. Suraphan was pissed off – and that was before he learned about the hefty fines he was expected to pay. But a leadership change was looming in Thailand, and the candidate Suraphan backed ended up winning.

"Within one month after that, they dynamited the fuck out of that mountain – got a road through there and everything," Martin said. "And Suraphan only got fined five-hundred baht, or twenty bucks."

Thailand would prove to be a perfect training ground for working in China.

When Wang Libo was a young boy, his grandfather would tell him stories about his years in Malaysia. He captivated Wang with descriptions of tall cement buildings with flat walls and square windows. "My grandfather told me modern buildings like that were everywhere over there," Wang recalled. "And when he came back to Hainan all he saw were small stone houses with dirt floors and tiled roofs. He said people outside were living better than in

Hainan. Hainan was very backwards back then." Forty years had passed and Hainan villagers were still living in those one-story houses made of lava rock, just like they had for centuries. Wang, not yet a teenager at the time, dreamed of the day this would change. He thought the stone homes were dark and depressing. He wanted to live in a house where you could brush against a wall and not draw blood.

In 2000, at the age of twenty-seven, Wang realized his dream. He and his wife of three years moved out of his parents' lava stone house, the house he had grown up in, and built a new home on a different plot of family land. The house was not large, but it had smooth walls and square windows. It was made of red brick and cement and was situated near the cement road. Cement was a status symbol in Meiqiu. People talked of saving up to build a "cement home" near the "cement road" and Wang was one of the first in Meiqiu to live in a house built using cement.

Wang said that while he admired the resiliency of the old stone homes – lava rock walls can last generations – he didn't miss living in his old house at all. Life was easier in cement houses. And since villages were still closed to most vehicles, being close to the cement road meant he could get where he needed to go much faster. "Old stone homes are a reminder of old tough lives," Wang said. "When everyone lived in old stone houses, we had to trade coupons for rice. There was no meat to eat. Now you can buy anything you want."

Before passable roads were built in the late 1970s, everything was carried on the shoulders of people traveling on foot. In fact, many villagers still commonly use the unit of measurement *dan*, literally the amount of weight a grown man can carry over his shoulder. Old men in Meiqiu recalled hauling sacks of coal to Haikou, a three-hour trek, hoping they could trade it for just one yuan. And then they began their journey back to the village, fearful that bandits would steal the only coin they had. Until the late 1980s, water was fetched from wells thirty meters deep. In the winter months, the wells would often run dry. What did the villagers do? "We didn't use much water in the winter," one longtime Meiqiu resident said wryly.

Meiqiu was the only home Wang had ever known. And, he figured, it would be the only home he'd ever know. Very few people
leave the village, and those who do usually go just a short way
down the road to Yongxing. Wang's great-grandfather had told him
that his ancestors probably arrived on the island several hundred,
maybe even a thousand, years ago, from Fujian province in southeastern China. Everyone in the village, and several surrounding
villages, shared this origin story. That explained why they were
all ethnically Han Chinese and not part of the Li or Miao minori-
ties native to Hainan. It also explained why everyone carried the
same family name, Wang. Wang Libo assumed that if you looked
far enough back in the family tree you'd find that everyone in
Meiqiu was related in one way or another. And he'd later learn,
as anyone with a large extended family will tell you, that this can
be both a blessing and a curse.

Most villagers assumed their ancestors felt the area had auspicious *feng shui*. Meiqiu and the neighboring communities sit
slightly east of what's now a 27,000-acre national geological park.
The park surrounds an extinct volcano crater and has earned the
reputation of the "green lung of Haikou." Locals say their air is
cleaner than the surrounding parts of the island, that their primitive forests are more lush, that their location is less susceptible
to wind and rain. The villages are also perched on a ridge, higher
than many other parts of the island, which is thought to be more
advantageous for burying and honoring the dead.

Wang's family had been farmers for as long as he or his relatives could remember. The area's rocky terrain was not suitable
for most crops, including rice, but fruit trees thrived in the black,
nutrient-rich volcanic soil. Wampee, guava, jackfruit, banana and
longan are grown in family farms and harvested from the wild.
But it's the local lychees that are famous, and everyone brags
about how big they are. Lychee season begins in May; jackfruit
and wampee start to ripen in June. And while the fruit seasons
are finite, the money they produce needs to last the entire year.

There have been plenty of interruptions to life on this island
paradise, some of them rather severe. Things got so bad for Wang's
grandparents, they fled to Malaysia and lived there for several years

before his father was born. "At that time, Hainan was in chaos," Wang said, recalling the story he was told. "I'm not sure, maybe it was the Japanese War." Hainan has seen its share of chaos. It has been ruled by many masters: dynastic generals, pirates, foreign imperialists, missionaries and feudal warlords, to name just a few. And then, of course, there were the Japanese, the Nationalists and the Communists, who arrived in succession during a turbulent, often terrible three decades, starting in the late 1930s.

Before the Japanese invasion of Hainan, which began in February 1939 and didn't end until the close of the Second World War in 1945, Wang's family lived in a village called Cangdao, just over two miles from Meiqiu. Cangdao was the largest village in the area and its residents had a reputation, compared to other villagers at least, for having large amounts of money and land. Wang said many men in Cangdao, intent on defending their possessions, formed citizen militias and bandit gangs after the Japanese invaded. Perhaps it was Cangdao's size that caught Japanese attention. Perhaps it was its fight. Today, many believe it was a combination of the two, coupled with its hubris: Cangdao was one of the few villages in the area not to construct a protective exterior wall. It was an easy target, and Japanese soldiers burned it to the ground. The surviving Cangdao villagers limped off to seek refuge in neighboring villages. Most ended up in Meiqiu. "Some older villagers told me there were one thousand villagers in Cangdao before the Japanese came," Wang said. "When we moved to Meiqiu, Cangdao had no more than one hundred people."

According to stories told in the village, Meiqiu was a comparatively safe place to be during the Japanese occupation of Hainan. It was small enough to be ignored, and a wall of lava rocks, as tall as ten feet high in some places, encircled the village. The walls also came in handy later, when Chinese Nationalist forces controlled the island. "They would rob you," one elderly Meiqiu resident said. "And if you didn't give them what they wanted, they would threaten you with guns. But they weren't like the Japanese, who took all your things, burned down your village and raped your women. They were Chinese. They just took your rice and your chickens. They didn't kill farmers."

The Meiqiu wall was knocked down decades ago, but Wang always felt fortified by the place. This was home. His father had lived in Meiqiu his entire life; Wang had been born and raised here. Over the past century his family had survived the same horrors as everyone else in the village. He never felt like an outsider, and thought he never would. But that was before anyone in Meiqiu had heard of the "Red Line" or Project 791.

2

FIRST CLUB

Zhou Xunshu's parents had always dreamed of having a police officer in the family. In 1995, at the age of twenty-three, Zhou enrolled in the Guizhou People's Police School in Zunyi, a large city about six hours east of Bijie by bus. The school's name was deceiving. It had been a state-run police academy, but by the time Zhou arrived it was a privately owned vocational college that churned out security guards. Most students didn't stay the full two years, opting instead to sign on with an agency, arranged by the school, that placed them in low paying jobs throughout southern China.

During Zhou's first few months in Zunyi, the mornings were filled with exercises: *wushu* (Chinese for "martial arts"), self-defense, bodybuilding. It was akin to basic training. But there was little to do the rest of the time, and Zhou became bored. The curriculum seemed poorly managed, the school disorganized. When they did have classes – on topics like fire prevention theory – he couldn't see how they were relevant to his career. In late October, after six months, he dropped out. He took a job guarding an aluminum factory in Guiyang for 350 yuan ($42) a month.

Zhou hated the job. It was tedious, and the fumes from the factory floor made him sick. When he learned there were jobs available in the southern boomtown of Guangzhou in Guangdong province, and that thirteen of his former classmates were dropping out and leaving for the city the following day, he saw his chance. He was desperate to escape. He didn't tell his bosses at the aluminum factory he was leaving. He had worked there only two days.

No one in Zhou's family knew he was heading to Guangzhou. They didn't even know he'd left police school. Zhou had no phone at the time, and it would take at least ten days for a message to reach his remote village by regular mail. He wasn't in a hurry to discuss this decision with his parents anyway. They had paid his tuition – five thousand yuan, a lot of money for peasant farmers in Guizhou. They had saved it up for several years, and now it was gone.

Qixin – stuck on the side of a remote mountain, elevation six thousand feet – is perhaps the poorest village in Guizhou, perhaps the poorest province in China. Of course, there's no way to prove this, but although the villagers aren't starving these days, as they were a generation or two ago, there's no denying life in this tiny collection of crude stone homes is harsh and antiquated.

The road to Qixin is narrow, barely a single lane, with tall walls of rock and earth on one side and a steep cliff dropping off the side of the mountain on the other. There are no guardrails on the road, and storms often render it impassable. But there's only one other way to the top of the mountain – a four-hour hike. In the past, visitors not up for the trek would hop on the back of a horse. Today they must climb into the back of a beat-up blue dump truck. It was hard to imagine why people would choose to live in such a place. "In old China, life was very tough," explained the young driver of one of the trucks as he navigated the road, which was more rutted and muddy than normal. "Those with power would just kill the people they didn't like. So many people got scared and ran for the mountains. Later on, those with money or those who became government officials left the mountain. Now, the only people who remain are the poor ones, like us."

In the back of the truck, the driver's passengers stood, gripping tight to the bed's side rails, bracing their bodies as the vehicle lurched back and forth like a rowboat in rough water. At one point, as the driver waited for a van to unstick itself from the mud, his human cargo swallowed an uncomfortable view of the valley floor as the truck leaned towards the cliff's edge.

The landscape was bleak – everything the color of a brown

paper bag. The entire mountainside had long ago been carved into a series of dramatic terraces for farming, the only way people could subsist in such a harsh environment. Down below, on one of those perches, a farmer in mud boots used an ox to work the brown earth back to life, tilling the cold soil for the first time that year. Soon, he'd be planting tomatoes. In the distance beyond the farmer there was a wall built into the mountainside – a series of uniform circular pipe openings, too many to count, stacked atop one another.

These were crucibles, remnants of the dozens – maybe hundreds – of rudimentary zinc smelting furnaces that had been active on the mountainside in the 1990s. "They did not allow them to do it in the town, so they moved to the mountains," the driver said. "Now, the country does not allow them to do it here any more, either. Too polluted."

Reminders of the once-booming industry are everywhere. From the heights of the road, the remains of the demolished dome furnaces look like alien crop circles – and redundant graphite and terracotta crucibles, known as retorts, are ubiquitous. Rounded cones, about the size of an adult human thigh, they are now used by the villagers to build walls, reinforce walking paths and stave off soil erosion on their terraced farms. But most retorts go unused, littering the forest in piles that resemble spent artillery shells.

Who knows what else the zinc smelters have left behind? Their methods of distilling metallic zinc from its ore (the end result is used in the production of brass) were crude, not much different than the process used in China hundreds of years ago. They've been known to contaminate soil and waterways with lead, cadmium, mercury and other heavy metals.

Today, the zinc plants are rubble, and other industries are eyeing the region for its rich natural resources. Villagers on the mountain say a coal company from Shandong province has expressed interest in buying their land. There is also rumored to be gold in the hills. But residents can't agree on a selling price. And some villagers aren't interested in selling at all. They can't imagine living anywhere else. They feel too much of a connection to their crops. Zhou Xunshu doesn't understand these people at all.

A word that Zhou often uses to describe his childhood is *ku*, which means "bitter." Qixin didn't have electricity until the early 1990s, and despite China's "opening up" under Deng Xiaoping, the effects of the planned economy days lingered in the village over the next decade. Even today, the average rural family in Guizhou earns less than a hundred dollars a month – just 4,753 yuan ($780) a year. Zhou remembers sharing a bed with two of his brothers. Many days he would grow hungry looking at the family's boxes of government-provided potatoes, knowing they wouldn't last. How could those boxes feed two parents, six children and various in-laws, aunts and uncles through the winter?

They were hard times. Sometimes, in the coldest months, Zhou didn't have shoes to wear. "When we traveled into town we could see other people had better lives than us," he said.

The family home was a short, steep walk up a muddy trail from the road. The house had been expanded in piecemeal fashion over the years. The main structure was a single-story box made of gray concrete, twenty feet wide at the front. Two worn wooden doors were hung on either side of three wood-framed casement windows. The window frames and doors, painted red some time ago, were faded, stained, peeling. By the time Zhou left to go to the police school, this main building had been bookended by two taller brick structures with sheets of corrugated metal covering their tiled gable roofs, and growing off of both of those were two newer shelters made of cinder block. A few steps back downhill was the family pigpen, with a sloped roof and extra insulation provided by a layer of empty plastic rice sacks. In the middle of all of this sat a large cement courtyard, which also served as the roof for an ox shed dug out underneath it. At the far end of the courtyard, a crude lean-to covered two stone slabs and a hole in the ground: the family's only toilet. Squatting there, one could gaze on a deep forest; in the winter the leafless branches revealed a view of the terraced valley. On clear days, the mountains were never-ending. Songbirds trilled in the trees.

As a child, Zhou attended Qixin's school, studying by the light of kerosene lamps and seeking comfort from the heat of the coal furnace in the middle of the classroom. The primary school featured two classrooms, housing up to thirty students, grades one to five. This led to a lot of downtime for the children – when the teacher was giving a lesson to first graders, for example, all the other grades, as Zhou says, "did work on their own." Students sat on long wooden benches behind long wooden tables. Teachers wrote on boards made black by the dried sap from a sumac tree. After class, he went out to work in the fields, cutting the tall grasses with a sickle.

Neither of Zhou's parents had attended school, and Zhou got a late start to his education. He didn't begin primary school until he was nine, and he took another two years off after the fourth grade. He said it didn't feel too strange being older than most of his classmates; when he was in fifth grade one of his fellow students was twenty-five. And lots of people in the village just never went to school at all.

After Zhou finished fourth grade, the school was torn down. "The farmers in the village didn't think about the kids," he said. "Parents here only view school as a way to avoid being illiterate. They don't see education as a way to change their future and help them out of poverty. So they removed the school and split up the bricks, stone and wood among themselves." After that, he had to walk to a school in a village two hours away.

Zhou said his forced two-year break from school was necessary because he was "very naughty in class." He couldn't sit still. He had trouble concentrating.

Zhou eventually graduated from junior high school when he was eighteen. He spent four years studying to pass the senior high school entrance exam – his parents had hoped he would be the first family member to do so, following in the footsteps of the neighbors' son who had got into university – but schooling had never been Zhou's strong suit. Four years in a row he went through the motions in Bijie, and four years in a row he failed.

"I just couldn't really absorb anything," Zhou said. "When I was studying, I always thought about other things." He could only remember two of the English words he'd learned in school – face and apple – and claimed he "could never spell them right." Feeling he had run out of options, in 1995 he enrolled in the military police school in Zunyi. Perhaps Zhou could become something after all.

His family always had a chip on its shoulder. They felt picked on. They said that other people – those with power and money – were out to get them. Zhou's grandfather had ended up in Qixin in 1931 after years of wandering, years of running. They moved to their current home – the site of it, at least – in 1948, when Zhou's father was eleven. "They were very poor," Zhou's eldest brother, the only one of the family's four brothers to still live in Qixin, explained. "The family moved from village to village trying to find a place they could afford to live. Finally, they settled here."

There's a story about the family that's been passed down from generation to generation. An ancestor named Zhou Youming, from Hunan province, was supposedly a general during the Ming Dynasty, nearly seven hundred years ago, and Emperor Zhu Hongwu asked him to go conquer Guizhou. After doing so, General Zhou, so the story goes, settled near Bijie. "After the general's generation, we just went backwards," Zhou's eldest brother, known simply as First Brother to family members, said, an M-shaped crease forming between his eyebrows as he spoke.

Zhou, also known as Fourth Brother, had never been convinced there was a general in the family. "It's just a folk tale," he would say. "There are no historical documents to prove it. We've always been peasant farmers. Always."

Perhaps because of the perceived fall in the family's fortunes, they were especially conscious of the sting of rejection. "Let me tell you. It was because during my grandpa's time, our family did not have money, and so we were always looked down upon. They were bullied all the time and that is why we moved to five different places. Over and over again. Finally, they were barely able to settle down here," First Brother said. He took a long intense draw on his Huangguoshu cigarette, named after Guizhou's famous waterfall, the largest in the nation. His chain-smoking, combined with his jet-black pompadour hairstyle, recalled a 1950s movie greaser transported to rural China.

"This is why we've always wanted to have a policeman in this family – to avoid the family being bullied," First Brother said. "But Fourth Brother did not want to do this."

Nope – Zhou Xunshu was on a train to a new life in Guangzhou.

When Zhou and his classmates boarded the train, they might have been mistaken for soldiers in their police school uniforms, but for the lack of any badges. Tickets for the thirty-hour trip to Guangzhou were one hundred yuan, and Zhou was lucky to find a seat. The train was overflowing with migrants, all hoping to find work in the city.

Zhou was scared. He had fifty yuan in his pocket and no guarantee of a job. He desperately wanted to prove to his family that he could make it on his own. He didn't want to have to return to Guizhou and admit he had made a poor choice. In fact, he didn't want to return to Guizhou at all. He hugged his bag tightly. It contained all of his belongings: a toothbrush and toothpaste, a blanket, two pairs of underwear, one collared shirt, a T-shirt and a pair of trousers.

In Guangzhou, the boys stuck together. They booked rooms in the cheapest hotel they could find: ten yuan a night. Zhou had trouble sleeping that first evening; he knew he'd be out of money soon. There was no way he could return home a jobless, penniless dropout.

But if there was one thing Guangzhou had in the 1990s, it was jobs. After a decade of reforms on the mainland, many firms from Hong Kong had moved production to Guangdong, creating a huge demand for unskilled labor. By 2000, the Pearl River Delta was home to an estimated 22 million migrant workers. Fewer than 3 percent of them returned home permanently. In the previous decade, Guangdong's population had grown nearly 40 percent.

The day after the dropouts from the Guizhou People's Police School arrived in Guangzhou, all fourteen had jobs. "You all will start work at Dongguan Fengjing tomorrow," their contact at the employment agency said.

"Dongguan Fengjing – what's that?"

"A golf course."

Silence.

Finally, one of them asked bravely: "What's that?"

The boys were told golf was a game for rich people, mostly foreigners. That was it.

Their arrival at Fengjing, forty-six miles east of Guangzhou, near the manufacturing city of Dongguan, did not enlighten the confused security team. The Chinese word *fengjing* translates to "hillview," and that's all they could see: brown hill after brown hill, plus some bulldozers. The view went on forever. *How many rich foreigners does it take to play this game?* Zhou wondered.

Zhou would not find out – not at Fengjing, at least. He left after only five months, before the course was completed, before there was any grass on the ground. Five months was long enough for Zhou to prove himself as a security guard, however. He earned a reputation for being a leader, and was considered the de facto head of security, although he still earned the same six hundred yuan monthly salary as everyone else.

Ironically for Zhou, the young man bored by the fire prevention lectures at the police school, it was his performance in helping fight brushfires in the small mountains surrounding Fengjing that would change his life. The hills were ablaze, and the fire was threatening to spread to Fengjing's course. Zhou rounded up the team and organized a plan of attack. Armed with hand axes and machetes, they entered the smoke-filled woods, their mouths covered only by kerchiefs. For an entire day, the young men chopped and hacked, chopped and hacked. The result was a twenty-two-yard-wide firebreak that ran the length of the forest. It stopped the fire in its tracks.

His initiative caught the eye of a Fengjing manager who had grown to like Zhou through their daily conversations. When the manager left to work at Guangzhou International Golf Club, less than an hour's drive to the north, he suggested Zhou should have an interview for a security job there. He gave Zhou the contact details for Frank Lin, a businessman from Singapore. "It will be more money," the manager assured Zhou. "Meet with Mr. Lin."

Lin hired Zhou on the spot, at a starting salary of one thousand yuan a month – three times what Zhou had been making as a security guard in Guizhou. "I just got a good feeling from talking to him," Lin said. "The way he looked, the way he talked. He just came across as a very honest and trustworthy person."

Zhou had landed his second job at a golf course – and he still had no idea what golf was.

Martin Moore had already done his years of "shit duty" in rural Asia. He had paid his dues at Mission Hills Khao Yai, and was now headed for paradise. It was the summer of 1995, and Jack Nicklaus' team had already informed Martin he'd been tapped to be the project manager at a course set to break ground in Surfers Paradise, part of Australia's Gold Coast, starting that September or October. Martin was working a course remodel in Okayama, Japan, and he couldn't wait to start something new. What could be better than sun and sand Down Under? His shaper in Okayama had recently left, and instead of waiting for a new person to arrive, Martin got behind the wheel of the bulldozer himself and started shaping greens. "I wanted to get that project done," Martin said. "I was going to Surfers Paradise!" He was already daydreaming of topless beaches and snorkeling the Great Barrier Reef.

Then Martin received a call from Lee Schmidt, one of Nicklaus' designers back in the States. He warned Martin he should expect an unwelcome call – asking him to go to Kunming, China. Martin's heart sank. He had no idea where Kunming was, but knew it was nowhere near Surfers Paradise. And the reports Martin had heard from colleagues working in China were not positive. Everyone talked about the filth, the crowds, the yelling, the spitting. No one seemed to enjoy it.

"Do you remember, around two years ago, a guy named Arthur came to visit you at Khao Yai in Thailand?" Schmidt asked Martin.

"Well, he wants you to be the design coordinator on a new course. He specifically asked for you."

Martin did recall his one and only encounter with Arthur Yeo, a businessman from Singapore. Yeo had been introduced as a future client of Jack Nicklaus, and Martin had lunch with him, answered some questions and took him on a tour of the Mission Hills Khao Yai job site. It was a pretty standard site visit. Martin had done several of them before. He spent maybe five hours with Yeo, and never thought much about him again.

But sure enough, a few days after talking with Lee Schmidt, he received a call from Nicklaus' right-hand man, Bill O'Leary.

"Do you want to go to Kunming, China?" O'Leary asked.

Martin had been rehearsing his response for days. "Hell no," he said.

O'Leary chuckled and said, "Okay, I just thought I'd ask. Arthur wanted us to ask you. I don't blame you. I'd go to Surfers Paradise, too."

Three days later, Martin received another call. It was O'Leary again.

"Arthur keeps bugging me. He really wants you to go there," O'Leary said.

Martin stuck to his original response. Nothing was going to keep him from the beach.

Three more days passed, and another call from O'Leary.

"Martin," he said, "Arthur says he's not going to do a Jack Nicklaus golf course unless you're the project manager."

"Okay, Bill," Martin said. "Tell Arthur I'll do it for an extra three thousand dollars a month."

"Ha," went O'Leary. "They'll never give you that."

"I know. That's the idea."

Twenty-four hours later, O'Leary called Martin again. Arthur Yeo had accepted Martin's terms.

Martin didn't know what to expect in China, "other than, there wasn't much golf." And if the country as a whole was a mystery, the city of Kunming was a secret. While he knew people who had worked in China, he had yet to meet anyone who had heard of Kunming.

That wasn't too surprising. In the mid-1990s, foreigners who found their way to the capital city of Yunnan province tended to be either students or backpackers. "Westerners were looked at as if they'd just disembarked from a spaceship," one longtime Kunming resident said. Yunnan province borders Myanmar, Laos and Vietnam, and parts of it felt like an extension of Southeast Asia. Martin figured his experience in Thailand was the reason Yeo had been so insistent.

When Martin arrived, Kunming's population was somewhere around two million, but it still felt more like a town than a city. A few maze-like sections of old Kunming still existed – crooked lanes lined with rickety mud and wood-framed houses with tiled roofs that sprouted grass and flowers. But it was clear where things were headed: to wider roads, taller buildings, vanishing character. The bits of tradition that lingered among the city's attempts at modernity caught Martin's eye: old men, their skin wrinkled and dark from the sun, inhaling tobacco smoke from large bamboo bongs; street food hawkers crushing into spaces on nearly every sidewalk, the pungent aroma of their Yunnan spices – if Martin breathed too deeply, the hot chilies made his nose run – doing battle with the stench of the public toilets; members of Yunnan's many minority groups walking the streets wearing traditional clothing and jewelry, styles that, in many cases, haven't changed in centuries. Some women wore what Martin thought looked like intricately embroidered tapestries, with bold, bright colors, accented by elaborate silver jewelry that often covered large portions of their arms and chests. If the sun hit them just right, Martin suspected he might be blinded.

Martin saw nearly no private cars on Kunming's streets. Traffic consisted almost entirely of buses, taxis and bicycles. He slowed as a bicycle passed him, carrying a slaughtered pig, its split carcass stuck on a spike mounted above the bicycle's rear wheel, the pig's head and tail flopping with each push of a pedal. To be sure, Martin had not landed at a beach resort in Australia.

In the days before construction was set to begin, Martin settled into the Holiday Inn in downtown Kunming. It was a brand he recognized. "That Holiday Inn was the only place civilized at all in Kunming," he said. "You could actually order a pizza in there. And they had a bowling alley in there. Every couple weeks, Arthur and I would get together and bowl a few games, order pizza and drink some beer. But that was it. There wasn't anything else."

He had been called to Kunming to work on Spring City Golf and Lake Resort. It was prime, undeveloped land, situated on the eastern shore of Yangzong Lake, about thirty miles east of Kunming. Across the water from Spring City, there was one floundering resort, where Martin eventually moved to be close to the construction site, but otherwise the lake was fringed by farmland and a few small villages. At the far end of the lake, Martin could see a smoke-spewing, coal-fired power plant to the north and an aluminum plant to the west. He was told that local government officials had assured Yeo that both of these eyesores would soon be closed down.

Culture shock was less of an issue for Martin this time around. Like Arthur Yeo, Spring City's developers were from Singapore, and so were many of the staffers; most spoke English, so language was not much of a problem. The most common gripe was the remoteness of the project. There were a couple of "total shithole restaurants" they'd go to in the closest village, and sometimes they'd slurp a bowl of noodles in a tent on site provided by one of the contractors, but Martin would often cook something up on the two-burner stove back at his place.

Trips to Kunming were infrequent because the only way to the city at that time was a circuitous two-lane road that looped around most of the lake. The journey was a good ninety minutes if there wasn't an accident. But there were often accidents. One in particular, Martin will never forget.

The power plant was nestled on the edge of the lake because there was a coal mine nearby, and the road was often lined with creaky, overloaded blue dump trucks that created a sooty dotted line between the mine and the plant. There were tractor-trailers, too, which barely fit on the road and struggled to make it up the inclines. So Martin was used to slow traffic to and from the course, but this wasn't the usual traffic jam. Something was wrong. When his truck finally crawled up to the scene of the accident, he cringed. There was a truck so mangled it was hardly recognizable. Another car had rolled down an embankment. For some reason, a pickup truck on the side of the road caught Martin's eye. There was a blanket or tarp laid out in the truck's bed, with something protruding from underneath it, hanging out over the open tailgate. Suddenly, Martin realized he was looking at a human leg. The image stuck with him for several days – as did the actual body.

"On my way to the job site the next morning, he was still there," Martin said. "Left the job site that evening, he was still there. He was there for three days on the back of that pickup truck."

It seemed things operated differently in China.

According to Arthur Yeo, the political climate surrounding golf was "pretty good" when Martin took the Kunming job. Modern China had around fifteen golf courses by this point, and it would be another decade before Beijing announced that building new golf courses was illegal. As Yeo put it, "nobody knew what golf was about" in China. And in many ways, nobody knew what China was about, either.

Yeo said Spring City's developer, Straits Steamship Land Limited (now known as Keppel Land), insisted on the course being legal. "Being a Singapore publicly listed company, we don't take risks," he said. "But it wasn't easy. Nothing is easy in China. It took us a while to get it." Yeo maintained that Spring City was legal in the eyes of Beijing, meaning its business license specifically mentioned the word "golf." This is a status perhaps only a dozen courses in China today can lay claim to, although you'd be hard pressed to find anyone working in China's golf industry who could list such super legit courses with any certainty. For what it was worth, the local Yiliang county government was quite open about its involvement in Spring City – it owned a 20 percent stake in the project.

As Spring City was winding down, Martin knew there was something he had to do before he left: watch an execution. It wasn't something he particularly wanted to do, but he felt obligated to do it all the same. The mayor of Yiliang county had been very persistent, and the county's support had been instrumental to the project.

Perhaps, Martin thought, the mayor wanted to introduce his new foreign friend to some local color that never got mentioned in the guidebooks. "He kept inviting me the whole freaking job," Martin said. It's estimated that China executes several thousand people per year, more than the rest of the world combined, and Yunnan province accounts for a good portion of those deaths due to its close proximity to Southeast Asia's Golden Triangle, a hotbed of heroin and opium production. Drug trafficking is a capital offense in China. "'Come on down and watch us execute a drug dealer.' He asked me at least twenty times during my year and a half at Spring City," Martin said.

They got drunk before they went out to watch the men die. Normally, Martin tried to avoid the mid-day drinkfests with local officials, but this was one liquid lunch he was happy to partake in; the beer and *baijiu* might dull his senses before the main event. He didn't realize it at the time, but in a way he was watching history. Death by firing squad had been China's modus operandi for executions since 1949, but starting in 1996 Yunnan province began experimenting with lethal injection as an alternative, and formally adopted it as its primary practice in 1997, even introducing mobile killing units called "execution vans." One of the stated rationales for the change was to lessen the spread of HIV from blood splatter.

That day, Martin didn't see much blood. He didn't see much of anything. He and the mayor stood gazing out onto an empty field, empty save for a single wooden stool located about half a football pitch from them. Five uniformed men holding rifles waited as a prisoner wearing what looked like a white pillowcase over his head was guided to the stool and lifted on to it. (Martin was thankful he couldn't see the man's face.) Then the execution happened: a thud of simultaneous rifle fire followed fast by the thud of a body hitting the earth. The dead man was carried off, and another live prisoner was placed on the stool. And it all happened again. Then it was time to go back to Spring City. "We all went back to work," Martin said. "I remember finishing up the day. It didn't seem to bother me that much at all."

There was little pomp and circumstance. It all seemed unusually routine. Still, Martin was sure the viewing was bestowed upon him as an honor. "He was a very nice guy," he said. "He was one of the reasons we didn't have any trouble."

But that was not to say everything at Spring City went smoothly. As Martin's first experience dealing with Chinese contractors, it was "an eye-opener." "It was like, *Jesus*," Martin said. "Just contractors lying to you. Lying and cheating and trying to cut every corner and, you know, just doing poor work. If you rode them hard, they'd try to backstab you. It was tough."

For the most part, they weren't contractors Martin had chosen as project manager. They weren't contractors he could replace, either. It was all pre-ordained through back-room handshakes and side deals that happened long before Martin arrived on the scene. "They'll flat out tell you, 'We've already chosen the dirt contractor. It's a government company,'" Martin said. "It happens a lot. It's black and white." Occasionally a contractor seems to have a stranglehold on local business. Or maybe somebody's cousin runs the state-owned firm. Sometimes it's clear that certain permits or approvals are granted more swiftly to a specific contractor.

In golf course construction, "dirt contractors" play an important role. They're the initial earth movers. They do the bulk grading, the cut and fill. They dig out the lakes and build the hills. If they don't do their job well, it slows the whole project down. "Usually they're absolutely horrible," Martin said of the Chinese crews. In Kunming, he realized, "you can't tell them what to do – and you're told that. They're a government company. They hire us as the management company, but good luck managing that."

Martin learned rather quickly that much would be beyond his control, and that there were local rules he'd need to navigate around. Like, for example, the unofficial toll stops that would often delay truck deliveries. In China, golf courses are commonly thought to be magnets for local business development. What they don't say is how much of that business is outside the scope of the project itself. Everyone wants a piece of the action, a fact Martin observed one day as he pondered why a large shipment of sand had yet to arrive on site. He heard the contractor's trucks were not too far down the road, held up by the local cops. The trucks were forced to stop and negotiate for a permit to display in their windows to be allowed to complete their deliveries. Otherwise, deliveries would stop until the police moved on. "There were times when the deliveries would go good for a month and then, suddenly, they would stop again," Martin said. "Well, the trucks got stopped by the police again." And they'd have to wait for the roadblocks to be cleared.

It reminded Martin of Thailand, where, before major holidays, or any other time of the year when the police were running low on money, they'd set up random roadblocks that most people knew to be a kind of forced donation line. Martin learned to stay silent and keep his passport hidden. Back in Thailand, he'd just roll down his window, hand over five hundred baht and go on his way, no questions asked.

Martin longed for the simplicity of Thailand.

Unlike at Fengjing, when Zhou Xunshu arrived at Guangzhou International Golf Club, the course was finished. There were bunkers instead of bulldozers, and more grass than Zhou had seen in his life. His first day there, Zhou inspected every corner of the course. He found the green hills and lush lawns calming, and for the first time in months he thought of Qixin, with an unusual sense of nostalgia. "It felt like I was grazing my cows in the village," he recalled.

Zhou's early days at Guangzhou International were carefree. For a short time, he was a man unburdened by aspiration or expectation, unencumbered by any knowledge of golf whatsoever. When a colleague brought a camera to work and suggested he and Zhou take photographs on the golf course, Zhou did what came naturally to him: in his khakis, black loafers and a bright yellow "Marlboro" windbreaker, he acted out maneuvers he had learned in his *wushu* training. At a tee box, he chose a "horse-riding" stance; near the main gate he did a "flying kick"; and in a sand trap he posed as "golden rooster standing on one leg," raising the bunker rake like a weapon. "Those photos of him doing *kung fu* moves on the golf course make me laugh," said Zhou's wife Liu Yan, years later. "He's so thin, and he has hair! It seems he lived a happy life back then. Happier than now."

When Guangzhou International opened, it was one of the most exclusive clubs in the region. Memberships sold for 240,000 yuan ($28,500) – more than a poor peasant boy from rural Guizhou could fathom – and mostly businessmen from Hong Kong and Taiwan snatched them up. In a way, Zhou already felt as though he had "made it," though he was only twenty-three. He was earning more money than anyone he knew back in Guizhou; his "office" was the most beautiful place he'd ever seen. Every day, though club rules didn't allow him to interact with the clientele, there he was, standing in close proximity to men worth millions of yuan – men worth more than everyone in Qixin, probably worth more than a dozen or so neighboring villages, combined.

The course was one of the area's nicest, designed by the international firm Nelson & Haworth. But it was emblematic of the Guangzhou boom, an island of luxury surrounded by industry. Guangzhou International was sixty miles east of the city, in Xiancun town, part of greater Zengcheng city, which was home to mainland China's heaviest concentration of cement factories – and, according to some, the worst air quality in all of Guangdong province. There were hundreds of factories in the area, each spewing a noxious mixture of smoke and cement powder from their redbrick kilns. After playing eighteen holes, golfers would sometimes return to the clubhouse looking like ghosts, their bodies coated in gray dust.

Zhou didn't care about a little cement dust. He was taken with his new surroundings. He called back home to inform friends and relatives of the fascinating new world he had discovered. "You must come," he said. One of Zhou's brothers did a stint working in the club's cafeteria. Eventually Zhou's security force was composed entirely of Guizhou exiles. Lu Zhan, a classmate from police school, was one of them. Lu's career move was a lateral one – he left a security guard job for the one at Guangzhou International – but he saw it as a step up. "Even though there weren't many golf courses," Lu said, "we all knew golf as a noble sport – a game for rich men. We all felt that by just being in that environment, we had already raised our social standing."

Soon, just being in the environment wasn't enough for Zhou. He was drawn to the game, and desperately wanted to be part of the action. This had nothing to do with money or fame – the concept of "pro golfer," which had existed as an official vocation in China for less than two years, was still unknown to him. Instead, he wanted the challenge. Zhou had always been athletic – he grew up playing basketball on a dirt court in his village – and he was fiercely competitive. He wanted to give this golf thing a try. But he couldn't: security guards were forbidden to play.

It's not uncommon for people from mainland China to speak openly about their distrust of the Taiwanese. Taiwan, the orthodox line goes, is a breakaway province, and the Taiwanese are traitors. This is what many are raised to believe, even if they've never actually encountered someone from Taiwan. Zhou thought differently. Sure, he held an irrational hatred of all people from Taiwan, but for Zhou it wasn't political. It was personal. The one Taiwanese person he'd met in all his life – the general manager at Guangzhou International – was the only thing standing between him and golf.

Guangzhou International was a private club with a wealthy clientele, and keeping up appearances was important. Thus, the club's manager made it a rule that non-managerial staff were not allowed to play the game or even use the driving range. Zhou, despite overseeing a large portion of the security force, was not officially a manager, and the rule proved torturous for him. One of Zhou's duties was following playing groups around the course, and reporting their whereabouts back to the clubhouse via walkie-talkie. He studied the golfers carefully. The shapes their bodies made when they hit the ball. The way they dressed. The way they interacted. The strange etiquette of it all. He was fascinated. The more Zhou watched, the more he appreciated the nuances of the game. This was more than grown men hitting a white ball into a hole in the ground, more than trying to see who can make the ball go the farthest. There was strategy, and Zhou appreciated this. He started taking note when golfers reached into their bags to select a different club, and used his binoculars to try and make out the number printed on the bottom. He didn't quite understand what it meant, but he knew it must be important.

Zhou spent his days watching other people play the game. "I loved it crazily," he said. "I even dreamed of hitting balls in my sleep." Often, his dreams were so vivid he could feel the softness of the fairway grass beneath his feet, the texture of the club's rubber grip in his hands. Backswings gave him goosebumps, and the moment of impact – when clubface and ball would collide – was an explosion of excitement he could feel move from his fingertips to his arms to a place deep in his chest cavity. The elation would often jolt him awake. He'd sit up in bed, out of breath and sweating. Then Zhou would spot his security guard uniform hanging in the dormitory window. He'd see the cement floor and walls, the mosquito nets, the three roommates asleep nearby, the metal fan that did little more than move hot air around the room. He'd lie back down and close his eyes, hoping to be transported once again to a world where he was allowed to play.

"It was like having a delicious piece of meat in your mouth, but not being able to eat it," Zhou said. "So bad."

For two long years, Zhou walked and watched, hoping one day he'd get a taste of the game that captivated him so. Then, in 1998, representatives from PING, an American golf club manufacturer, visited Guangzhou International. At the driving range, the PING reps, the club instructors and the club's executive team – led by the Taiwanese general manager – tested out some top-of-the-line drivers. Zhou, dressed in his security guard uniform, looked on as the men tried to hit the ball over a tree-covered hill about fifty yards behind the yardage marker that read "225." A small crowd had formed, including Zhou's immediate boss, Wang Shiwen, a serious-faced but friendly northeasterner. Nobody could clear the trees. Not even the Taiwanese GM, who often boasted about his credentials as a professional golfer.

Then, a voice from the distance. It was Zhou.

"Leader," he said, addressing Wang. "Can I have a try?"

Several in the group responded by laughing. *The security guard wants to take a swing?* The general manager teased Zhou: "This is a really expensive club," he said in a sarcastic, sing-songy tone usually reserved for children. "If you break it, can you afford to pay three thousand yuan on your salary?" Everybody in the crowd knew the answer to this question, especially Zhou, who worked the numbers over in his head: it'd take him a quarter of a year to earn the value of the club.

Wang knew of Zhou's desire to golf. "If he breaks it, I'll buy it," he jumped in. "Give the boy a try." Based on Wang's tone, this was not a request; it was an order.

Years later, Wang would admit his actions that day were fueled in part by nationalistic pride. "At that time, for people like us, people from the mainland who worked at golf courses but didn't have lots of money, it was rare to see such a good club," Wang explained. "And if we did see one, no one would let us play with it. Usually we only played with old discarded or reassembled clubs."

Zhou was a fixture at the driving range. Whenever he had free time, he'd carefully watch the instructors as they practiced. But Zhou had never hit a ball before. He was very much a novice, a greenhorn. And now he was going to take his first swings of a driver in front of a crowd? A snickering, unforgiving crowd? This was a gamble, to be sure. There was little chance that anyone would be losing three thousand yuan – something would have to go horribly wrong for Zhou to actually damage the club – but a loss of face seemed guaranteed.

This did not deter Zhou, who was just ignorant enough about golf to fail to understand how substantially the odds were stacked against him. Vegas would have had him a long shot even to make contact. But Zhou, seeing this as his only chance, stepped forward. He removed his hat. He removed his tie. He loosened the collar of his white button-down shirt. He took the three-thousand-yuan club in his hands, which were shaking.

Zhou's world became distorted. Everything seemed so much bigger now. The driver was massive and unwieldy. The 225-yard marker was barely legible, it was so far away. The tree-lined hill seemed like a distant village, and the crowd surrounding him now numbered in the thousands. Everything was huge! Everything, that is, but the ball. The ball was a white speck of dust on the green mat beneath Zhou's wobbly legs. How could he possible hit *that*?

"Come on, security guard, what are you waiting for?" the general manager taunted.

Zhou blinked repeatedly, trying to bring his world back into focus. He took a deep breath and settled himself the best he could. He lined up his shot, and swung.

Whiff.

Zhou missed the ball completely. He heard chuckles in the crowd. But he picked the ball up and carefully placed it back on the rubber tee. He swung again.

Whiff.

More laughter. Zhou felt his face go flush. The hill was no longer the goal. Contact. *Just make contact*, Zhou told himself. Again, he lined up the ball.

Whiff.

Baseball was another sport Zhou was unfamiliar with, so three strikes didn't mean he was out. Although some in the crowd said they had seen enough, Zhou wasn't going to leave unless someone forced the club from his hands. He had waited so long for this chance. He had to at least hit the ball. He couldn't let Wang down.

Zhou called on his *wushu* training, one of the only things he remembered from his short stint at military police school. He focused on his *yi*, or intention, remembering something his instructor had said: *It is the thought which guides the movement.* He blocked out the crowd from his mind. Blocked out the jeers, the yardage markers, the hill and the trees. He focused only on the small white target. He just wanted to hit the ball. He stared at it with so much intensity his entire field of vision became white and dimpled. He saw nothing but the ball.

Zhou raised the driver and swung. At the bottom of his motion, he heard a pop. Suddenly, Zhou felt as though he had been transported to one of his dreams. His hands tingled. His body filled with warmth. He wasn't exactly sure what had happened – but he knew he wanted to feel this again.

At first there was silence. Followed by a gasp or two. Then cheers. Any laughs were now those of disbelief. The security guard had done it. He had hit the ball. Long. Straight. And over the trees. No one, including Zhou – who stood there, dumbfounded, his hands still welded to his three-thousand-yuan weapon – could believe it.

"I was happy, and I was proud," Wang recalled, nearly a decade later. "I was right about choosing him. But none of that matters. The most important thing is that he hit the ball over the hill! He had so much explosive force. To hit the ball past the trees on the hill, more than 280 yards – I've worked at the course for ten years and I've only seen three to five people do that."

Some in the crowd thought it was just dumb luck. That's what the general manager from Taiwan said. He told Zhou he'd never be able to do it again.

"I didn't dare take another swing," Zhou said. "To be honest, I was scared I'd have to pay for the club. It was much too expensive for me."

Zhou retrieved his hat and his tie and floated all the way back to the workers' dormitory. He sat on his metal bunk bed, his body still trembling.

"That was the moment I started thinking that, if I worked hard, maybe one day I could become good at golf," Zhou said.

But there remained one problem: Zhou was still forbidden to play. He was determined not to let that stop him, however. He had caught a fever.

He started building up an arsenal, scouring the course's wooded areas for lost balls, collecting broken clubs discarded by members. He dragged a worn-out driving range mat back to the workers' dormitory, where there was a narrow swath of grass just outside Zhou's ground-floor window. It was a secluded area. On one side was the faded green wall of the dorm, on the other was a wall of thick tropical trees and foliage. Beyond that, well, that was no longer the club's property. In his free time, Zhou would steal back there with his mat, his balls and some clubs he'd repaired. He'd spend hours chipping and pitching in that constricted space, the fear of losing balls and breaking windows teaching him to drive the ball straight. This, of course, did not always happen – especially early on – and Zhou worked out an arrangement with the maintenance staff: He'd fix any windows he broke, in exchange for their silence.

At night, Zhou would hop out of his dormitory window and sneak over to a practice green with just a ball – no putter. Under the moonlight, he'd roll the ball, again and again, and study how it moved atop the curves of the closely cropped grass. He read any golf book he could get his hands on, and watched golf videos (John Daly's *Grip It and Rip It*, to name one) in the driving range office when he was off duty. He may never have been a good student, but Zhou taught himself golf.

He took every opportunity to watch the golf instructors as they practiced at the driving range. He'd scrutinize their mechanics carefully, and then race back behind the dormitory and try to mimic them. On Monday evenings, club managers gathered at the driving range to drink beers and hit a few balls. Zhou, while not a manager, would often tag along, like a dog waiting for scraps of food to fall from the dinner table.

"He always went with me, and he always asked me to let him have a try," Wang said. "I knew it disobeyed the rule, but I'd let him take several swings. At first I did not really see his talent – I only knew he had explosive power and could hit the ball very far."

Even then, Zhou had a very compact, aggressive swing. Much of his power came from his strong legs, which he'd bend in an exaggerated fashion. This unique stance wasn't something Zhou had picked up from a book or a video. It was a technique borne of necessity – many of the second-hand clubs he was using were much too short for him. He also swung with a certain amount of anger and resentment. He hated that other staff members were allowed to play golf, yet he had to practice in secret. During his infrequent opportunities to hit balls at the driving range, Zhou would picture the Taiwanese manager and swing with fury.

"I still didn't know what a professional golfer was at that time, but everything about it was so interesting to me," Zhou recalled. "The leaders sometimes played videos showing a guy called Tiger Woods. I said, 'Wow! Look at the atmosphere.' So many people watching. I wanted to be under the spotlight like Tiger Woods. I knew I couldn't reach his level, but I wanted to attend my own tournaments. I wanted to have that feeling."

In early 2001, when Zhou returned home to Qixin for the first time in more than five years, he brought back ten golf balls, and the villagers looked at the strange foreign spheres with wonderment and curiosity. His mother bounced one, and everybody clapped. Then some neighborhood children took the balls, and they played with them like marbles. Zhou figured he'd choose another time to explain his new dream to his family.

Martin Moore's team had put the finishing touches to the Mountain Course at Spring City in December 1996. The driving range and clubhouse were completed the following year, and in November 1998, Spring City celebrated its official grand opening, with leaders of the Yunnan provincial government and the prime minister of Singapore in attendance. Construction on the club's Lake Course, designed by Robert Trent Jones, Jr., began that same month. In 1999, *Golf Digest* magazine named the Mountain Course the No. 1 golf course in China and Hong Kong.

It was a nice thing for Martin to be able to put on his resumé, but by that point Spring City, and China to some extent, were already in his rearview mirror. Throughout the '90s, China had remained a mystery to most Westerners in the golf scene. "It just wasn't on people's radar," Martin recalled. "Nicklaus was actually very active then, but there were definitely a lot of people in the industry that wouldn't have a clue." After Spring City, Thailand and the Philippines were still seen as the boom markets, and Martin was fully on board to go back where things were easier.

He got jobs in both countries managing projects for Paragon Construction International, part of the mighty Nicklaus empire, for what promised to be a steady flow of work. But that came to a crashing halt with the Asian financial crisis of 1997. As Martin put it, "the whole shit hit the fan."

When the crisis hit, Martin was working on a Greg Norman course in the Philippines. The peso plummeted from 26 to the US dollar to 41. "We stopped getting paid by the client, and it just really fell apart," he said. Nicklaus shut down operations in the Philippines in 1998 and laid off everyone there, except for Martin. They offered him a gig in Mexico, but he balked at the opportunity – if he was going to move that close to home, he might as well *go home*, was his thinking. He had spent nearly a decade in Asia. He had met his wife in Thailand. They now had two sons. His eldest boy was almost old enough for school. It seemed like a good time to move the family to the United States. There'd always be golf courses to build there, he thought. And at that time, he seemed to be right – more than 750 new courses would open between 1999 and 2000, the biggest golf construction boom in history.

In August 1998, Martin, his wife and his two sons moved to Gulfport, Mississippi, where Martin took a job as an independent shaper on a Nicklaus course while he figured out his next move. He began talking to two American golf course designers about a possible business opportunity. Lee Schmidt, who Martin had met in Thailand while they both worked for Jack Nicklaus, and Brian Curley, who at the time was president of golf design at Landmark Golf Company in Indian Wells, California, had worked together at Landmark in the '80s, and in 1997 they decided to join forces once again. Their partnership would eventually be known as Schmidt-Curley Design. They were looking to form a golf course construction firm that would focus solely on their designs, and Martin was the first person they reached out to. "I jumped all over that," Martin said. "I was shaping all day, and opening this company all night."

The trio formed Flagstick Golf Course Construction Management, and landed their first project in late 1998, in Indio, California (then called the Landmark Golf Club – today it's called

The Golf Club at Terra Lago). Within a year, the course was open and playing host to the 1999 Skins Game between Fred Couples, David Duval, Sergio Garcia and Mark O'Meara. Over the next few years, Martin, along with Schmidt and Curley, worked on a dozen or so courses in the American Southwest.

They thought this could be the start of something big. They had no idea just how big it was about to get.

Despite all of his stealthy preparations, Zhou Xunshu wasn't able to start playing golf regularly for years. Things began to look up in April 2001, five years after he had arrived at Guangzhou International, when the Taiwanese manager left the club. The rules changed, and after hundreds of clandestine practices, Zhou could finally see how his skills translated to an actual golf course. It was like a dream. But it only lasted three months.

"It was my fault," Wang Shiwen, Zhou's boss, said. "I made a mistake when I was playing on the course. I teed off too soon at hole No. 9. It didn't hit the members playing in front of me, but it scared them. The course punished me and the whole security department. Banned us from playing."

Bans like this would happen with annoying frequency. They could last anywhere from a couple of months to a half a year. And Zhou became extremely frustrated. "He was very depressed," said Lu Zhan, Zhou's old friend and roommate. "By then, his goal was to be a pro golfer. We talked about that a lot."

During one such low point, Zhou rounded up some shafts from broken clubs and fashioned his own set of practice drivers. To make the club heads, he'd cut water bottles in half, fill the bottoms with a concoction of cement, water and soil, and then stick the shafts in the mixture until it dried. To further bind the shaft with the cement head, he wrapped the joint with iron wire. Zhou was afraid of being laughed at, so at night he'd carry his weighted Frankenstein club up a metal staircase to the dormitory roof. "I wouldn't go to sleep without practicing a hundred swings," he said.

In autumn 2001, Zhou received his first partial set of proper golf clubs, after he'd led the security department to victory in the club's interdepartmental basketball tournament. As a prize, Frank Lin, the Singaporean who had hired Zhou in 1996, offered Zhou a barely used set of MacGregor clubs he'd originally purchased for his wife. He told Zhou he could have them for whatever price he wanted. Zhou was too proud to take the clubs for free, so he offered eight hundred yuan, more than half his monthly salary.

"I cherished those clubs," Zhou said. "I used to watch the instructors clean their clubs with a special foam. It made them so shiny. I didn't have access to that foam back at the dorm, so I used a toothbrush and soap. And then I polished them with a rag. I did this almost every day."

At this point, he was allowed to play on the course twice a month. He considered this unacceptable. How could he become a pro golfer by playing only a couple of dozen times a year? He approached his bosses with a proposal. He'd work without pay in exchange for free access to the course. His younger brother, who was working as a cook at a nearby construction site, had offered to pay Zhou's daily expenses, which were minimal. Zhou said he'd do any type of job they wanted – caddie, gather balls at the driving range, clean them – all he wanted to do was golf. He made the offer twice. Twice he was turned down.

In spring 2002, Zhou approached Wang with an ultimatum: *Let me play, or fire me.* Wang had always liked Zhou. He admired his determination and realized, although he was very good at his job, Zhou had little interest in being a security guard for the rest of his life. "Okay," Wang said to Zhou. "This is what we are going to do. But you have to promise not to tell anyone."

Zhou started working the night shift. Every morning after his shift, at 6:30 a.m., before most of the customers would arrive, Wang and Zhou would play a round. Because they didn't use caddies to carry their bags, it was obvious Wang and Zhou weren't members, so they had to sneak around the course like cat burglars. Wang was risking his job with the arrangement.

"Sometimes, if someone was coming, I'd have to go hide in the bushes," Zhou said. "And before each swing, I'd have to look around to make sure nobody was looking. If the coast was clear, I'd swing quickly and race after the ball." After a year of racing around the course like this, he was hitting in the 70s.

"He made great progress," Wang said. "At that time, we were developing lots of players, including some teams, and they were all jealous of Zhou's fast improvement."

Zhou started playing in amateur tournaments, putting even more strain on his work schedule. Lu often covered for him. "We are like brothers, so I'd do anything to support him," Lu said. "We all hoped he could achieve something. Most of us had the same dream he had. But he was a little bit crazier than us, and he was also more talented. He was our hope."

But something always got in the way. In April 2003 it was local peasants. The club's tee boxes were marked with decorative metal golf balls, oversized and painted in a variety of colors. They were about the size of grapefruits and stuck into the turf with metal spikes. Late one night, a group of local farmers sneaked onto the course and stole the tee markers to sell as scrap metal. The entire security team was blamed, and Zhou was banned from golfing. He was crushed.

He again offered to work for free. "Just let me golf," he pleaded.

No.

"I can't live without golf. Leader, please reconsider."

No.

"If I can't golf, I'll have to quit."

Are you sure?

"Yes. This time, yes. Either I golf or I quit."

Then quit.

After seven years at Guangzhou International, that's exactly what Zhou did.

3

KEEP MOVING

Martin Moore was confused. He was back in China, in the thick of the most ambitious golf course construction project in history, and trying to figure out what the rush was. He had already assembled the largest team ever for a single golf construction job. He had already come up with the most aggressive schedule anyone in the industry had ever heard of. But it never seemed to be enough for David Chu and his son Ken, the men behind the massive Mission Hills golf complex near the southern city of Shenzhen. They were always pushing him to move faster, *faster, FASTER*. Martin knew every detail about the project – right down to each bulldozer and every grain of sand – but he couldn't help but feel there was a lot of information beyond his grasp. Why the unreasonable deadline? Why all the secrecy? Why the late night meetings and sleepless nights? It was as if the Chus knew something no one else did.

When Martin first learned of the job from his business partner Brian Curley he was intrigued, but he was also taken aback. Not only did Mission Hills Vice Chairman Ken Chu want to build five courses simultaneously, he also wanted them to be built in one year. Nothing like that had ever been done before. Not even close.

"I thought it was unbelievable," Martin said. "I mean, just to build five courses at one time, and then to say you're doing them in one year? Unbelievable."

Mission Hills already had five courses, which were built over a much more manageable nine-year period that started in 1992. For the second batch of five, Martin initially put together an eighteen-month plan for Chu, and he thought that was still a tad unrealistic. He explained to Chu that while building five courses simultaneously, especially under such strict time constraints, would normally be next to impossible, building one course in a year-and-a-half is a realistic goal. So, the only way they would be able to turn Chu's vision into reality would be to treat the five courses as separate projects. Five different teams building five different courses that happened to be part of the same golf club. Martin presented Chu with a spreadsheet listing the roster of talent he thought would be necessary to get the job done – it was the longest such list he'd ever seen in his life. Dozens upon dozens of names, representing much of the world's golf course construction industry. The cost would be colossal.

"Confirmed!" was all Chu had to say. "But I need it done in one year."

Martin still thought it was implausible. But he didn't know "Mission Hills' style" yet. And he certainly didn't know what to expect from the twenty-nine-year-old Ken Chu. Martin told Chu that the ball was in his court. There were approximately forty million cubic yards (thirty million cubic meters) of dirt that needed moving before Martin's guys could get started.

"When the contractor pulls out three hundred dump trucks and sixty excavators, you can get anything done," Martin said. "They're working twenty hours a day."

Martin had always held up what his team did with Landmark Golf Club in Indio, California, as a benchmark. They broke ground on the thirty-six-hole layout in December, and finished construction in nine-and-a-half months. By the following November, the course hosted a nationally televised tournament. That feat was beginning to look like child's play compared to what he was witnessing at Mission Hills.

"Probably three or four months into it, it's like, 'Wow,'" Martin said. "That's when I started to become a little bit of a believer in it." Chu could not be stopped.

At a press conference in November 2002, Mission Hills announced its plans to expand from five to ten courses, a move the club claimed would vault it past North Carolina's fabled Pinehurst Golf Resort – where eight courses were built over more than a century – as the largest golf resort in the world. A few months after the press conference, in early 2003, the Mission Hills website stated: "Pinehurst, currently the largest golf club of the world, will soon be replaced by Mission Hills, the only private golf club in the world to own 180 holes. Mission Hills has made a name of itself in the world of golf and has created its own legend."

Indeed, there is a little legend (and perhaps some myth) behind Mission Hills' story. The tale starts with Hong Kong entrepreneur David Chu, who is commonly credited as the mastermind behind the operation. By most accounts, he was a self-made man. He owned a successful cardboard packaging factory in Hong Kong and, according to family members, began operating in mainland China even before Deng Xiaoping's economic reforms, which kicked off in late 1978. Many say it was during these early years operating in Guangdong province that Chu learned the rules of *guanxi*, or connections, that determine who is able to do business in China, and who is not. No one would take the word of a stranger, but the word of a friend or relative of a Party official – that was another matter entirely.

In the 1980s, David Chu had decided to move his family to Toronto, buying a house in a golf community, Glendale Golf and Country Club, despite having little interest in the game. But something about the experience must have clicked with him, because by the end of the decade he was itching to build a golf community of his own, less than an hour north of Hong Kong in the Chinese city of Shenzhen, which in 1980 was named China's first "special economic zone" with lenient free-market-style policies designed to attract foreign investment. "Back in the early nineties, prior to China taking over Hong Kong in 1997, Deng Xiaoping wanted to expedite Shenzhen's development," Ken Chu explained. Shenzhen was seen as the "first door to Hong Kong" – the place where East and West would meet. Traditionally, associates in China would congregate with karaoke, or "do business [at] the mah-jongg table," Ken said, and the new wave of investors arriving in Hong Kong, and even the special economic zone, didn't fit comfortably into either setting. In Toronto, David Chu had seen how business-men used golf as a networking tool, and although only a handful of people on the mainland played golf, he figured it was only a matter of time before the practice would become commonplace. *Guanxi* and golf seemed like a perfect fit. But land in Hong Kong was scarce. Shenzhen was the ideal location for his golf venture, within reasonable driving distance for 150 million or so people, including wealthy Hong Kongers.

Mission Hills occupies a large swath of mountainous woodland in Guangdong province that spills over into Shenzhen and another major manufacturing city, Dongguan. The entire sprawling complex takes up 4,950 acres, nearly six times the size of New York City's Central Park. The resort even has its own public transportation system, with a bus system shuttling members, guests and employees from one side to another.

When David Chu identified the tract of land that would become the home of his golf empire, many were highly skeptical. "Yeah, today everyone compliments us as visionaries, but back then people thought we were crazy," said Ken, years later, who was just a teenager when his father purchased the remote expanse in one of the poorest parts of Guangdong. "I also thought it was crazy. Why choose this land? It's so underdeveloped. You hardly see people on the street, even in nearby Guanlan town. There were less than ten thousand people in the town back then." And none of them played golf.

Indeed, that posed a big problem for the site – there were no major roads connecting Mission Hills with… anything. "Shenzhen city to here used to take four hours," Ken remembered. "Back then, in the early nineties, it was all bicycles. Definitely, we had really hard times in the earlier days. I mean, as low as a hundred players per month." Ken crammed four years of study into two at Western Ontario University so he could race back to Hong Kong to help his father steer the fledgling golf club.

The Chus said the club's growth was organic. "We built as the demand grew," Ken recalled. "We did not build it for the ego. Purely for the market demand." But he also doesn't shy away from saying that Mission Hills played a large role in driving that demand. The family likes to claim that the number of golfers in China doubled after the World Cup of Golf was played at Mission Hills in 1995, and that the number doubled yet again after they brought Tiger Woods to China in 2001.

Tiger's first trip to China, back when he was just twenty-five and coming off his second win at the Masters, almost didn't happen. It was scheduled just two months after the 9/11 terrorist attacks, and security concerns had already forced the cancellation of an Evander Holyfield–John Ruiz boxing match scheduled for Beijing in late November. It was determined, however, that China at that time was just about the safest place in the world to be. So the show went on, much to the relief of the Chus, who had been planning the spectacle for nearly eighteen months.

The weekend event, scheduled to coincide with the announcement of China's ascension into the World Trade Organization, was intended to stimulate the growth of golf in a country barely aware of the sport's existence. "We wanted to spark interest in the game, especially among junior golfers," explained John Cappo, former managing director of China operations for IMG Golf, one of the event's organizers. "It was our belief that to do that, you must first create major golf events in China, so people have something to aspire to."

On the first day, Tiger held a clinic for a few dozen local golfers and played in an exhibition stroke-play match against four of the top pros from mainland China, Hong Kong and Taiwan. The following day, he played another round, this time paired with a different group of amateurs at each hole.

It proved to be a hot ticket – and a pricey one. Entry was around $130 per day, and while it's unclear how many of the 100,000 or so attendees (estimates vary greatly) actually paid face value, local news reports called the exhibition the most expensive sporting event in Chinese history.

Tiger received some $2 million for his time, and paid $500,000 in local Chinese taxes, according to media reports. The following year, it was widely reported he was the top taxpayer in Shenzhen for 2001. Many thought the statistic was more a commentary on the rampant tax evasion among wealthy Chinese, than on the size of Tiger's paycheck.

To be sure, Tiger was not the only person at Mission Hills that weekend with deep pockets. Well-heeled amateurs paid as much as $80,000 to play a single hole with the world's best golfer. Wealthy parents paid anywhere from $30,000 to $50,000 per hole to give their children a chance to go toe-to-toe with Tiger. And Duan Yongping, chairman of Guangdong-based BBK Electronics, signed his company on as title sponsor of the event with the stipulation he could golf all eighteen holes with the superstar. (Five years later, Duan would make headlines for spending $620,100 to have lunch with Warren Buffet.)

There were distractions galore for anyone carrying a golf club. Mission Hills was a madhouse. Traffic was backed up for miles on the highway leading to the golf club. Parking lots were overflowing, and hundreds of ticket holders raced to the venue on foot.

The scene inside was just as crazy. Golf in China was only seventeen years old at the time, and golf etiquette was just as foreign as the game itself. Spectators barreled through bunkers. Kids rolled down hills and played in the sand. If people weren't snapping photographs, they were shouting into their mobile phones. Organizers made repeated announcements pleading with the fans to settle down: You don't want to embarrass China, they said.

This was all part of the Mission Hills legend. But there are other aspects of the company's story that are rarely discussed. There is the scandal from 2002, when, according to the *South China Morning Post*, an investor called Harry Lam Hon-lit was "executed" just two days before a "hearing of a multi-million-dollar legal dispute between Lam's Digger Holdings and the Mission Hills Golf Club in Shenzhen." Lam was killed "gangland-style," according to the AP's report, with a single shot to the head as he took his breakfast at his usual teahouse in central Hong Kong. He had recently filed a request to stop construction at Missions Hills, citing a fight over the valuation of his shares in the development. It was very bad timing. The Chus found themselves fielding calls from reporters, and with the legal case still moving forward, chose to make no detailed public comments. Rumors spread that the killers were linked to the People's Liberation Army, or a *kung fu* movie actor-turned-tycoon. Eventually, six people were convicted – including the tycoon – but no motive was ever established for the murder.

Other omissions are less sensational. Nowhere in the official Mission Hills history will you learn about the club's Thailand connections, or its two additional founding partners, men who appeared to be just as integral, if not more, to launching the club as David Chu was. They've been erased from the official record. For instance, a *South China Morning Post* story from early 1993 says it was Elmer Yuen, described as a Shanghainese man "who made his money from a digital electronics business in Hong Kong," who acquired two thousand acres of land near Guanlan town in 1992 with the goal of creating the "best suburb of Shenzhen." Yuen told the paper he estimated an investment of $700 million would be necessary to develop the golf course and luxury housing development.

The story mentioned Yuen's successful golf venture in Thailand, Mission Hills Golf Club in Kanchanaburi, which opened in 1991 with a Jack Nicklaus-designed track "touted as one of the best courses in the country." Thailand is where the third piece of the Mission Hills puzzle resided, a former Hong Kong boarding school classmate of Yuen's who is credited with convincing him that "golf was synonymous with riches." That man, the other original partner, was a wiry Thai-Chinese tycoon with sunken cheeks and a temper: Suraphan Ngamjitsuksri.

In fact, David Chu gets third billing in the story. A 2001 court document related to Yuen's divorce from his second wife, on the other hand, paints a different picture. It states that the Mission Hills development in China was Chu's idea, and suggests the trio's initial investment totaled ten million dollars, with 55 percent to come from Chu, 30 percent from Suraphan and 15 percent from Yuen. The document also mentions that "relations between the partners were becoming strained" by the end of 1994. The reasons for this were partly due to "a dispute over the timing of the sale of properties built at Mission Hills, but also because the project had cash flow problems." (Harry Lam Hon-lit allegedly held 3 percent at the time of his murder – or so he was claiming to the court.)

Given the order in which the Thailand and China Mission Hills projects opened, even the origin of the club's name is up for debate. Ken Chu maintains it was inspired by the Shenzhen property itself. "We had a vision, we had a mission, and then there's lots of hills," he offered. "We pasted that together." Whether spawned in China or Thailand, many in the golf industry always assumed the name was inspired by, if not outright copied from, well-known golf courses in the United States. There's Mission Hills Country Club, founded in 1926, in Northbrook, Illinois, a suburb of Chicago. And then there's another unrelated Mission Hills Country Club in Rancho Mirage, California, that since 1983 has been home to the Kraft Nabisco Championship, one of the five annual major tournaments in women's professional golf.

It's not uncommon for Chinese clubs to borrow the names of well-known golf courses from the West. For example, China has its own Pebble Beach and Pine Valley – but Ken says his club's familiar name was a coincidence. "Back in the early 1990s, internet was inaccessible," he said. "We did not even know that club [in California] existed."

Still, it's clear the Mission Hills name and logo were in use in Thailand years before the brand ever landed in China. Indeed, Martin Moore had helped build one of the original Mission Hills courses for Suraphan in Thailand – Mission Hills Khao Yai, his first job in Asia.

Martin recalled a day in 1992 in Thailand when Suraphan pulled him aside and said, "Martin, come have dinner with me tonight in our village home. I have some friends from Hong Kong I'd like you to meet." Elmer Yuen was the first person Martin was introduced to. The other man in attendance, Martin was told, owned a cardboard box factory in mainland China, just outside of Hong Kong. It was David Chu.

Martin's first impression of David Chu was unremarkable. He just seemed like a regular Chinese businessman. He didn't carry himself as though he had a lot of money – there was no hint he'd one day be one of the biggest golf developers in the world. In fact, it was clear to Martin that Suraphan was the driver of this particular train. Yuen and Chu appeared to occupy secondary roles.

"I want to build a Mission Hills in Shenzhen, China," Suraphan later confided in Martin. "With those two men you met last night."

He paused, then added, "Do you want to go to China?" He was trying to steal Martin away.

"I'm staying in Thailand," Martin said definitively.

The first course at Mission Hills Shenzhen, the World Cup Course, was a Nicklaus design, and many of the workers on the project reported that Suraphan was the one primarily calling the shots. But once the World Cup Course was complete, sources said, the trio began to butt heads – not difficult to believe with Suraphan in the mix. The Thai "enforcer" was forced out. The China operation got to keep the name and logo, and Suraphan, according to someone familiar with the deal, got "a boat load of cash."

Suraphan did manage to leave his imprint at Mission Hills Shenzhen, however. The original clubhouse there was designed by Suraphan's architect. In fact, it's almost an exact replica of the clubhouse at Mission Hills Khao Yai, the course Martin built for him.

Ken Chu acknowledged the existence of three original partners, but of Yuen and Suraphan he simply said, "They left." He added, "By 1994, when the club pretty much opened, they didn't have faith in this project." It's clear David Chu, now referred to by some as "the father of golf in China," was the last man standing. And that was all that mattered.

Ken Chu was attending the University of Western Ontario in Canada when the first course at Mission Hills opened, and was not yet thirty when they opened their fifth. By the time plans for the next batch of five came to pass, he wanted to make sure it was clear the torch had been passed. He wanted to be the guy calling the shots. Some onlookers felt Ken Chu thought he had something to prove, to his father and everyone else. The first five courses were built in nine years? Well, he was going to do the next five in one.

Ken was by far the most vocal and visible member of the Chu family during the project, but some suspected David Chu was still the mastermind behind the growing family business and that the desire to be the biggest and the best at everything started with him. It was rare to see David out on the work site during construction, however. Although he lived nearby and was bankrolling the project, he only showed up about once a month. Instead, Ken would meet with his father with daily updates. It was clear to Martin he was being groomed to take over the empire. "He would've been the most mature thirty-two-year-old you'd ever meet in your life," Martin said. "His father was polishing him early."

Ken Chu had a confidence and business savvy that belied his age. He was driven, photogenic, well spoken. He was always immaculately dressed, with a vast wardrobe of tailored suits, as well as luxury watches and designer eyeglasses matched to each ensemble. Even when he was just wearing trousers and a golf shirt at the job site he looked put together. When he walked into a meeting, he commanded – and frequently demanded – respect.

Ken was "a pusher," Martin said. He was the kind of guy who "expected eighteen hours a day from you." He was fond of calling last-minute, late-night meetings he'd routinely show up an hour late for. "I think he thrives on six white guys and ten other Chinese guys having to wait on him," another person familiar with the meetings said. It was not uncommon for him to arrive to these meetings in a designer suit. The rest of the guys, wearing shorts and T-shirts, would smile every time they caught him adjusting his tie in the mirror.

Ken mandated a record-breaking construction schedule that was difficult enough, but it was the mountainous terrain that really made things tough. Designer Brian Curley called it "one of the most brutal properties" he'd ever seen.

"Those sites, you couldn't even walk them," Curley said, noting the land's steep "up and down" slopes. "You've got to manhandle the property just to get it to something that resembles land that would tolerate golf. So you can argue that, sure, it was open space. Sure, it was covered in trees and all that, but now that we're done with it all, the thing is still open space and still covered with trees. It's just that you're playing golf through it."

Before-and-after photos of the property are hardly recognizable as the same location. Curley said it wasn't unusual "to find a mountain gone overnight." A massive team of laborers, using heavy machinery, moved thirty million cubic meters of earth in just eight months. Curley said the site often required dynamite blasts three times a day and that "it would rain rock for huge distances."

Martin recalled that Curley impressed Mission Hills with master-planning and "big picture stuff." Few architects could manage the mammoth challenges that came with working with a client like Ken Chu, where everything needed to be big – bigger than anything else in the world – and done yesterday. Curley was efficient, adaptable and fast as hell. "Brian will pull out a fucking napkin at lunchtime and route eighteen holes," Martin said. "If that guy would have given him a 'topo' right there on that table, Brian would've given him about two routing options during lunchtime. He's just got an eye for that."

Then Curley would go back to his office and have one of his assistants draw it up in color, complete with cart paths, roads and housing, and have it delivered to the potential client in twenty-four to forty-eight hours. Martin said Curley had been successful in China because of this approach. Other foreign designers might say, "We'll get that to you in thirty to forty-five days." Chinese businessmen don't want to wait that long. People who can turn around plans in a day or two have a decidedly upper hand. "In China, they want that shit, man," he said.

But Brian Curley's speed alone could not handle every obstacle Mother Nature threw their way. From May to September 2003, Martin's crew had to work through southern China's summer monsoon season and large amounts of rain. To make matters worse, the construction calendar also overlapped with the outbreak of the SARS epidemic. At least three people on the work site came down with the virus.

The Mission Hills mythology even goes so far as to credit SARS for helping the game gain traction in China. Ken Chu likes to tell the story that during the outbreak, golf courses, thanks to their fresh air and open spaces, replaced boardrooms as places where business deals went down. This, the Chus say, was just one more reason Mission Hills *needed* to expand.

Part of the plan was to have the five new courses designed by some of the biggest names in golf. The five original courses at Mission Hills had been attached to names like Jack Nicklaus, Vijay Singh, Jumbo Ozaki, Nick Faldo and Ernie Els. Those eighteen-hole layouts were completed over the course of nine years, a timeline that allowed for a good bit of back-and-forth between the big-name designers and Mission Hills regarding the look and feel of the course.

This was not the case with the following five courses, which had to be built in a fraction of the time. There was little way the celebrity designers would be able to have much input into the courses that would bear their names. And, for the most part, they didn't. Using his handy napkin as a start, Curley and his partner Schmidt routed and designed all ninety holes. Construction began even before the involvement of Annika Sörenstam, David Duval, David Leadbetter, Jose Maria Olazabal and Greg Norman was finalized. A few of the celebrities made some site visits and talked strategy with Curley. But others rarely even looked at the plans, only showing up for the grand opening and to pick up their check. Despite what the signposts read, these were all Schmidt-Curley designs – except for one.

David Chu insisted that Greg Norman be one of the names attached to a course, a move that threw the construction schedule somewhat of a curveball, because Norman was the sole designer to demand considerable say on the actual design of his course. Normally this wouldn't have been much of an issue, but the courses were nearly halfway complete by the time Norman got involved.

Norman, who was given first pick of the courses, sent his top designers to Mission Hills to scope out the property and determine which track deserved the Greg Norman name. Norman's team did not appear to be in a hurry, and their relaxed Down Under temperament did not mesh well with the project's manic timeframe. They spent a few days moseying around the place, but instead of making an immediate choice, said they had to go back to Australia to talk things over. The clock was ticking.

After several weeks, Norman's team made its choice: perhaps the most picturesque and challenging layout available, it snakes through steep ridges, severe hills and dense forests. They asked for some slight changes to the routing, and indicated that they would provide a new plan for grading the land (which, for the most part, had already been graded according to a different design). One month went by. Two months. Three months. In this building frenzy, it felt like an eternity.

When the grading plan eventually arrived, Mission Hills learned that Norman's team wanted the course to be as many as five meters lower than it currently was. That meant three million cubic meters of dirt had to find a new home. That's a lot of dirt, a whole golf course's worth. It was moved to a nearby layout, one bearing David Leadbetter's name. That course had to be completely reshaped to take on the dirt. Everyone was feeling the pressure.

Mission Hills was determined to avoid any more delays, and hoped there wouldn't be any last-minute changes coming from the course designers. So, after one of the final site visits by Norman's team, a construction crew was ready to pounce. It wasn't the typical golf course construction crew – it was the largest one ever assembled. Two thousand people were assigned to that one course, and they worked on it almost nonstop for two months straight. What would normally have taken months happened in mere days. Mission Hills was keeping to its deadline, no matter what came its way.

Twenty-one days later, grass was growing on the entire course. When Norman's team returned, they were amazed. They expected to see a landscape of dirt. Instead, all they saw was green.

The reasons behind the hurried timetable remained a mystery to almost everyone working on the project, and the niceties-be-damned approach to getting things done sometimes led to crossed wires. Midway through the project, Martin learned that a group of Mission Hills' security guards had started spying on his workers in a bizarre effort to make sure they were putting in enough time on the job. The guards kept logbooks, documenting the hours each person worked – or at least that is what they thought they were doing. One day a dumbfounded Martin got chewed out for not being organized, for having a lazy team. Martin had no idea what they were talking about, so out came the notebooks. It turned out none of the numbers in the books were accurate – the guards couldn't tell the Thai shapers apart. The worksite was hot and dusty, and the shapers often covered their faces with scarves. Even Martin, who had known the workers for years, had to yell, "Who's that?" before approaching someone behind the wheel of a bulldozer.

Martin wasn't sure where the distrust stemmed from. "I guess it's a China thing, I don't know," he said. "These guys were working their asses off. We're already seven or eight months into the project and we're on track to break the record for building five golf courses. What is there to complain about?"

When Zhou Xunshu first arrived at Yiganxing Golf Club in Guangzhou, workers there assumed he was the boss's new bodyguard. That was before they saw him put on a display at the driving range. "Back then, my irons were very accurate," Zhou said. "I think they were impressed." Not long after he walked away from Guangzhou International, Zhou scored a job as Yiganxing's driving range supervisor. It wasn't his dream job, but he viewed it as a step in the right direction. *Keep moving forward*, Zhou told himself. *Keep moving*.

Zhou soon learned that the China Golf Association had two official designations for golf professionals: "pro golfer" and "pro coach." The titles had only existed for a decade in China, and either one represented another step up for Zhou, with the promise of a better job and better pay. "Pro golfer" was the more prestigious of the two, and while there were a variety of ways to achieve this coveted status, most seemed unrealistic for someone like him. You could become a pro by being selected to represent China in an international team event like the Asian Games, but Zhou thought, at thirty-two, he was likely too old to be considered for something like that. Or you could earn the title by finishing in the top three of an official CGA-sanctioned tournament, but Zhou wasn't aware of too many of those open to domestic players – it seemed far-fetched, out of reach. There was a third option, however, and that was to take a test.

The test was expensive, and notoriously difficult. It was four rounds of play on one of Guangdong's toughest courses, and it was almost always scheduled during monsoon season, when wind was often a factor. Golfers who averaged a score of 74 or better for the four rounds passed the test – a very rare occurrence. Zhou didn't have much money at the time, so he decided instead to take the test for pro coach certification, which was both easier and cheaper.

He passed. He was officially on his way.

Zhou's new distinction was followed quickly by a new job. Dragon Lake Golf Club, a beautiful course nestled amongst lush mountains about an hour north of Guangzhou, had recently opened, and Zhou was among its first hires. He was given a dual role: golf instructor and manager of operations. His new salary, which included housing, was five thousand yuan a month, five times more than he was earning as a security guard just two years earlier. The extra cash would come in handy, because soon Zhou would have someone else to spend it on.

Zhou and Liu Yan started work at Dragon Lake on the same day, but they didn't really talk until later in the summer. It was July 21, a Wednesday, and the sun was bright in the sky. Liu Yan was a caddie, still in her teens, more than a decade younger than Zhou.

Zhou's boss had asked him to take photographs of every hole on the course that day. A caddie was expected to travel with him to hold an umbrella and protect Zhou from the powerful sun. That morning another girl had been scheduled to hold the umbrella, but she was nowhere to be found. Liu Yan happened to be stand-ing nearby, and a foreman asked that she accompany Zhou. She protested at first – holding an umbrella for a boss on such a hot day did not sound like fun – but the foreman insisted.

As it happened, this was not the first time Zhou had taken notice of Liu Yan. She stood out among the other female caddies: tall, slender and beautiful, with a big friendly smile that put him at ease. The two started chatting during their trip around the course, and, hole by hole, Zhou got slower and slower at taking the photos so they would have more time together. At the end of the day, he asked Liu Yan for her phone number. Not one to play games with personal matters, that night he sent her a text message asking if she wanted to have dinner with him. Liu Yan knew Zhou was technically her boss, and she thought it would simply be a meal between coworkers, a thank-you for filling in for her AWOL colleague. So she brought a friend along – might as well have Dragon Lake pick up the tab for both of them, she thought.

"I did not expect we'd start dating," Liu Yan said. Later, she would say that being assigned to the last-minute photo session was *yuan fen*, or fate.

Liu Yan was more independent than many Chinese girls her age – she had gone off on her own in search of a job, after all – but she was from a small village in Hunan province, and wanted some aspects of her life to have a traditional feel to them. The courting process lasted months. When Zhou and Liu Yan would go on "dates," usually dinners near the course or shopping trips to Guangzhou, they were never alone. Even though it was now clear they were more than colleagues, Liu Yan always brought one of her friends along to chaperone.

"I spent lots of money!" Zhou recalled good-humoredly. "I had to buy dinner every day, for three people."

To add to Zhou's frustration, their three-person outings were always cut short by the 10 p.m. curfew in place at Liu Yan's employee dormitory. The dorm was only five hundred yards or so away from where Zhou lived, but after curfew she might as well have lived in Hong Kong. The nights grew longer and longer for Zhou, who anxiously awaited each dawn and the chance to lay eyes on the caddie he was falling in love with.

By the autumn, it was clear to both Zhou and Liu Yan where things were headed, and during a conversation – between just the two of them, finally – they decided to make their relationship official. They became boyfriend and girlfriend. Their talk was on November 11 – 11/11, celebrated by young people in numbers-obsessed China as "singles day." The following day, Zhou sent Liu Yan ninety-nine red roses.

Half a year after an umbrella brought them together, Zhou and Liu Yan decided they had had enough of tradition. Without telling either set of parents, Liu Yan moved in to Zhou's apartment in the curfew-less managers' dormitory, which had air conditioning and laundry facilities, luxuries not available in the caddies' quarters.

The couple were now living together, but there was much they had yet to learn about each other. For example, much of Zhou's past remained a mystery to Liu Yan. He seemed reluctant to talk about where he came from, or what he had done before he came to Dragon Lake. It seemed out of character for such a straightforward person.

"When we asked him where he was from, he seemed embarrassed," Liu Yan said. "But we kept asking him. He just smiled and asked me to guess. So I said, 'Hunan?' And he said yes. But I didn't believe him – he's the kind of person that it's easy to tell when he is not telling the truth."

Ken Chu pushed Martin and his team hard until the very end. And he made it clear each and every day that what they were doing was "top secret." They weren't supposed to tell anyone what they were building. It didn't matter that the Mission Hills website, for the better part of 2003, had proudly proclaimed that, with 180 holes, Mission Hills would soon overtake Pinehurst as the largest golf club of the world. Or that in November 2002 Mission Hills held a press conference entitled "Mission Hills Golf Club on the Road to World No. 1 – Champion Golf in China."

Martin's crew finished the five courses – all ninety holes – in fourteen and a half months. Faster than he ever thought possible.

Not long after, Mission Hills held a lavish press conference and ceremony in which the *Guinness Book of World Records* proclaimed the ten-course facility the largest golf club in the world. Within months, the Chinese government would announce its ban on the construction of new golf courses.

"Those guys amaze me," Martin said of the Chus. "Dr. Chu, he seems like he knows shit like a fortune teller."

David Chu is said to have played an integral role in helping secure the 2008 Olympics for Beijing, and most who knew him assumed his connections within the Party were significant. One person who worked on the project said it was widely assumed the Chus were tipped off about the government's plans for a moratorium, which led to the project's mad dash to the finish line. "I think somebody said something to them," said the source. "'There's going to be a crackdown, so if you are going to do something, do it – and do it big.'"

4

PLAYING THE GAME

NOTICE FROM THE GENERAL OFFICE
OF THE STATE COUNCIL ON SUSPENSION OF
BUILDING NEW GOLF COURSES

(No. 1 of the General Office of the State Council,
promulgated on January 10, 2004)

*"The people's governments of all provinces, autonomous regions
and municipalities directly under the Central Government, all
ministries and commissions under and all institutions directly
subordinate to the State Council:*

*"Since the reform and opening, golf courses have been devel-
oped rapidly in China, which played an active role in improving
sport facilities and developing golf sport. However some serious problems have arisen in recent years. In some places, golf
courses have been built excessively, taking up a large amount
of land. In other places, the collective land of the peasants has
been requisitioned and occupied in violation of the legal provisions. Unauthorized occupation of cultivated land has seriously
damaged the benefits of the state and the peasants. Additionally,
in some cases real estate development has been conducted surreptitiously under the guise of building golf courses. For the
rational use and protection of land resources and to curb the
blind construction of golf courses, the State Council hereby noti-
fies relevant issues as follows:*

*"I. New golf course construction shall be suspended. From
the date of issuance of this notice up to the time when new*

relevant policies come out, no local people's government at any level and no institution under the State Council shall approve the construction of any new golf course project. Projects already in progress that were started without following the standard procedure of obtaining approval of planning, project initiation, land-use and assessment of environmental impact, etc., must stop construction immediately. All planned projects that have not yet started construction must be canceled. As for golf course projects with approved project proposals and feasibility study reports, but without approvals for land-use or project initiation, approvals for land-use or project initiation shall not be granted. For those projects with approval of planning, land-use and project initiation, but whose construction has not yet started, those projects must be abandoned.

"II. Cleaning up golf course projects that have been built or are being built. The local people's government at all levels should immediately clean up and thoroughly inspect the golf course projects that have already been or are currently being built within their respective jurisdictions. The emphases of the cleanup and inspection lie in: whether the procedures for approval of golf course construction projects are complete, whether the construction project conforms to the overall planning on utilization of land and urban planning, whether the land use conforms to relevant laws, regulations and provisions stated in the 'Notice of the Central Committee of the Communist Party of China and the State Council on Further Strengthening Land Administration and Earnestly Protecting Cultivated Land' (No. 11 [1997] of the Central Committee of the CPC).

"III. Regulating the operation of completed golf courses. We should regulate the golf courses that have been built and put into operation based on clear and verified information, and in accordance with the relevant laws, regulations and policies of the state. The local people's government at all levels shall take effective measures to strengthen the management of existing golf courses, to strictly control the consumption of water resources by golf courses and to supervise and implement the construction of peripheral environmental protection facilities, so as to ensure

*environmental protection in accordance with the relevant laws
and regulations.*

*"IV. Strengthening supervision, inspection and guidance.
The local people's government at all levels should strengthen the
cleaning-up and regulation of golf courses, where unauthorized construction and illegal use of land are to be punished
by the law. The people's government of all provinces, autonomous regions and municipalities directly under the Central
Government should submit the results of the cleaning-up and
inspection of golf courses to the State Council by February 15,
2004. The Development and Reform Commission shall, in joint
efforts with the Ministry of Land and Resources, the Ministry
of Construction, the State Administration of Environmental
Protection, the General Administration of Sport, the State
Tourism Administration and other departments, pay close
attention to research and propose measures on regulating and
guiding the healthy development of golf sport and construction
of its facilities."*

This was not the first time China had banned the construction
of golf courses. On May 26, 1995, the "Circular of the State
Council Concerning the Strict Control of High-End Real Estate
Development Projects" introduced a series of measures intended
to curb what the government saw as a looming luxury real estate
bubble. One of the document's directives stated that the odd
trifecta of "new golf courses, replica ancient cities and amusement parks" was to be "strictly forbidden." But then, two years
before that, Nicholas Kristof had written in the *New York Times*
that, "Pressing ahead with its clampdown on runaway economic
growth, the Chinese Government has banned new golf courses
and announced that work on some luxury hotels and villas will
be halted even though they are already partly built." It was all
beginning to sound rather familiar.

In fact, the 2004 ban was merely a rehash of a ban already in
place, one that had gone largely ignored for more than a decade.

Still, it signaled a shift. While the previous prohibitions had lumped golf courses in with a variety of other luxury developments, the 2004 directive targeted golf specifically. It appeared the government was ready to get serious. And this time, when news of the moratorium got out, "everything went cold," Martin Moore said.

Well, not quite everything. This was China, after all. One course designer, who'd been working in China since the early '90s, said his client told him to ignore the ban and carry on with his work. How could the client be so brazen? "My client was the central government," the designer explained. The course was part of a resort in southern China known to be a holiday retreat for government officials. "I was working on a pet project of the central government, right while they were doing the moratorium," the designer said. "They were talking out of both sides of their mouth."

Few in the industry were spooked by the moratorium. According to Martin, there was an assumption there'd always be someplace building golf courses. Who cared about China? Martin himself had a few projects going forward in Thailand, and golf development in the United States was still "booming full speed." "I didn't think much of it," he said. "I didn't even think I'd make a career in China. I had no idea I would even do any more courses there."

Building golf courses in China was a headache. Thailand was easy by comparison. So, in the years following the big job at Mission Hills, Martin's focus turned elsewhere. He worked on Schmidt-Curley and Nicklaus jobs close to home, in California, Nevada, Montana and Nebraska. Business wasn't going gangbusters – he never had more than a few jobs going at once – but it was steady. "I didn't pay any attention to China," he said. "I don't think anyone in their right mind had any idea that China was going to boom. I thought it was all over. I wasn't going back over to Asia, other than to just vacation."

Zhou Xunshu started 2005 with a partial sense of satisfaction. Some months, once he tacked the coaching fees on to his base salary, he earned as much as seven or eight thousand yuan, a fortune to those he'd left behind back in Qixin village. He was living with the woman he loved, who loved him back. It didn't hurt that he also thought she was the most beautiful employee at Dragon Lake Golf Club.

But it wasn't enough. There were still pieces missing, some more jagged than others, and they stabbed at his backside like spurs, pushing him forward. First, there were his parents, with whom he'd had his differences. He'd always blamed the village for that. They are a product of their environment, he told himself, their harsh, antiquated environment. And he desperately wanted to get them out.

Then there was Zhou's deep-seated desire to become a certified pro golfer. He knew it was just a title, but if golf was to be his profession, Zhou wanted to be considered among the top in his field. He wanted to compete with the best. Zhou considered himself an athlete, a fighter. He knew how quickly he had advanced in the three years he'd been playing regularly, and he was convinced that if given the opportunity, he could match the country's top players stroke for stroke. It might take him a few years, but Zhou believed he could win a tournament in China, or, at the very least, finish in the top three, which would earn him his pro card. But there were only a handful of tournaments a year, and they were often poorly organized, with little advance warning.

When Zhou was feeling hopeless, there was someone he could look to for proof that being a successful Chinese professional golfer was actually feasible. For most of China's recent history, one man had been known as the nation's best: Zhang Lianwei. Zhang, like Zhou and many other first- and second-generation Chinese golfers, had stumbled into the game relatively late in life. In 1985, his javelin career over, he was working for the government sports bureau in Zhuhai, Guangdong province, painting lines on soccer fields, racking up snooker balls and doing other odd jobs. He was then presented with the opportunity of working at a new enterprise in the city – the second golf course in Communist China. For three years, Zhang caddied, mowed lawns, raked bunkers and practiced, practiced, practiced. Nearly twenty years later, in 2003, Zhang, who says he is "90 percent self-taught," became the first

Chinese player to win a European Tour event, fighting off Ernie Els to take the Singapore Masters. In 2004, he became the first Chinese player to tee up at the US Masters.

Zhang may have been a pioneer for golf in China, but he often felt the country did not give him the support he deserved. In April 2005, Zhang got emotional during a press conference following a round of the BMW Asian Open, an international tournament in Shanghai. He announced to the assembled media that he'd never received any state funding during his career; he'd had no domestic sponsors, either. "It's such an ordeal playing golf in China over the years," he said, his voice cracking. "It's tough, it's difficult, and it's lonely. I know golf is not an Olympic sport, but I think the sports authorities should at least have shown some kind of support, like air tickets or something, to show their appreciation of my contributions." Zhang went on to propose that the sport's governing body in China allocate 10 to 20 percent of its budget to supporting golfers. "Over these twenty years, I have made a lot of money if you look at the checks," he said. "But you don't know how much money I have spent to support myself. My sponsorship all comes from foreign companies. In fact, I don't feel comfortable being supported only by foreign brands. Wherever I go, people look at me and think I represent China. But they don't know that I haven't received support from China. With this opportunity, I call for sponsorship from Chinese enterprises." Zhang closed by saying he felt he "had nothing to lose" by making the statement. His remarks came in response to a question about what life was like outside of China's state-funded sports system. (Moments later, the same question was posed to twenty-six-year-old Liang Wenchong, then a rising star. Liang – perhaps calculating that he had more to lose than Zhang – declined to comment.)

Zhou knew it was possible. Zhang proved it. He just needed his own chance.

It was hard for Zhou to contain his excitement when he heard from a friend that a new professional golf tour geared exclusively toward domestic players like him was expected to launch during the summer of 2005. It was called the China Tour, and, a partnership between the China Golf Association and Singapore-based sports marketing firm World Sport Group, it was intended to be an answer to all of the big-ticket international golf tournaments that were popping up in China that rarely featured any Chinese players. "The future for golf in China – the real, long-term future – is not paying large sums to bring the world's superstars to play here. It is creating our own stars," the CGA's vice president, Hu Jianguo, declared to the media.

The tour, reported to have $8 million in funding, planned to host four events that year, with $100,000 in prize money for each event – a huge amount for Chinese "pros," even when split across the top players. "There was a need to find a place for China's golfers," the senior vice president of World Sport Group, Nick Mould, said. The goal was to make it possible for Chinese players to make a living at the game. The bigger picture was also important: the China Tour was "an investment in the future development of golf in China." With a population of more than a billion, and fewer people playing golf in the United States and elsewhere, the industry desperately needed a new emerging market.

Zhou was intent on getting his piece of the action. He knew a limited number of spots would be open to pro coaches like him, and that the official entry form would be posted on the internet "some time in the future." He wasn't good with computers or the web. He didn't understand how people could sit at a desk all day, and he had little patience for technology. Plus, he couldn't type well – and his stunted education meant he had a limited knowledge of *pinyin*, the standard system of romanized spelling for transliterating and typing Chinese. In text messages he often got the characters wrong. Even his spoken Mandarin was sometimes less than perfect.

But Zhou could at least press "enter," and for a chance at the China Tour, he was willing to put in a little screen time. Liu Yan helped him call up the web page that was supposed to have the registration form on it someday. Every day, without fail, Zhou would refresh the page – again and again – waiting for the download link to appear. When it finally did, he got goosebumps. He felt as though he'd won the lottery, and he hadn't done anything yet. He and Liu Yan hurriedly filled out the form and submitted it.

His persistence paid off. He earned one of the final thirty spots in the China Tour. His competitive golf career was finally on the move.

In June 2005, Zhou and Liu Yan packed up and moved to Chongqing, the massive megalopolis in southwest China. Zhou had been a member of the management team at Dragon Lake for just one year, but it was long enough for him to realize the role – and perhaps the place – were not the right fit for him. He felt out of sorts. He butted heads with leadership. He found the people shrewd and calculating. Off the golf course, Zhou is not one to play games. "How can I get along with people in Guangzhou?" he asked. "I'm a very frank person, more like the people in Chongqing, I think. Things are more straightforward there. Simple and easy."

Golf was just starting to catch on in Chongqing, and Zhou thought he'd have more of a chance being a big fish in a small pond, rather than trying to survive in Guangzhou's crowded golf waters. He landed a job at the Haoyun Golf Club, a driving range in a new development area that had sprouted up around the Chongqing Olympic Sports Center, a sixty-thousand-seat stadium that opened in 2004 and had absolutely nothing to do with the 2008 Beijing Games. Liu Yan got a position working in Haoyun's pro shop.

In many ways, Chongqing, famous for its hills, fog and spicy food, encapsulated China's economic rise. Some called it "Chicago on the Yangtze," a broad-shouldered gateway for the country's relentless westward expansion. In another nod to Chicago, Chongqing was infamously corrupt – mafia-style gangs ran many aspects of the city, aided and abetted by crooked local cadres and a double-dealing police force. In 1997, Chongqing joined Beijing, Shanghai and Tianjin as the only municipalities directly controlled by China's central government. By far the largest of the four, Chongqing covered an area approximately the size of Austria.

Chongqing was a nation within a nation, a city on the move. When Zhou and Liu Yan arrived, it was the world's fastest-growing urban center, and perhaps its largest construction site, as well.

Its deputy mayor told the Urban Land Institute that Chongqing was "just like Shanghai, only ten years behind"; *Travel + Leisure* magazine had dubbed Chongqing the "city of the future." In 2005, the city's population was more than thirty million, with just under half of those people living in its urban core. Some estimates had Chongqing taking on as many as one million new urban residents each year.

The month Zhou and Liu Yan moved into their new home, the city's first Wal-Mart opened. Later that year, Chongqing welcomed its second golf course, Sun Kingdom Golf Club, which the government said was part of a "green tourism" push in the southern part of the city. Zhou was heading where the action was, just as he had done when he boarded the train to Guangzhou a decade earlier.

Zhou played in two China Tour events within months of his move to Chongqing. In September he traveled to Kunming, and, fighting off his nerves, he made the cut, finishing thirty-sixth out of one hundred or so golfers. His score was relatively high – he didn't shoot par in any round – but so were the scores of all the players finishing outside the top ten. That wasn't surprising in a country with only two decades of golf under its belt.

Then, in November, he made his way to Hainan island. He'd heard that there were great courses there, and rumors that there were many more to come. Again, he made the cut, this time finishing thirty-seventh. His prize money didn't even cover his travel expenses. But Zhou didn't care. He was in the game.

Martin Moore's vacation from Asia ended much sooner than he had expected. In 2006, Ken Chu and Mission Hills were eager to make history again, this time in Yunnan province, a site not too far from Spring City, the course that had first brought Martin to China a decade earlier. On this occasion, the goal was even more audacious: twelve courses, built simultaneously on a tough site, but to be completed in a "generous" thirty-six months. Supposed moratorium on golf course construction be damned.

Martin knew from past experience that it was useless telling Ken Chu his plans were quixotic. So he tried to figure out a way to make them happen. He assembled another A-team of golf course builders, but this time he recruited one twice the size as the crew that made history building Mission Hills in Shenzhen. Fifteen shapers. Five project managers. They all adjusted their schedules to take part in the biggest golf undertaking anyone had ever heard of. Some had turned down other jobs to work at Ken Chu's beck and call. And Martin was beginning to admit that the scope of the project had him "freaking out."

He was careful to get everything in place, the best you ever could in China, so the project could get off to a solid start. He had visited the site four times. He had the construction calendar carefully mapped out. He asked some members of the team to arrive in Kunming early so they could get used to life in China. He had done everything that could be done.

And then it was announced that twelve courses had become eight.

And then the project was on hold.

And then it was completely canceled.

The local government had got cold feet. The project was so big, so bold, it was bound to show up on Beijing's radar. They couldn't risk the central government cracking down on them.

Martin went to the members of his A-team and asked if they had a plan B. "I lost money, but more importantly I lost face," he said.

The experience taught Martin valuable lessons about operating in China's legal gray areas: Make sure your employees know everything can go belly-up at any moment. Never guarantee anything.

Later that year, Martin started to get "the vibes." Business in the United States was cooling down, and the China market was perking up, despite the supposed moratorium on golf course construction. In the United States, the unprecedented golf course boom – which had peaked with nearly four hundred new courses built in 2000, and well more than sixteen thousand courses in total – was coming to an end. Golf course openings and golf participation were declining sharply. In fact, in 2006 golf course closures in the United States (146) outnumbered golf course openings (119.5) for the first time in sixty years.

Some in the industry tried to paint the statistics as good news, saying it was just an expected leveling-out after years of overbuilding. For too long the US golf scene had been spurred more by the desire to sell country-club housing than by any increase in demand for the sport. It was simply golf Darwinism, they argued: weaker courses were closing, and golfers in the long run would be better off with a smaller number of higher-quality places to play. But that logic, while perhaps accurate, did little to ease the concerns of those, like Martin, who made their living building golf courses.

Which explains why Martin was so excited when, in October 2006, he started hearing from developers in China again. First, it was a lead about a course in the mountains. Two months later, it was a course along a beach. The projects couldn't have been more different, but they shared one thing in common: they were both located in Hainan. Martin didn't read too much into it. He was just happy that, somewhere on the planet, there were jobs to be chased – and that China's supposed golf course moratorium was apparently lacking in muscle.

A half a year later, his suspicions were confirmed by perhaps the most incredible bit of news Martin had ever heard coming out of the Mission Hills empire.

"You have to think like a businessman," Zhou Xunshu said. "Itemize everything."

But a quick look at his books would suggest the business side of Zhou's competitive golf career was, to put it simply, failing.

By a friendly accounting, Zhou estimated he had lost nearly 20,000 yuan playing on the China Tour in 2006. Although he made the cut in four of the six tournaments, he had never placed better than twenty-first, and never earned more than 10,800 yuan ($1,350). He had finished on average twenty-six strokes behind a tournament's winner – a mountain in golf numbers. With tournaments taking place in all corners of China, his travel expenses trumped his winnings. If the trend continued, "I try to find more students," Zhou said, matter-of-factly.

As a golf instructor, Zhou's methods – specifically how he charged for lessons – might, if he were lucky, help him break even. He rarely charged by the hour. Instead, he'd assess your abilities and ask you your goals. Then he'd quote you a lump sum, and he'd be your coach until you attained those goals. "That way, I am less bothered and I don't need to keep track of how many hours and how many lessons," he said. "My price may be a little bit high, but I don't want too many students. I just want several dedicated students." One student paid Zhou ten thousand yuan, and once he starting shooting in the 70s, he was so happy with the results that he gave Zhou another thirty thousand yuan on top of it.

So why even bother competing, since the odds were so surely stacked against him? He was too old to be starting an athletic career. He had no sponsors, no coach and a mounting deficit. "Even if I lose, I want to join the competition," Zhou explained, "because I want to have something to look back on when I quit playing. I want to be able to tell people, 'Look, I played in that tournament against the best in China.'" But he knew he needed some pragmatic goals for the coming year. He wanted to finish 2007 ranked in the top twelve on the overall China Golf Association money list. That would earn him his "professional player" classification. "And then I can attract some sponsors," he said. "Being a certified pro golfer is the highest honor in golf in China, and once that happens, sponsors will find you and sign a contract with you."

If Zhou were to finish near the top of a tournament or two, there was little doubt in his mind what he'd put the winnings toward. He wanted to buy an apartment, so he and Liu Yan could start a family. And he felt the pressure to buy soon – property prices in Chongqing, like many cities in China, were rising fast.

Only a handful of Chinese golfers had traditional sponsorships – money from a major brand in exchange for using a product or wearing a logo – like those enjoyed by golfers in the United States or Europe. In China, usually a sponsorship came in the form of free gear or clubs, but no money. Cash sponsorships would come from a golf course that employed the golfer, or simply a rich businessman who happened to take a liking to a certain player. Most of these sponsorships covered only the golfer's tournament travel expenses, maybe 80,000 to 160,000 yuan a year. That was a drop in the bucket for a wealthy business owner, but a potentially career-changing sum for someone like Zhou, desperate to have his mind focused on golf and not the bottom line. "If I could find someone to support me financially, my performance will improve in a straight line," he said, pointing his finger up and to the right.

Sponsorship or no, almost all the golfers on the tournament circuit needed a second job to survive. They also had to be conscious of every yuan they spent. For the season opener of the 2007 China Tour in Nanjing, Zhou had traveled to the tournament via a two-and-a-half-day train ride. Had he traveled by plane, he wouldn't have been able to bring his own caddie, a luxury for most Chinese golfers, who usually use a young female caddie assigned to them by the course. He also never stayed at the official tournament hotel. He rarely ate his meals at the clubhouse restaurant; too expensive. "This place is very cheap, right?" he would say after dinner in a town or village outside the golf course grounds. "Four of us can eat for the same amount one person would pay at the clubhouse." Little victories like this seemed to keep him going.

Zhou was not the only one. In the days leading up to tournaments, a separate competition would inevitably break out among the players – who could find the cheapest hotel? Word would spread around the practice green that one golfer found a room somewhere for thirty yuan a night, including hot water, and dozens of other golfers may try to follow him to the same place that evening. It was not uncommon for Zhou to change hotels one or two times in the lead-up to an event. Wasn't this distracting? "It's no problem," he always said. "I only have one bag. I just put it on my back and go."

When playing with one eye on the bank balance, the seemingly mundane could turn into migraines. For example, in the days leading up to the Shanghai leg of the China Tour – which was about thirty-seven miles to the west in Jiangsu province, since no Shanghai course wanted to give up a week of business for the domestic golf tour – Zhou noticed that the sole from one of his Nike golf shoes had come unglued, so much so that it flapped when he walked. For most pro golfers this would be no problem. Just go back to the hotel and unbox a new pair. But these were the only golf shoes Zhou had with him on this trip. He wore them off the course, as well.

"These were one thousand yuan," he noted ruefully. "They're not fake."

The concern on Zhou's face was obvious. He couldn't afford a new pair of shoes. The tournament started the following day. How was he going to compete?

The small, country towns that bordered most Chinese golf courses – the places where Zhou usually stayed during tournaments – may have been ugly and boring, dirty and unrefined, but they featured an abundance of practical conveniences unavailable to those who paid the extra cash for the official tournament hotel. Out on the street, he found a cobbler, an old man sitting on a stool, wearing an apron, ready and willing to put his shoes back together – although the man may have never dealt with golf shoes before. Zhou left his shoes with the man, who assured him he'd have them fixed and ready for action by the time Zhou got back from dinner.

When Zhou returned, the cobbler was nowhere to be found. A vendor nearby said the shoe repairman wouldn't return until 6 a.m. Zhou started to get anxious. He headed back to his hotel, wondering what he'd do if he couldn't find the cobbler in the morning.

The man at the front desk stopped Zhou and said, "I think these are yours." He handed Zhou a plastic bag containing his mended shoes. "The old man wanted to make sure you got these tonight. You can leave his payment with me."

"How much is it?" Zhou asked, relieved.

Zhou's tournament was saved for two yuan.

"My girlfriend's mother always asks me how much money I make, and whether I can afford to buy an apartment or car," he said during that year's tour. "I'm honest with her and tell her I will try my best. But anyway, it's free love. My girlfriend has the right to leave me if I don't have enough money for her."

Money, Zhou said, was not really the main thing that concerned Liu Yan's mother. "Her real worry is that we have been together three years and we aren't married yet."

The Omega China Tour symbolized just how new the game of golf was to China. Each stop on the tour came with a total purse of only 800,000 yuan, or $100,000 dollars, a paltry amount by the standards of the PGA Tour, but far more than Chinese golfers had seen before. The prize money helped recruit a ragtag group of fresh-faced golf pros.

There was Zhou, of course. His rise from farmer to security guard, to obscure competitive golfer, mirrored the random trajectories of his competitors on the Chinese golf circuit. Many had spent their formative years swinging a harvesting sickle, not a 6 iron, out in the provinces. For most, their first job working at a golf course or a driving range had just been a convenient way to make money, an attractive alternative to some other form of menial labor. At one of the fancy pre-tournament welcome meals thrown by a sponsor, a Chinese guest, watching the way the golfers attacked their bowls of rice, whispered, "They eat like *farmers!*" At heart they remained, as one first-generation Chinese pro golfer put it, "blue collar workers."

There was Liu Anda, who was working as a sushi chef in Dalian, a city in northeast China, when a regular customer who happened to be a Japanese golf coach persuaded him to come and work at a new driving range. Until then, Liu, who grew up in a small farming village, had never heard of golf. "After I finished my work duties, I watched them on the driving range, and I said to myself, 'That doesn't look hard at all,'" Liu recalled. "I picked up a 7 iron and took a swing. The ball went very far. Then I hit about five or six more balls and I did not miss. All of them went very far. I asked the Japanese coach, 'I can support my family doing this?' He said, 'Yes.'" Two years later Liu had been hired as the head pro at Tiger Beach Golf Links, in Shandong province. He owned a small Chinese barbecue restaurant on the side. He believed his golf career wasn't a stroke of luck, but a work of fate. "I am a Christian and I believe in God. He led me to golf," he said.

Another of Zhou's competitors was Wu Kangchun, who grew up in Zhuhai, in southern China, close to one of the early golf courses of the Communist era. He remembered all the lost golf balls he collected in the hills as a child. To make some extra money for the family, he would sell the balls back to the course. "Back then, I did not know golf," Wu said. "I only knew the balls." By chance, another golf course went up right beside his village, and his sister got a job there as caddie master. His older brother worked there, too. Told there was a Singaporean coach looking to train young golfers, he decided to leave school at seventeen to sign up. "I was bad at school, so it didn't make that much difference if I kept studying," he said. "There weren't many other ways out for me." Most of his income didn't come from playing, however; it came from gambling on golf matches with local businessmen.

Zhou often also met Chen Xiaoma on the circuit. Chen's given name, Xiaoma, means "pony," and he came from the countryside – from the age of ten until he was twenty, he worked in his family's rice fields along the Yangtze. Tired of that hard living, he asked his uncle to help him find a salaried job. Chen's uncle, the only relative with a college education, was an engineer who worked in the construction of golf courses. As with everyone else on the China Tour, Chen had not heard of the sport, but he thought that he might get a good job at a course, as a laborer. Instead, he ended up working at a driving range. "At first I thought it was a pretty funny game, and that only big bosses would come and play," Chen said. "We weren't busy on weekdays, and that is when I got a chance to play."

Some had a more athletic, more worldly, background. The son of an army cook, Yuan Tian had already worn many different hats by the time he was twenty-five. At age eleven, he had enrolled in martial arts school because he wanted to be the next Bruce Lee. At the age of twelve, he joined a touring acrobatic stunt motorcycling troupe called the Flying Dragons. (His parents made him quit when he was fifteen, after too many broken bones.) He spent five years doing odd jobs – stints as an electrician and as the man who slaughters oxen no longer of use to farmers – before he ended up in southern China at an aunt's home that just happened to be near a golf course whose employees just happened to be on strike. Soon he talked his way into a job as a golf instructor, despite having never played the game. Three years later he was teeing up in his first China Tour event. "I have always been good at sports," he explained, "but I also worked very hard. I'd play from morning until night, only taking breaks for lunch and dinner." He was also one of the China Tour's flashiest players. At each tournament in 2007 he arrived with his hair dyed a different color.

After graduating from university and going to work for his father's construction company, Wu Weihuang traded his fifteen-year regimen of morning *wushu* for rounds of golf. "I wanted to grow my business, and I knew wealthy and well-connected people played golf," Wu said. "I never thought I would become a pro golfer. But after playing for seven months, I was shooting in the 70s. In two years, I was the best golfer in the city." Wu, like most of his peers, was self-taught, and it showed. His swing was stiff and stabby, reminiscent of a hockey slap shot. He tended to choke the shaft, swinging with such fury that all the muscles on his slight but sinewy frame would ripple and pop. But "homemade" was good enough to go pro – good enough, in fact, to leave the construction business to his father and start a golf equipment company.

One of the strongest men on tour, Qi Zengfa, had been a world-class youth rower in China's state-funded sports machine before quitting at the age of eighteen. A couple of years later, in the late 1980s, he had learned that a new golf course in Shanghai was looking to hire and train out-of-work athletes. "I had never seen a golf ball or club before," Qi said. "When I left rowing, a body-building coach saw me and my build and asked me to become a body-builder. But ever since I was a kid, I always liked ball games, so I went with golf." In 1994 he became one of the first Chinese golfers to achieve "pro" status.

And finally, there was Xiao Zhijin, who had worked as an entertainment manager at a hotel on Hainan island. He was intrigued when his bosses bought an indoor golf simulator for the hotel's guests to use. It was his first introduction to golf, and he soon discovered he had a knack for the sport, or, at least, the computer-simulated version of it. Before long, no one at the hotel, guest or employee, could beat him. Over one of those rounds of simulated golf, a customer – the owner of a golf course in northeast China – offered to double Xiao's pay if he'd be willing to pack up and move to become his course's caddie master. Xiao accepted the offer, and when he arrived at his new place of employment, it was the first time he had seen a real golf course. Though, soon enough, Hainan island would have its share of them.

With these men on board, it was clear the China Tour had soul. The game was so young in China – nine years younger than Tiger Woods, in fact – that the players lacked pretense. Golf was so unpopular in China that those who ground away at the game for a living had yet to assume the affectations usually associated with professional athletes elsewhere in the world. China Tour golfers drank. They smoked. They cursed. They said what was on their mind. They came from a far different rung on the social ladder than the elites who had thus far monopolized the country's courses.

A small number of players were managing to cash in, but most were forced to hold down second jobs. At the tournaments, where a finish outside the top twenty meant a player probably wouldn't be able to cover his expenses for the week, a fraternity atmosphere prevailed. Golfers shared rooms at the cheap hotels and crowded tables at the cheap restaurants. They'd smoke cigarettes and down tall bottles of cold local beer; if it looked as though they were going to miss the cut, then several shots of that foul Chinese firewater, *baijiu*, were ordered. While most players got serious once they hit the course, tournament life away from the game had the feel of an extended boys' night out.

One Friday night, in the middle of one of the 800,000-yuan tournaments, China's golf trailblazer Zhang Lianwei threw himself a forty-second birthday bash in the clubhouse restaurant. Most of the other players attended. At the press conference earlier that day Zhang had closed by saying, "Come to my party and drink alcohol. If you don't drink alcohol, drink tea." Zhang himself opted for the alcohol, again and again, and he took the stage to perform several karaoke songs in Cantonese until very late in the evening.

With a slight hangover, Zhang went on to win the tournament by two strokes.

Everything was a bit rough around the edges. In its own way, the China Tour, and the men who toiled along its route, shared much with the early days of professional golf in other parts of the world, even places like the United Kingdom, where golf had gone through its growing pains more than a century before. Take, for instance, this passage from Mark Frost's *The Greatest Game Ever Played*, which describes the pro golf scene in late nineteenth-century Britain. Change a couple words here and there, and it's not too far from the recent situation in China:

> ...professional golfers were considered common laborers in Britain, sons of the working class, admired for their playing or teaching skills but in the narrowed eyes of the gentry predisposed to drinking binges and petty larceny. Professionals who harbored any hope of advancement in the game all lived an itinerant existence, traveling by third-class rail and hitching rides on farm wagons to remote tournament sites, bunking in cheap rooming houses, eating common meals, and closing the local pubs. They occupied a lowly rung on the social ladder shared by nomadic music-hall performers, a station somewhere between traveling salesman and migrant farmworker. Most were rough characters, poorly educated if at all, with thick regional accents that grated on a gentleman's ear. Their legendary weakness for the demon rum appears to have been more than rumor, and they weren't sipping single malt scotch; many of them brewed their own backwoods moonshine, bottles of snake venom with a razor-blade chaser.

There was no petty larceny on the China Tour, but the alcohol did flow. Indeed, Zhou often drank in the days leading up to a tournament. He also drank in the days during the tournament. One could say that beer seemed to be an integral part of his training regimen. He drank when he played well. He drank when he played poorly. He rarely drank to excess, but he'd enjoy a couple beers with dinner, and then one or two more before bed. (The one time Zhou sat at a table where red wine was served, he mixed it with Sprite in an attempt to make it more palatable.)

Beer, Zhou said, was a necessary ingredient to a good night's sleep. "The night before last I couldn't sleep because I did not drink any beer that night," he said during one tournament. "I need alcohol to relax." Another time, he complained of a restless night, this time not because he didn't consume any beer, but because the beers he drank only had a 2.8 percent alcohol content. The next night, when a call to the front desk confirmed the hotel had cold beers available for purchase, he celebrated like it was Christmas. When the bottles arrived at his door, he inspected the labels carefully. The brand was Sedrin, and the alcohol content was 3.6 percent. These would do.

"*He pijiu, hao shuijiao*," Zhou said with a smile as he opened his first bottle. "Drink beer, sleep well." A little less than an hour later, he was snoring, the TV remote control still in his hand.

Zhou was friendly and polite with many of his fellow players, but he rarely let anyone get close. He admitted to being a bit of an introvert, and on tour he often appeared to be a loner, but he had cultivated a reputation for being honest and straightforward. The worst thing anyone said about him was that he was the loudest snorer on the China Tour.

Secretly, Zhou found most golfers on the tour to be arrogant or "putting on airs." He wasn't too concerned with clothing, and was perturbed by golfers who seemed to treat the China Tour as a fashion show. "If it looks okay and is comfortable, that's enough," he said. "I do not need to think about what to wear or how to dress to attract the camera everyday. Not necessary!"

He had personal grudges against several other players, some of whom he felt were two-faced, and others he believed had slighted him in some way. He didn't always like how they passed time after the day's play had ended, either. At one tournament, when a fellow golfer asked Zhou if he wanted to go into town with him to get a massage, Zhou politely declined. After the other golfer left, Zhou said, "Frankly speaking, he is going out to find a prostitute, and that is why I never go with those golfers, no matter where they say they are going. In a rural town like this, it is hard to find a real massage parlor, because only bosses go to places like that. Here there are only farmers."

Zhou felt he had more in common with those farmers, or with the workers picking weeds on the course. "I like pure, simple people," he said. And while Zhou knew many golfers on the tour had also grown up poor, he was convinced none of them had grown up as poor as he had. None of their paths to golf was as wild and random as his was. He also suspected that approximately 90 percent of the China Tour's golfers had finagled some kind of external financial support, whereas he was struggling to make ends meet.

He had a chip on his shoulder. And it was sizable.

Admittedly, Zhou had made little effort to find a sponsor. He was not a good salesman, especially if selling himself. He didn't believe in boasting, and didn't like listening to others do it, either. He wanted to be recognized for his actions, not his words. "I don't know how to ask people to sponsor me," Zhou said. "It feels just like begging people for money. I can't do that."

5
NO CHOICE

"At night there are mosquitoes."

From Zhou. A text message. And by his standards, a lengthy and informative one. He had sent it from the driving range, two hours before his 10 a.m. opening round tee time. So there were mosquitoes in the hotel in Qingdao – but still no word on where the hotel was. Or its phone number. Or its name. The message did represent progress, however. In the days leading up to his second stop on the 2007 China Tour, Zhou's electronic missives had been even shorter. He had sent word that the hotel was "bad" and then "very bad," but no more than that.

In Qingdao the odd communications continued: 华山洗浴宾馆. *Huashan Xiyu Binguan.* Huashan Shower Hotel. It didn't sound good, in English or Chinese. And first you had to get there.

Zhou had discovered early on that finding transportation to golf courses in China is rarely easy and often expensive. Because they are so new, the courses, like China's airports, are almost never close to a city center. Qingdao's Liuting International Airport was twenty miles north of the city, and Qingdao Huashan Golf & Resort was twenty miles further to the northeast, where all you'd find otherwise was farmland and factories. No Chinese taxi drivers earned enough to play golf, and they rarely knew how to get to the far-flung courses. If a Chinese cabbie knew one thing about golf, it was that it's a rich man's game – and rich men in China have their own cars and drivers. They'd often refuse the long trip, because they knew there wouldn't be a passenger available for the return fare.

One China guidebook says visiting Qingdao is like "stepping

into a replica of a nineteenth-century Bavarian village." The city had been a German concession from the late 1800s until the early 1920s, and many Teutonic buildings still stand. But for anyone participating in the Qingdao leg of the China Tour, there was no need to visit Qingdao. Instead you had to go to Huashan.

Huashan hadn't aged well. The town had only officially been around since 1992, and the buildings along Zhifu Road, intended to serve as its "Main Street," were all less than ten years old. Yet the whole scene looked worn and depressed. The tan tile exteriors of the buildings were coated in a permanent layer of dust – the road was not yet fully paved – and the steps leading up to their entrances were cracked and crumbling. The facades of the buildings were split in half by large plastic billboards announcing garishly what was inside: a bank; a clothing store; an insurance agency; a mobile phone dealer; a man who would fix your eyeglasses or your wrist-watch, or both. Some shop signs were so big they made it difficult to see out of the windows on the second floor.

In a way, downtown Huashan and its dusty main drag was noth-ing more than a modern version of a frontier town in America's Old West. It seemed as though it had been cobbled together hurriedly, in anticipation of the rush of people to come. There was a hint of lawlessness. In an effort to ward off intruders, every ground floor shop window was veiled with jailhouse-like metal bars (though many were beginning to rust). The occasional street lamp lit Zhifu Road, but beyond its parallel rows of tiled buildings, it was pitch black. That darkness was deceiving, however, because out in the unlit distance was where all the life was: the countryside villages, where most of the area's fifty thousand residents lived. Maybe some day that rush of people would come, but in 2007, Zhifu Road felt like a deserted, bankrupt strip mall.

The Huashan Shower Hotel was on Songshan Road, the only Huashan side street that glowed, thanks to the buzzing purple, red and yellow signs announcing the Arc de Triomphe (*Kai Xuan Men*) Music Bar. Kai Xuan Men occupied the same new three-story pastel-green building as the Shower Hotel. It was a karaoke bar, or "KTV," the widely accepted Chinese genteelism for "brothel."

The bar's entrance faced the road, and the door was always open, revealing what could have been, to the casual observer, a sparsely decorated Chinese living room. Placed conspicuously near the doorway was a red sofa decorated with large white cartoon paw prints. Next to the sofa was a Christmas tree. It was almost June. Usually, one or two girls – they looked like they could have been in their late teens, but it was hard to tell – sat atop the sofa dressed in clothes one would wear to go shopping on the weekend. They lounged listlessly, staring at the opposite wall as if they were getting ready to watch a rerun of the evening news. Occasionally, a toddler would be seated with them. They'd all giggle when the rare foreigner walked by.

The bar and the hotel shared the building with Xiang Yun Ge Restaurant, a banquet-style Chinese restaurant boasting plenty of private rooms and enough space to host a large wedding reception. On the first day of the tournament, the dining hall was filled to capacity for a private party, or so the hostess claimed. It didn't seem she was lying, given the number of cars scattered about the street. The restaurant – not the pro golf tournament down the road – was the hottest ticket in town that day. According to the hostess, their customers were mostly government officials or executives with local state-owned enterprises. But this was still the countryside, and the men filing in and out had an agrarian glow about them – crew cuts, weathered brown skin and dirt on their shoes.

The lobby was cold, in both temperature and ambience. The floor was faux marble. The walls were cement and painted white. One side of the lobby was decked out with oversized living room furniture upholstered in imitation leather that had begun to blister long ago. Above the sofa hung a large painting of a waterfall. The other half of the lobby boasted the day's fresh ingredients – arranged in more than forty white plastic and Styrofoam containers on the floor. Huashan is close to the Yellow Sea, and the selection of creatures and animal parts on offer looked like lab prep for a university biology course. Chicken gizzards, pig kidneys, silkworm pupae, plump bamboo worms, entire freshly plucked chicken carcasses, quails, squid two feet long, shrimp, cuttlefish, stingrays, octopuses with bulging, translucent eyes, chickens' feet, conches, snails, coagulated pig's blood, and various fish, mollusks, tendons, hearts and other entrails. Each item was sitting in its own fluids or juices or blood or slime, all waiting to be cooked up and served as lunch.

In most Chinese cities or towns, regardless of size, there is usually someone willing to take you where you want to go, for a price – whether it's in a Volkswagen, a motorized rickshaw, or on the back of a motorcycle. But despite all the cars outside the Xiang Yun Ge, not one was for hire. No taxis. Nothing. The only option, it seemed, was to walk. The course was about twenty-five minutes away by foot. How were the golfers staying at the Shower Hotel getting to the course each morning?

Walking north along a newly laid road – almost all of the roads in Huashan were new – you were quickly surrounded by farmland, but signs of the inevitable change soon to come to the area were visible in the distance. The farms were being phased out. Next to each brand-new, multi-story building stood a cluster of construction cranes, ready to erect more new buildings. In 2001, the Shandong provincial government had declared Huashan one of six "high-tech industry development zones" in the province. Multinational companies from Singapore, South Korea and Japan had moved in and opened factories. Toiling in the fields was a thing of the past. The local people now worked on electronic gadgetry: computers and MP3 players.

Nonetheless, Shandong, together with Hebei and Henan provinces, still accounts for nearly 10 percent of the world's wheat production and 50 percent of the domestic harvest. What arable land that remains is farmed intensely. Fields don't lie fallow for long. As soon as the winter wheat crop is harvested in May and June, corn is planted. Peanuts, green beans and other vegetables fill in the gaps, planted in long, straight lines, the young leaves protected by plastic sheets over the soil. The carefully aligned crops felt incongruous with the haphazard manner in which the rest of Huashan was being developed.

Another new road signaled the way to the golf course. In contrast to the orderly efficiency of the crop rows, this route was a chaotic blank canvas, two very wide lanes separated by a wide median and flanked by a sidewalk. No one had got around to painting lane markers. It didn't matter. There were no cars in sight, except for a rickety blue Dongfeng dump truck that was cruising down the wrong side of the road. Tall, modern-looking lamps lined the street, as did several sapling trees, one planted every twenty feet or so along the sidewalk. But the soil around the trees was overgrown with weeds and tall grass. The median was the same way. The road appeared to have been laid recently, but it already felt abandoned.

In the distance, a woman was pacing barefoot along a yellow blanket of wheat. She had spread out thousands of tiny, amber-colored kernels on the flat concrete. The woman had a stocky but solid build, like a retired gymnast. Middle-aged, she sported a short, asexual haircut and was wearing black polyester trousers and a polyester blouse with a drab tan and mauve floral print. Her pink plastic sandals had been placed beside her patch of the road, the boundary of which she had marked with a dozen evenly placed large stones. Slowly, she walked the length of her section of wheat, back and forth, hands behind her back, shuffling through the kernels, her feet rubbing them against the road below.

"I'm rotating the kernels so they all get sun," the woman explained in a thick local dialect. She smiled, flashing a chipped front tooth.

Not too far away, on the other side of the median, another woman was doing the same thing.

By the time the wheat makes it out to the street in Huashan, it is nearing the end of its journey from the farm. It has already been threshed, the wheat literally separated from the chaff. Nowadays this is done mostly with machines, small threshers and occasionally large combines. Grain acreage has decreased in recent years, partly due to better opportunities with other crops, but also because of urban encroachment, so the government has encouraged the adoption of improved technologies, often with subsidies, to keep production levels high. But for some steps in the process, bare feet and concrete are all that's needed.

In the past, most farms had a naked piece of land, called a *shai chang*, set aside for drying the kernels before the grain was stored for the summer in a warehouse, or in large clay crocks in the home. It's said that for every acre of wheat a family has, they'll need around 240 square meters set aside for drying. But now that farmland was growing increasingly precious – and only 12 percent of China's land is arable to begin with – most farmers agree this isn't a very practical use of their tillage.

So, as much as they can, farmers try to use development, particularly the introduction of paved roads to their rural communities, to their advantage. Wheat kernels dry several times faster on cement than they do on a traditional *shai chang*. Naturally, using the roads in this way can be dangerous, sometimes deadly. Accidents often happen when cars swerve to avoid the swath of grain. Around the time of the winter wheat harvest, a car collided with a cyclist as its driver tried to maneuver around a road-top *shai chang* near Qihe, a city in the province's northwest – the cyclist died in the wreck. The aftermath provided some insight into how much value the locals place on kernels of wheat (the driver could easily have just driven over the grain) and how much value local authorities place on human life (for causing the fatal crash, the farmer paid only a $1,400 fine).

Further along the road to Qingdao Huashan Golf & Resort, two workers were napping in the cab of a small rusty combine. Further still, sixty-year-old Wang Zhongkui was tilling his sorghum field with a spade near the sidewalk. He had been a farmer his entire life. He lived on the opposite side of the road, in a village just beyond a row of single-story brick grain warehouses, with doors adorned with a square-shaped red and gold sign featuring *fu*, the Chinese character for good fortune. Wang had a round, friendly face and his crew cut showed only a few specks of gray. Beyond Wang, in the distance, the golf club was now visible – you could just make out the roofs of luxury villas peeking out over a wall. "I have seen it," Wang said of the course, resting his chin on his sturdy hands, which he had stacked atop the nub of his spade's wooden handle. "But I have never been inside."

He thought about his response for a moment, and then corrected himself. "Before it was a golf course, I often visited that land. When the golf course was built, nobody was allowed inside."

He smiled. "I have less land now." Then he got serious. "Villagers here used to have two *mu* of land each, but now they have only a third." Wang forcefully raised two fingers, and then three, for emphasis.

"It is because of the golf course. The golf course used to belong to us."

He said that the villagers had seen no financial benefits from the course. "No one is happy about this. But there haven't been any conflicts. Most now go to work in the factories," Wang said. "My family eats most of the crops we grow here." He pointed to his land, split up into rectangular patches of peanuts, corn and sorghum. "We sell whatever is left over."

Then Wang closed the topic with one of the most vexing and frequently heard phrases in the Chinese language. "*Mei banfa*," he said. "There's nothing we can do."

Often you hear "*mei banfa*" used in its defeatist form – when someone is trying to shirk responsibility. The person is unwilling to put in the necessary effort to perform a task that, in most situations, falls within his or her job description. Saying that they have no choice takes it out of their hands.

But Wang was telling the truth. There really was nothing he could do.

The final stretch of the journey ran along Route 204, a multi-lane highway that stretches 130 miles from Qingdao to Yantai, a busy seaport on the Bohai Strait in northern Shandong. The road, which opened in 1990, cut the travel time between the two tourist cities in half. And since 1996, when drivers on Route 204 look to the east as they pass through the town of Huashan, they'll see the province's first golf course. Or at least they'll see the wall that protects Qingdao Huashan Golf & Resort from riffraff like Wang Zhongkui.

Beyond the resort's wall the large luxury homes were mostly vacant. "TAO OF BUSINESS IN HEAVENLY VILLA" a billboard on the wall proclaimed in English. The advertisement featured a heavily Photoshopped golf fairway and three people: a bejeweled woman in a lavender evening gown holding a gold masquerade mask; a cocksure man in a double-breasted suit using an inverted 9-iron as a cane; and, closest to the green, a woman in a black dress, seated and playing the cello. The ad's Chinese text was no less obtuse: "Leading the dance of business philosophy, one villa can conquer the world."

A few other billboards were more straightforward, with contact information for the King's Palace development, which promises buyers a "Unique Villa," a "Unique Lifestyle" and four luxurious master bedrooms. And above the chimneys and tiled rooftops was a bright red sign announcing that weekend's China Tour event.

"The most important event in golf, Heroes gather in Huashan."

Five golfers were pictured. Zhou Xunshu was not one of them.

"A long day."

Frank Chen, the China Tour's Chinese media director, seemed to exhale the words in a sigh. He was staring at the media center leaderboard – a Hisense flatscreen TV. He shook his head.

"Lots of blue." And blue was bad.

Blue numbers meant bogeys, or worse. Bad scores. Black numbers signified par. Red was used for birdies. The rare eagle was highlighted in yellow. But on this day, the board was awash in blue. Only five golfers had finished the day under par.

Late in his round, Zhou had managed to splash some red beside his name to turn what could have been a horrible day into just a bad one. He scored birdies on two of the final three holes to finish 6 over par with a 78. He was in a tie for sixty-first place, and was at risk of missing the cut. One golfer Zhou was tied with, Dong

Caihong, had made history on the Qingdao Leg – she was the first female player to tee up for a China Tour event. Zhou could not be pleased.

In the nearly three weeks between the season opener and the Qingdao tournament, Zhou had played on an actual golf course only once. He was too busy teaching, trying to save enough money for the coming month. He knew the tournament schedule – packed, by Chinese golf standards – would have him away from his home, his girlfriend and his paying job for several weeks. After Qingdao, he would fly to Beijing for a non-China Tour event sponsored by China Unicom, a state-owned telecommunications company. Then it was down to Guangzhou for the third leg of the tour at Dragon Lake Golf Club, Zhou's former employer. Because of his familiarity with the course, Zhou was putting pressure on himself to perform well there. Friends and former colleagues would be in attendance.

But it's hard to perform well when you don't have time to practice. Zhou's training schedule was dictated by his teaching schedule. He squeezed practice in before and after his students. And he was doing both at the public driving range, which didn't have a playable putting green. It wasn't ideal. Not even close. This, however, was the lot of a pro golfer in China. He had bills to pay, plane tickets to buy, a girlfriend to support. There were no sponsors beating on his door offering to chip in. When he was away from home, on the road at tournaments, for a full month, there was no income. "*Mei banfa*," Zhou said. "If you don't play, you can't win. I'd never get better."

Zhou had changed out of his golf shoes and into a rather garish pair of lace-up brown loafers. They were shiny, and a section of their thin soles was made of metal. They surely didn't go with his outfit – the same fading maroon trousers and pilling baby blue golf shirt he had worn during his round.

Standing there in the Qingdao Huashan clubhouse lobby, he pointed to the large gold clock from Omega, the China Tour's title sponsor, which was mounted to a red plastic display stand. He urged a young golfer from Chongqing, making his China Tour debut, to pose for a photograph next to the clock. "It will be a good souvenir," Zhou said, his gruff voice making it sound more like an order than a suggestion. Zhou lined up the shot – "two steps back, one step to the right" – and then snapped the picture. He looked at his work on the camera's display screen and nodded, satisfied. "*Bu cuo*," he said. "Pretty good." Then it was Zhou's turn. They were both still tourists.

The ride back to the hotel was in a Chinese classic, the box-like minivan known throughout China as the *mianbao che*, or "bread car," because of its loaf-like appearance. Despite their tiny 1.3-liter engines, the vans are workhorses, and wildly popular, thanks to their versatility and price tag – they start at around four thousand dollars. On any given day, you might see a *mianbao che* overflowing with schoolchildren, watermelons, furniture, livestock, or, in this case, Chinese professional golfers.

The van belonged to the owner of a small grocery store near the Shower Hotel. Zhou had met him during his first day in Huashan; he had needed to find a ride to the course, and saw that the grocer also owned a car. A weeklong relationship was born. Zhou saved the man's phone number in his mobile phone, and the *mianbao che* became his taxi for the duration of the tournament. The price: ten yuan each way. Expensive, but much better than walking every day. Zhou had learned quickly that, upon arriving at a China Tour event, securing a reliable ride to and from the golf course was second only to finding an affordable hotel. At the driving range and putting green, the golfers would gossip about who had negotiated the best deals.

Two rows of seats had been ripped out of the grocer's *mianbao che* to make more room for passengers. In their place he had put tiny plastic stools, which slid along the greasy exposed metal of the van's floor every time he made a turn.

Before getting back to the Huashan Shower Hotel, the grocer stopped the van at his shop, so people could stock up on mosquito coils and food. He knew his market.

Zhou, who had a 7 a.m. tee time the following day, chose to buy his breakfast in advance: three cans of Red Bull, two juice boxes of whole milk and three chocolate pastries. He seemed happy, bubbly even, the day's bad round seemingly behind him.

He ran out into the empty road, closed his eyes, and took a deep breath.

"Fresh air," he said with a comfortable smile. "Not like the city."

Zhou then turned his attention to an apartment block on the other side of the road. It had a bright orange tile roof and a surprisingly clean white exterior. Windows were spaced uniformly across the width of the structure. The building was new, three stories tall, boxy and boring. Zhou, still standing in the middle of the road, put his hands on his hips and took in the scene, nodding slowly, right to left.

"The countryside here is not bad," he proclaimed. "They even have buildings like this!"

Huashan Shower Hotel wasn't the worst hotel in China. Indeed, there are much, much worse. As a bare-bones, downmarket hotel, it was typical. At the Shower Hotel, 120 yuan – about fifteen dollars – a night got you a double room with ceramic tile floors, two hard single beds, a small color television and, a special surprise, a private bathroom with intermittent hot water – thus, the name. No toiletries were included, not even towels or toilet paper. But all necessities were available to buy downstairs at affordable prices, if not top quality. The bath towels for sale in the hotel lobby and the street-side shops were thin, and the size of washcloths. There was no kind of barrier between the shower and the rest of the bathroom, no door or curtain or ridge in the floor – and the shower nozzle was affixed to the wall facing the toilet and sink. Instead, the floor was purposefully higher on one side and angled slightly, so water would flow to a drain between the toilet and sink.

The screens in the windows had large holes, providing a warm welcome to the mosquitoes. Outside, there was commotion. Several tall construction cranes were busy erecting a group of six-story apartment buildings, twice the size of the one Zhou had marveled at. A small dog barked as it raced around the large pieces of concrete piping that littered the vacant lot behind the hotel. Zhou went to bed early, keeping his tee time in mind. Shortly after midnight, a loud truck arrived at the construction site. Its horn beeped repeatedly, perhaps warning that for the next fifteen minutes it would be dumping large quantities of rocks, one on top of another. Two hours later, the dog was barking again. At 4:44 a.m., dawn light flooded the east-facing rooms, and a rooster began to crow. Around 6 o'clock, the public address system from a local school began blaring its musical morning calisthenics instructions: "Stretching exercise! Ready, and go! 1! 2! 3! 4! 5! 6! 7! 8!"

Zhou's tee time was in an hour.

The nighttime noise did not seem to bother Zhou. He followed his 78 with a 76 on Friday, an even-par 72 on Saturday and a 75 on Sunday. He was 13 over for the tournament. Not exactly the kind of numbers that would have sponsors beating down his door, but at this tournament, on this course, which had the entire field befuddled, it was good enough. Qingdao, or Huashan, ended up being the best result of Zhou's young career. He finished twelfth, seven strokes behind the legendary Zhang Lianwei. After phoning Liu Yan back in Chongqing, Zhou celebrated what he called a "breakthrough moment" in his career at a tiny, empty restaurant in Huashan town. His companions were two people he barely knew, an American journalist and his translator, and a round of cold Tsingtaos.

"Today, my plan was even-par," Zhou said. "If I got even-par, I'd definitely be in the top ten. Then my name would be on the leaderboard. Today, I made so many mistakes on my tee shots, but I still saved a lot of pars, so I felt I improved a lot." It was one of the first events in which Zhou actually turned a profit. After taxes and travel fees, Zhou's total earnings for the tournament were around eight thousand yuan – one thousand dollars.

Zhou fiddled with the cap to his bottle of beer. He still had the hands of a farm worker – that would be true no matter how well he played golf. They were covered in scars, as though he'd used a porcupine as a punching bag. "It's from cutting the wild grass in the village," he explained. "We used sharp sickles. I started when I was ten." Zhou started to count his scars. He lost track after thirty.

He pointed to the biggest one, on his left hand, which drew a curved line between the middle and base knuckles on his index finger. "You could see the bone," he said. But they'd never use stitches in the village, he said, just "put the flesh back on" and wrap it up.

"There's also this one," Zhou said, pointing to a divot above his left eyebrow.

In the spring, before there was grass to cut, Zhou and his childhood friends would attach sickles to long pieces of bamboo, and then use the contraptions to cut leaf buds off of the tallest trees. One of Zhou's friends took a wild swing, missed a tree completely, and connected with Zhou's forehead instead. He almost lost an eye.

Zhou seldom went back to the village these days. Just talking about doing so could change his mood, and he'd often try to change the subject. "Life in the mountains was pretty rough," he'd usually say when asked about his youth. It was, he said, a page in his life. "Conditions were bad, and there was nothing we could do about it."

Now he simply wanted to get his elderly parents out of the village.

"My father has arthritis in his leg," Zhou said. But there was more to it than that. "He also believes in Jesus. My parents are home alone and they needed to find something to attach to, and there are some people in our village who are believing in that," he continued. "So my father started to believe, too. He gets on his knees every day and prays. He's got a cross and reads the Bible every night."

Zhou was not pleased with this development. He said he realized older people in China may search for some kind of meaning "because they suffered from the old traditions in the old society," but he was worried. It seemed his father was starting to rely more on prayer to heal his leg than on medicine.

"Last time I went back for Spring Festival I tried to teach him that science is what he should really believe in," Zhou said, referring to the Chinese New Year, the biggest holiday of the year. "I said, 'Look at the planes in the sky, do you think Jesus made that happen?' I gave him some medicine that made his leg feel better, and I thought he understood what I had told him. But after I left, he could walk again because of the medicine, and so he went out and met those people in the village, and he started to believe again. I think it will be fine once I get them to Chongqing."

Zhou said his parents, who were in their seventies, didn't have much longer to live.

"They've never taken a plane before," he said. "I want to get them to Guiyang so they can take a plane to Chongqing."

In the village of Meiqiu, on Hainan island, nearly any event of any significance takes place under the phoenix tree, which sits in the clearing where three of the primary paths out of the village converge. Concrete Chinese chess tables are arranged near the knotty trunk of the old tree, the branches of which cover much of the open area like a giant parasol. For Wang Libo, and many of his fellow Meiqiu villagers of a certain age, walking past the big phoenix tree is like being on an episode of *This is Your Life*.

When he was just a teenager, Wang had led the construction of the cinder volleyball court that takes up much of the courtyard. This new, bigger court (he still knows the exact dimensions – twelve meters wide by twenty meters long) replaced a smaller, shabby, dirt playing area. Wang's team laid the bricks to mark the boundaries of the court. Then they installed the posts and the net, which were all paid for by the village committee.

Volleyball was a big deal. Each village had a team, and every summer Wang and his Meiqiu cohorts would play home and away matches with other squads from the area. They'd line the court with powdered limestone, and large crowds would cycle for miles to watch the action. "We gambled on every match," Wang said. "I remember one day we lost seven hundred yuan. That was a lot of money!"

Just on the other side of the phoenix tree stands one of the most important relics from village history. It looks like a pile of vine-covered lava stones – not exactly an uncommon sight on this part of the island – but it's actually one of Meiqiu's original entry gates. Closer inspection reveals a trapezoidal section of stone wall with a rectangular opening in the middle. No one knows for certain how old the bit of wall is – lava rocks appear to be ancient even when they're "new" – but "hundreds" of years is what most people say. Typically no one pays it much mind, until somebody from the village gets married or dies.

There are three such old entryways in Meiqiu, each denoting a specific section of the village. Every family belongs to one entryway, and that is where they congregate on the occasion of a wedding or a funeral. All weeds and vines are removed from the stones, and the married couple – or on bad days, the coffin – is walked beneath the lintel. "The old men in the village say this village gate is the only way to welcome new people in, and to send daughters and the dead out," Wang explained. "When these important things happen, people must walk through the old village gate. It means God will bless you in the coming days. If you walk around the opening, it is not auspicious."

Wang and his wife walked through the old gate behind the phoenix tree when they got married in 1997. The whole village was there to wish them well. They set off firecrackers. They killed pigs and goats and chickens in their honor. It was a day of celebration for everyone.

But ten years later, in August 2007, Wang found himself and about one hundred other villagers gathered under the phoenix tree for a decidedly different occasion. And no one seemed to be in a celebratory mood. The blood-red flowers of the phoenix tree had come and gone with the season, but the curved seedpods remained. In the gloom of the early evening sky, they hung from the tree like hundreds of dark sickles.

It was cooler than normal for the middle of the Hainan summer, but the crowd was hot with anxiety. For several weeks, rumors had been swirling around the local teahouses that a company was interested in renting land in the area. But no one seemed to have the details: What land, for what price? And who was the mysterious company interested in large swaths of rocky terrain previously thought only good for growing fruit trees? Meiqiu's residents wanted answers, and they were finally about to get some.

The village governor stood atop a cement bench next to a lychee tree and told the crowd that the rumors they had heard were indeed true. There was a developer interested in village land – in fact this company, named Junhao and based in Hong

Kong, was intent on buying up property from many villages in the area, not just Meiqiu.

The government had determined that each plot of Meiqiu land in question would fall into three categories, with three different prices: "garden," where most of the land was covered by fruit trees, at 29,000 yuan per *mu*, a Chinese unit of measurement equal to roughly one-sixth of an acre; "fruit tree land," where a portion is covered with fruit trees, at 26,200 yuan per *mu*; and *huangdi*, or "wasteland," earth covered in wild plant life, rocks and grass, at 12,500 yuan per *mu*.

The meeting went on for more than an hour. The governor did most of the talking, but the crowd did plenty grumbling, muttering among themselves as he talked through what he knew of the proposals. Some villagers flatly refused to sell their acreage. Some expressed disappointment with the prices. Others worried what the future would hold without large portions of their family land.

Wang didn't say much. He just listened. Conflicted, he agreed with some of what everyone had to say. He admitted that the numbers being bandied about were tempting for a poor villager like him. It was more than he ever thought someone would want to pay for his "wasteland" near Meiqiu. But when he learned that land laden with fruit trees was also to be included in the deal, his mood changed. The fruit reaped from one *mu* of fruit trees could fetch around ten thousand yuan at market in one year. "Do they think we're stupid?" he asked. "We can make back the compensation money in two or three years selling fruit."

The villagers also didn't agree with the "Red Line," the literal red line that encircled the entirety of land planned for development on the proposal map. They felt it came too close to their village. They didn't want to feel surrounded. Wang noticed that some of the land he owned fell right inside the Red Line.

He thought about his children, and their children. These lands had been passed down from generation to generation. Meiqiu people took pride in private land ownership. They felt it set them apart from other parts of rural China, where land is typically owned by a collective. Wang felt a duty to hold on to his family's land legacy. His initial inclination was to refuse to sell. But as the governor continued, it became clear to Wang and everyone else in the crowd that the decision to sell or not to sell had already been made for them. This deal was going through, whether the villagers liked it or not.

"The situation became very chaotic," Wang said. "The governor said we had to sell. He said the prices were not negotiable. So why assemble the entire village for a meeting when nothing is open for discussion? He may be one of us, but the village governor is just a mouthpiece for the government."

The meeting came to an end, but the village remained abuzz. There was too much information to take in. Too much to think about. Too much change, too soon. Lost in all of the chatter was the village governor's off-handed, and perhaps off-script, remark that the land the villagers were required to sell was to be turned into golf courses – probably because no one in Meiqiu knew what a golf course was. There was also no reason for the villagers to know that Junhao, the company purchasing the land, also had an English name: Mission Hills.

None of the villagers signed off on the land deal, but the government had. And the bulldozers were soon on their way. While talks between Mission Hills and local government authorities had no doubt been ongoing long before that meeting under Meiqiu's phoenix tree, most agree the "Yangshan District Land Consolidation and Ecological Restoration Project" was officially launched on September 1, 2007. Many villagers assumed the numbers associated with that date explained the project's code name: Project 791.

Ken Chu and Mission Hills were at it again. And this time they were determined to go bigger and bolder than ever before. In July 2007, Chu reached out to a small circle of associates with news of a project so ambitious it far exceeded almost anyone's wildest dreams. Mission Hills was looking at two sites, both in Hainan, and had plans to build forty-eight courses, three times the number of golf courses that existed in the province at that time. The smaller location, where just twelve of the courses would go, was forty-five miles up the east coast from Sanya, Hainan's southern resort city. The other plot was to the north, not far from the capital city of Haikou, and it was massive. Ken was intent on building thirty-six courses there – and he wanted construction on all the courses to be simultaneous. The Haikou project was currently on standby, he said, but it might start moving by the autumn. His people were already working on a plan to get 1,500 pieces of heavy machinery to the island. Ken noted that the Hainan government was especially keen to work with Mission Hills, given the company's reputation and track record for aggressive thinking. The government, he added, was eager to see the world-record-setting project completed in eighteen months.

Thirty-six courses. Eighteen months. When word finally made its way to Martin, the numbers hit him like a tsunami. He was excited – this had all the makings of a historic, not to mention wildly lucrative, project – but he was also cautious. He didn't want a repeat of Mission Hills Kunming, which had fallen through a little more than a year before and left Martin red-faced, trying to explain to dozens of foreign workers why the big job he had promised them was no more.

"What are my chances of calling these same guys back and telling them now I've got thirty-six golf courses I'm going to build?" Martin thought. "They're going to look at me, and I'm going to be the laughing stock of the world."

On top of that, the schedule seemed impossible. Martin spent days crunching the numbers, and the fastest timetable he could come up with for the construction was thirty-two months. And even that was working at an unprecedented pace. "We don't have near this much time," was the response from Ken Chu.

Ken reminded Martin of the logic that had made the five courses a reality in Shenzhen in 2003. "If someone asked you to build two courses in eighteen months, would you tell them you could do it?" he challenged Martin, who saw where this was going, and said yes. "Okay, well, just treat this like eighteen separate two-course projects," Ken explained, making it sound simple. Too simple?

Martin started doing the sums in his head. He'd need eighteen project superintendents. He'd have to have four shapers per project. "We'd need sixty-four shapers," Martin told him.

"Confirmed!" Ken exclaimed.

"Ken, I don't know if there's sixty-four shapers in the industry."

Martin spent the better part of the next two months at his desk in Scottsdale, Arizona, trying to wrangle the army required to meet Ken's audacious demands. He called everyone he knew in the industry: project managers, superintendents, irrigation specialists and, of course, shapers. He called them all. "If a guy knew how to turn a fucking key and run a bulldozer, bring him on," Martin joked.

But with each call, Martin made sure to remind everyone that this was China. Building golf courses there was a tricky business. Everything could fall through at any moment. He couldn't make any guarantees. The new hires would soon realize what he meant.

It was a "huge undertaking" getting all the foreign workers to Hainan, as Martin expected it to be. But he didn't expect the headaches that continued once everyone had arrived at the job site. He'd usually spend around six days at a time on the site. Two of those days would be consumed by dealing with, as he called it, "the white guys fucking whining," just like he did in his first days working in Thailand. Most of the crew had never worked in Asia before. And much of their whining had to do with the food brought to them in Styrofoam containers during lunchtime. *They sent me soggy French fries today. My salad and my spaghetti got all mixed together.*

"I have to get all the expats in one big group and tell them all to shut the fuck up and work," Martin said. "I said, 'I got a list of thirty other guys who want this job.'" He tried to explain that the conditions were good, really good, for a Chinese construction site. "I mean, I go down to a different job and they're fucking eating fish heads. Mission Hills did a very good job."

In fact, the Chus had a little cinder block village built just for their foreign workers. Cereal was served for breakfast in the morning. There was a karaoke bar, an internet café and a basketball court. "The only negative was that they'd pack six to eight people in one room," Martin said, remembering the conditions in the employee dormitories, which were pretty typical.

Even though nice hotels in Haikou were on offer, Martin would make a point to stay at the compound with the rest of the employees. Everyone would laugh and ask, "Why do you stay at that shithole?" Martin had his reasons. First, he worked long hours whenever he was on site, usually at least 6 a.m. to 9 p.m., and he had no interest in spending an additional two hours on the road. In the mornings, he could grab breakfast and a coffee and be out on one of the courses in a matter of minutes. In the evenings, it was just plain fun. All his Thai workers were there, and they often barbecued and cooked Thai food and sat outside, drinking beers, smoking cigars and catching up.

But Martin also had another, more business-minded, reason for staying on site. "I wanted to gain respect from other workers. I didn't want them to think I was a cocky bastard who had to go stay at a five-star hotel. That wasn't my style."

He also knew he needed to give some of his new hires a lesson in how things worked in China, and how their new bosses operated. Several of his coveted shapers were trying to dissect their contracts and make changes. "You're wasting your time," Martin told them. "What are you going to do? Take them to Chinese court?"

6

THE MOUNTAIN IS HIGH

Zhou Xunshu had all the physical tools. His swing looked home-made, but according to the American pro golfer Jim Johnson, one of the China Tour's official coaches in 2007, it was "pretty solid, pretty simple. It works. It may look a little funny, but it is tech-nically okay. He's got a short backswing, but he's really strong. His calves, they are like iron." When he hooked Zhou up to his testing equipment, Johnson rated him to be the longest hitter on the China Tour.

After Qingdao, Zhou rattled off a string of solid showings, including an eighth place finish at Dragon Lake. But things really started to click for him in Kunming. It was August, and he was two-thirds of the way through the season. He was ranked four-teenth on the China Tour order of merit and sixteenth on the China Golf Association money list for the year. He needed to break into the top twelve for the year, or finish in the top three of a single tournament, to earn his professional player certification. The top twelve seemed within reach, but only if Zhou could keep up the momentum and rattle off a series of impressive performances leading up to the tour's October finale in Beijing.

Zhou apparently didn't want to wait that long. He seemed intent on doing things the quick way. At the Nick Faldo-designed Lakeview Golf Club near Kunming, he fired off his best ever open-ing round, holing four birdies en route to a 3-under 69. He entered the clubhouse with a share of the lead, and for the first time in three years on tour, he saw his name displayed in big characters on the leaderboard. At the end of the day, he was in a five-way tie for fourth place.

The round led to Zhou's first ever in-tournament media interview, as well.

"Is not having sponsors difficult for you?" the female reporter asked.

"Yes, it is very hard. Some other golfers, after each tournament, they will have a rest and not leave until the next day," he told her. "I need to go back to Chongqing the night the tournament finishes because I need to teach the next day. If I do not teach, I cannot make money."

"How often are you able to practice?"

"Usually, I get up at 6:30 in the morning and go running as a way to maintain my fitness level. Then I eat breakfast at 7:30 and go to the driving range to practice until the noon. Then I start to teach in the afternoon, and sometimes I don't stop until midnight."

"Wow. So busy!"

"There is really not enough time in the day for me. Sometimes in the morning people will call me and ask for a lesson. And I can't refuse or else people will judge me. And if I give a lesson in the morning, the whole order of my day is disturbed."

"Have you thought about what you'd do with the prize money if you were to win the tournament?"

"I would definitely put it toward buying an apartment in Chongqing. But there are three days left – I can't really think about this until the tournament is finished."

And fortunes change fast in golf. One day you're feared, the next day you're forgotten. "Golf is the only sport I know of where a player pays for every mistake," 1946 US Open winner Lloyd Mangrum once said. "In golf, every swing counts against you." Sometimes, so do the trees. Friday started well for Zhou – he had carded three birdies on the front nine and was sitting in second place at 5 under par. Then a nightmare ninth hole took Zhou's name off the leaderboard. He hooked his tee shot, which ran dogleg left, and his ball was nowhere to be found. After a long, frantic search, it was concluded that Zhou's ball must have been lodged inside a knot of branches in one of the tall trees to the left of the fairway. So Zhou had to take a penalty stroke and tee off again. His following shot from the fairway landed in the sand trap before the green. He managed to chip a beautiful bunker shot, which landed three-and-a-half feet from the pin. But his putt lipped out and Zhou walked off the green with a 3-over 7. He slammed his putter into the grass, and then the pavement, repeatedly. He was out of the top ten. And then it started to rain.

That triple bogey stayed in his head throughout the back nine. He struggled with his driver, missing fairway after fairway. He found himself focusing on saving pars, and when he did give himself birdie chances, they barely missed. After six straight pars, he bogeyed the sixteenth hole after his tee shot sliced into the water. The rain really started to come down when he got to the seventeenth tee. He missed a fourteen-foot birdie putt on that hole, and on the eighteenth, Zhou put himself in an excellent position to enter the clubhouse at 1 over for the day, 2 under for the tournament. But play was halted before he could take a one-foot birdie putt. Thirty minutes later, Zhou's "gimme" putt spun out. He let out a shout, tapped in for par and, frustrated, launched his ball into the water nearby. The day, which had begun with such promise, ended with him tied for sixteenth place overall, nine strokes behind the leader.

The best golfers are the ones who are good at forgetting, the ones who realize the only thing they can control is their attitude toward the next swing. Zhou lets things linger and stew. "Sometimes my mind is a mess out on the course," he said. "I can get impatient and sometimes I just think too much. I let too many things into my mind. If I make a mistake, it's hard for me to let it go. I keep thinking about it, and then I make more mistakes, and then I get angry about them."

Zhou said golf was different than other sports, like basketball or football. To do well in golf, he believed, you first need to "conquer yourself." That had proved difficult for him – his head could put up quite a fight. But he managed to rebound from his rough Friday outing and finished the tournament in a five-way tie for ninth. It was his second top-ten finish of the year and earned him 12,860 yuan before taxes. On the Omega China Tour Order of Merit, he inched up to the thirteenth spot.

He was looking more like a certified pro golfer with each match.

★

Golf legend Bobby Jones said, "You swing your best when you have the fewest things to think about." With that golf truth in mind, it's no surprise Zhou wasn't swinging his best at the close of the 2007 season – his head was overflowing.

"We're going to have an Olympic baby," Zhou announced over dinner on the eve of the opening round of the tour's late-September stop in Xiamen, a picturesque port city on China's southeastern coast. Liu Yan was two months pregnant, due in April 2008. It was auspicious – but the news required some changes in their situation. "Also, we're getting married. Probably in November, before she gets too big," he said.

Zhou had cobbled together enough money – through their own savings, and loans from friends and relatives – to buy an apartment in a Chongqing high-rise. So they were moving, too. Liu Yan's parents had only slowly warmed to Zhou, and a house was a prerequisite for getting married.

"He is too old," Liu Yan's father had said once he met his daughter's boyfriend for the first time, when Zhou had traveled to her village in Hunan for Spring Festival in 2005. In China, an age difference of three or five years was acceptable. The twelve years that separated Liu Yan and Zhou was too much. Zhou was very nervous on that visit. He was afraid Liu Yan's father wouldn't approve of the relationship and would kick him out. So Zhou behaved himself. He washed the food, and he washed the dishes. He worked very hard to win over her family. Yet Liu Yan's father didn't talk to him during the visit. Not a word. "Why bother talking to him?" Liu Yan's father told her. "I don't like him."

Her father was more opposed to the relationship than her mother. Her mother's greatest fear, according to Liu Yan, was that if Zhou's finances didn't improve, they might not visit Hunan very often, especially after they had a child. And Liu Yan knew her parents wouldn't want to move to Chongqing. Hunan was their home.

One day, Liu Yan called her father in tears, knowing he still didn't approve of the relationship. He responded with an ultimatum for Zhou. "If you want to marry my daughter, you need to buy a house first. And you can't move back to your hometown," he said. Her father was especially suspicious of the fact that Zhou came from Guizhou. He had traveled through the province during the 1970s, and said he never wanted his daughter to live there. "I know that place," he said. "Not good!" Her father said until Zhou bought a house he would withhold the family *hukou*, or household registration certificate, a document necessary to get married in China. And so Zhou scrimped and saved and borrowed so he and Liu Yan could get married.

After that, Liu Yan's parents started to change their minds. Liu Yan's brother, Liu Jun, had a lot to do with it, she said. Zhou was "honest and nice," he insisted. It was *yuan fen* for Liu Yan and Zhou to be together. Zhou was "not the kind of guy who would play tricks," he told them. Eventually, her parents decided to just let it go. However, Zhou still had to buy a house for their daughter.

So, as play began in Xiamen, Zhou's focus was elsewhere. If the profanity spewing from Zhou's mouth wasn't sign enough, his body language declared he was a man ready for the season to be over. After one of his seven second-round bogeys, he kicked an empty water bottle angrily down the cart path. It was only Friday, but he went ahead and booked his return flight for Sunday, the last day of play, choosing an early departure time on the assumption that he wouldn't be among those in the late groups battling for the title.

"What if you end up winning the championship?" another golfer asked Zhou.

"If I win the championship, I wouldn't care about the money I wasted on the ticket," he replied. Then Zhou turned his golf cap to the side and added, "But look at me. Do I look like a champion?"

Zhou didn't feel like a champion, and that is what mattered. Later, on his way back to the hotel in a taxi, he sighed and said, "I need to figure some things out."

Zhou didn't need to worry about rescheduling his flight. He finished tied for twenty-ninth, his worst China Tour finish since the season opener in Nanjing. At the airport, Zhou was antsy. He couldn't sit still. He stood in front of a glass fire extinguisher case on the wall and practiced his swing in the reflection. "I really hate waiting for flights," Zhou said. "I'm too impatient."

So, too, it seemed, were all of his fellow passengers. Before any rows were called for boarding, and despite the fact that all seats were pre-assigned, everyone rushed the gate and an anxious mob formed around the ticket taker. Zhou, now a seasoned traveler, remained seated and looked on disapprovingly.

"*Nongmin*," he said shaking his head at the crowd. "Peasants."

The 2007 season finale, the Omega Championship, took place in Beijing just a few weeks before Zhou and Liu Yan's wedding. It was cold and windy, with gusts reaching more than thirty miles per hour. Yellow and brown leaves fluttered across the tournament fairway; the seasons were changing, and Zhou's golf season, for all intents and purposes, was already over. Zhou shot an 83 and an 82 and missed the cut for the first time all year. Mentally, he had checked out.

In the weeks leading up to the event, Zhou hadn't been practicing as much as usual. The collective stress, which had been simmering for some time, began to boil over, causing little trivial tiffs back home with Liu Yan.

"Sometimes I think being single is best for a professional golfer," he said. "You don't need to think about anything, just spending the whole day practicing and at night have fun and relax or whatever. But having a family is just different. Sometimes even when I hear my phone ring I become very uneasy. It doesn't mean her calling me is annoying, it is just that little things start to add up, and indirectly this affects my mood."

Zhou's poor finish to the season pushed him out of the top twenty on the China Tour's money list. He failed to earn his elusive pro card.

"There were some successes and some failures," Zhou said, looking back. "The good part is I am improved. Kunming was a pity. That tree. I let one ball affect my mood the rest of the way."

He hadn't learned to let go.

Originally, Zhou and Liu Yan had wanted to schedule the ceremony for November 11, the anniversary of the day they officially professed their love for each other, back in 2004 at Dragon Lake Golf Club. But the restaurant they were looking at wasn't available that day, so they had to settle for November 10. "I was very irritated," Zhou said. "Just little things like that really bother me."

They didn't expect many people at the wedding. Many of Zhou's friends in Guangzhou couldn't make it, and they hadn't lived in Chongqing long enough to have a large group of acquaintances. He wasn't sure if his parents would be able to attend. Liu Yan's father had already told them that he couldn't get away – he was too busy overseeing the remodeling of the family house. He'd bought the materials himself and hired workers, and didn't trust them to use the materials correctly without his oversight. "No time. No other way. *Mei banfa!*" he had told Liu Yan. Her mother made the journey from Hunan with Liu Yan's brother and his wife.

Zhou and Liu Yan were married in a large private dining room in a downtown high-rise. It was a small yet colorful affair, a Chongqing take on a Western-style wedding, if some aspects of the evening seemed to happen in reverse. The couple arrived in a rented white Mercedes-Benz. The guests waited outside the building entrance, armed with confetti and streamers, pieces of which stayed attached to the bride and groom for the remainder of the afternoon. In the lobby, the couple welcomed their guests in a receiving line of sorts, with Liu Yan lighting cigarettes for all.

The dining room, which served as a setting for both the wedding ceremony and the celebratory meal, was awash in pink. At the back of the room stood an archway covered in fake flowers and pink chiffon. The front of the room was all pink curtains. The showpiece was a large portrait of Zhou and Liu Yan, framed by a ring of pink feathers and accented by strings of white holiday lights.

There were seven tables for the fifty or so guests, among them just a couple of Zhou's fellow golfers from the China Tour. At the center of each table the guests found a bottle of Sprite, a bottle of Pepsi, a bottle of Changyu Pioneer red wine, a box of *baijiu*, a pack of Double Happiness cigarettes and a bowl with an assortment of peanuts, sunflower seeds and candy. Loud English-language pop music billowed from several speakers.

Zhou wore a black pinstriped suit with a yellow shirt and silver tie. Liu Yan looked lovely in a lacy white wedding dress with a veil and dangling crystal jewelry. But this was, by and large, not a formal affair. Many guests wore jeans. Some had sneakers on.

When everyone was seated at their tables, the couple walked down the aisle together, from the pink archway to the wall of pink curtains. The marriage ceremony was conducted via microphone by an offstage emcee. This was followed by a traditional tea-drinking ceremony and a series of modern additions: a champagne tower; a bouquet toss; a bubble machine; a wardrobe change; more confetti; and dinner. Then the *baijiu* flowed. A couple of the guests passed out before dark.

Zhou and Liu Yan couldn't have been more in love. Unfortunately, not everyone was able to be there to see it. Zhou's parents couldn't make the journey from Qixin.

Zhou and Liu Yan's apartment was 1,300 square feet on the ninth floor of a thirty-story building. Zhou would have liked to buy a flat on a higher level for the resale value, were he not deathly afraid of heights – strange for a guy who grew up on the side of a mountain. "Even with a balcony or a window," Zhou said, "when I get closer to the edge I just feel like my flesh is falling off my body, one layer at a time." The ninth floor was high enough for Zhou, who, if he stood on his balcony a safe distance from the rail, could crane his neck and see a sliver of netting and green grass on the driving range where he worked. The rest was obscured by another high-rise apartment building. There were high-rises everywhere, tall, boxy and new. Just a few years earlier, this area had been all but empty.

With all the changes in his life, Zhou hadn't been able to practice all winter. Decorating his new apartment in Chongqing turned into a long ordeal. For several months he was forced to monitor it on his own. That was because Liu Yan had returned home to her parents' village, Tanzishan, in Hunan province, for their baby's birth.

Liu Yan's childhood had been pretty happy, so it was hard for her to imagine what life had been like for her father when he was young. He was born in the 1950s and came of age in Chairman Mao's China. He would tell Liu Yan about those days, and how hard they were. His family often didn't have enough wheat, so they ate the chaff. It wasn't just his family that was so hard hit; everyone in the area was relying on the chaff to survive. Liu Yan's mother told her this was because corrupt local officials kept all the real food for themselves. Sometimes, as a child, Liu Yan's father was so constipated from not eating enough fiber that his father had to use a finger to dig the feces out of him. "When I think about this, it makes me want to cry," Liu Yan said.

He'd had no childhood. He had started working when he was five years old, pulling his father's cart in the fields. He quit school after the third grade and left home at a very young age to earn money. When he was ten he found a job as a laborer on a reservoir construction site, carrying sand and rocks from one place to another. He worked every day but Sunday.

In his teens, he had bounced from one job to another. He sold lumber, medicine, chickens; he even sold ice cream for a while. To do business, he traveled across China, to places like Guangdong, Guangxi and Zhou's family's province, Guizhou. When he was twenty he saw that there was money to be made selling eggs wholesale. Every day, he'd take eggs from Hunan across the border, to cities like Zhanjiang in Guangdong province. After about ten years selling chicken eggs, he'd saved enough – sixty thousand yuan – to build the only house Liu Yan could remember from her own childhood. It was three stories tall, one of the nicest buildings in the village at the time.

Liu Yan's parents told her that things started to get better in 1979 and 1980, when the land was divided among the people. People in the village started to build more houses, and very few of them were made of earth, as was common before. The main road, which had once been very narrow, was widened. Soon enough, it would run all the way to Guilin, in Guangxi. In 1994, Liu Yan's father and seven friends took advantage of Deng's "opening up" reforms to start a small business. They built a red brick factory on some old farmland. Business was good for a while, but then the area's earth no longer produced the clay to make the bricks. Now, her father kept chickens on the land near the factory, but it wasn't enough to support the family. So he started to sell fertilizer and collect recycling – mostly bottles and cardboard. He also fixed watches.

Liu Yan had come to realize her father had been worried about Zhou because it had been so hard for her family in the old days. Her father wanted the best for his only daughter, and this older man, from a poor family, with an unstable job playing a game he'd never heard of, was not the son-in-law of his dreams. If he was honest, though, Liu Yan's father saw a little bit of himself in Zhou. When he was courting Liu Yan's mother, he didn't have money either, and no one in her family approved of their relationship. Over the months, Liu Yan's parents had come to respect Zhou's drive and determination. And now that she was expecting a baby, Liu Yan felt sure she could count on her father's support.

She was due in a couple of months, and she already knew she was expecting a son. She'd had two ultrasounds, and the doctors weren't supposed to tell her the baby's sex, but, she said, "This is the countryside, and things are a little different."

There was less pressure in the village. The pace of life was less intense. She was going to stay in Tanzishan for a month or two after the birth, following the tradition of *zuo yuezi*, or confinement. During that time, her mother would take care of her and the new baby. Plus, although Zhou was insisting that he and Liu Yan take care of their baby on their own, he was busy – decorating the apartment, yes, but also teaching and training. And the 2008 China Tour would start up right after the baby's due date.

Still, Liu Yan was eager to get back to Chongqing. "Every day here is kind of dull. Sometimes I help my mother in the kitchen. Sometimes I just stand on the balcony and stare at the road and the train tracks, and the smokestack from the chemical factory. After nine o'clock at night, you can't see any lights on the road.

By that time, most of the people here have already gone to bed," she said.

"The city is more convenient, more exciting. In Chongqing, I can go out shopping for fun. I can read books. The village doesn't even have a book store."

Liu Yan's mother said that Tanzishan hadn't grown as fast as other villages nearby. She blamed the local government officials for this – they were corrupt, she said, one thing that hadn't changed since the old days.

Despite Beijing's golf course moratorium, some big developers continued to show a remarkable ability to manage and massage *guanxi* with local government officials. Without the right connections, it would never have been possible to operate on the grand scale needed to build a golf resort. And managing and massaging *guanxi* was often a very tangible business. Sources familiar with one company said that before launching a large golf course construction project in Guangdong, the developer outfitted the local police department with a new fleet of motorcycles. On Hainan island, it was said the company built the county a brand new government office building during the negotiations over another large golf-related development. That land deal fell through, but the building, or at least the shell of it, remained. "It's sitting there like a big old white elephant," a local source said. "That's development in China right there."

Most successful developers have at least one person, if not a team of three or four, whose only job is to maintain solid relationships with – if not blatantly pay off – the local officials who sign off on various aspects of development projects, regardless of the directives from Beijing. These staffers call themselves CEOs, "chief entertainment officers," because they're constantly picking up the tab for meals, drinks and trips to the local karaoke joint ("chief enticement officer" might be a better title). First, there's the money that changes hands while a project is trying to get approved, and then there's the money that changes hands while the project is trying to avoid being shut down. "It's just to keep the trucks going, keep the villagers out of the way, secure the land," a source said. "It's just one thing after another."

There was one project on the mainland where the owner didn't play the game well with the local government, and to onlookers it was clear from early on that "the job would go on forever." Relatively minor land issues with villagers went unresolved because the owner was "tighter than hell" and "always trying to negotiate down to nothing." Everything with the owner "just takes forever and ever and ever," a source said. "He will always have problems," the person added.

Some successful developers, on the other hand, weren't afraid to throw money at problems. They often realized that a big outlay of money now would likely save them from expensive delays later. "At the end of the day, they're doing it the right way – for China," a source said. "I mean, it's just the money they'd lose by having all these people out there and delaying the project and all. You know, they've done it. They've been there. They're the experts on it."

Developers have been known to name a local village head as a subcontractor on critical projects. The village head makes somewhere on the order of five yuan per day for every villager he brings onto the project as a laborer, and that quickly adds up – at certain points during construction, a massive development can have thousands of local villagers on the payroll. The village head is indebted to the developer, and the developer knows it has someone who will defend the project if and when land issues arise. When disputes with villagers escalated at Haikou, one call from Mission Hills was all it took to get busloads of local officials on the scene to work things out.

Developers "know all the games to play," one contractor said. "That's just the China way."

Of course, there are times when problems don't get worked out, regardless of how much money gets thrown at them. A prime example was a monster project that Martin Moore had worked on. The owner was a billionaire real estate tycoon, one of the richest men in China. He had dreams as big as his bank account, and set his sights on a prime piece of land, a spot so beautiful that it could have been part of a national park. It had everything – steep cliff faces, stunning mountain views from almost every angle and, at the center of it all, a large meandering lake that would bring water into play on nearly every hole. He hired one of the world's most celebrated golf course architects to draw up a signature design. And he was busy buying up decaying resorts all over the area. He hoped this would be the first of as many as six golf courses he'd build there. Big numbers like this were becoming common in China – everyone was chasing after the Chus.

But Martin's experienced eye saw problems lurking at the site from the start. Right where the course's first three holes would be, there was a well-established village, whose residents also claimed some ownership of various other sections of the course. When Martin first arrived, he noticed several villagers had begun to build new, taller homes – a sure sign they were trying to score larger relocation settlements. Martin could tell these villagers were well informed, and canny. They weren't going down without a fight.

Then there was the rest of the course, hugging the lake, which happened to be connected upstream to a large reservoir. At the moment, the land was dry. The water was about five yards lower than what was considered "safe" for the course from a flooding perspective. But Martin had taken a look at the historical records and found that about a dozen years earlier the lake had risen to around ten yards above the "safe" level. The tycoon assured Martin and his crew that he had an arrangement with the local authorities: should the water start to flood the course, they'd open up the dam at the far end of the lake and draw the water down to a manageable level. Martin was skeptical.

The course ended up being one of the most drawn-out construction projects of Martin's career, spanning nearly five years. The delays were partly due to the weather. Brutal winters froze the ground and covered the course with snow, completely shutting down construction for several months each year. But the biggest issue was the land disputes that bedeviled the project from day one.

It was a story Martin had heard several times before. The owner says he paid the government for the land. The villagers say they didn't get paid, or that they weren't paid enough. "I know the owner is just out millions [for the land]," Martin said. "Say he pays a million out, and he gives it to his two or three people who deal with the government. How much do they take? And they go and pay the government. How much does the government take? By the time it gets down to these villagers, I mean, you know, two-thirds, three-quarters of it's gone. And those guys don't get shit."

Not far from the existing village, the owner built what Martin described as "a whole city" with "US townhouses." The villagers refused to move to them.

"I don't blame them," Martin said. "Better or not better, it's not their home. Some of these little villages, they're fourth or fifth generation."

While the bickering between the local government and the villagers raged on, Martin's team built "temporary" versions of holes No. 1, 2 and 3 in a valley far enough from the village to be considered untouchable. But the rest of the project was a constant game of stop-and-start. They waited for the tycoon to say which parts of the land were approved for construction. They would get word that the spats had been settled and it was time to go ahead. Then Martin's crew would find protesters waiting for them at the job site.

"They would block the roads," Martin said. "As soon as you went out there and had equipment running, they would all come up." The confrontations didn't become physical, but they were effective nonetheless. Martin said he instructed his guys "to just do what they say, you know. Never told them to challenge them or anything."

Construction "came to a complete halt" after villagers took their case to the central government in Beijing. That move put the project, once hidden away in the mountains, in the spotlight – China Central Television even came out to report a story. The unwanted attention couldn't have come at a worse time. Beijing had just launched what looked like another serious crackdown on golf development, and the tycoon's dream course was an easy target for the capital's "golf police." The owner scrambled to get more approvals and permits to clear the way, but as Martin pointed out, "none of them were for golf, obviously." There were no official permits for golf courses being issued in those days.

Soon, Martin's crew noticed helicopters flying overhead with some regularity. "The owner's people told us to fill in all the bunkers and plant grass over them," he said. "They told us to put dirt over all the cart paths. They said they didn't want it to look like a golf course. I thought it was the stupidest thing – there's no way you're going to disguise this so it's not a golf course."

While Martin began to question whether the project would ever reach the finish line, the owner continued to dream the way only a billionaire can. His first course may be in jeopardy, but that wouldn't stop him from thinking about courses No. 2, No. 3 and beyond. He had representatives from every celebrity designer out to visit the site, from Greg Norman to Tiger Woods. "Give him credit," Martin said of the tycoon, "he's got an imagination. He can sit there and think." Sometimes, though, imagination coupled with a seemingly endless budget can drive a person a little crazy. "Can we put a waterfall here?" was one of the owner's favorite questions. Waterfalls, unfortunately, couldn't hide a course from the golf police.

Although the village itself never moved, the land disputes and the scrutiny from the authorities eventually died down enough to where Martin's team could finish the course. The result was beautiful. Many who saw it thought it might be one of the best in China – and it had better have been. The owner had spent forty million dollars on the project, more than four times what was considered expensive in this country.

But then it started to rain. And the water began to rise, well beyond the "safe" level. The government didn't do a thing, and the entire golf course was submerged in four yards of water.

"It's ruined," Martin said. "Simply the opening of a gate would save him forty million dollars. And he obviously doesn't have the pull to make that happen. The government's in a bind. If the local government opens the gate and lets the water down to save an illegal golf course, there'd be some definite ramifications there."

The tycoon refused to give up, however. He hired the same designer to route another nine holes on the side of a mountain, six yards above the high-water mark. He thought another thirty million dollars would be enough to make it happen.

Ken Chu was certainly not the only Chinese golf course owner with high expectations. Take the golf course developer everybody called "the Chairman," whose boardroom antics made Donald Trump look like Donald Duck. The Chairman was a pedant for punctuality. If someone arrived a second late for a meeting, his security guards blocked them from entering via the main door to the boardroom. Instead, he or she would have to go outside and walk around the side of the building to an alternate entrance. That door led the person upstairs, then downstairs, before finally reaching the back door to the boardroom. That forced the latecomer to enter the room from behind the Chairman's custom-made leather executive chair, which extended two feet over the top of the Chairman's head. The twenty to forty pairs of eyes around the table would avoid catching the gaze of the late arrival as he or she slipped into the room.

The latecomer would take a chair at the table, but without any formal acknowledgment from the Chairman or the assembled senior staff. For a while the meeting would carry on normally, often with a PowerPoint presentation projected on a screen. The Chairman demanded all presentations come with visual aids, giving him a reason to use his beloved laser pointers, of which a multicolored collection was always lined up neatly on the table in front of him. And then, sometimes, the Chairman would issue a fine or two. For example, if some work wasn't completed because a fleet of trucks didn't make it to the site, the Chairman would single out the person responsible, slam the table and say, "You're fined! Two thousand yuan!" This was business as usual at the Chairman's weekly meetings.

Five minutes or so later, however, the Chairman would pounce on the latecomer. No matter the person's position within the company, or the country on his or her passport, the humiliation was the same. The Chairman would abruptly stop the meeting and "chew them out big time," Martin reported. At very least, the latecomer would be told to spend the remainder of the meeting, which would often go on for two hours, standing at his or her seat. Usually, however, the Chairman would tell the person to stand in the corner facing the wall "like you're in kindergarten." Staff being disciplined, with their backs to the rest of the group, would have to shout updates into the room's luscious wood paneling.

"Everything he does is like to show everyone, 'I'm the king. I've got all the power. I can do anything I want to do,'" Martin said. "They all want to look good in front of their whole staff, and if he can make a foreigner do what he says, he's really the king, you know."

The Chairman took aim at Martin's American project manager on a couple of occasions. Tardy for the weekly meeting, the manager had to take the walk of shame, knowing full well what would follow. He took his seat, and waited. Several minutes went by and then the Chairman, with the face of a disappointed parent, looked at the project manager and spoke. A young woman sitting next to the Chairman translated.

"The Chairman said because you arrived late to the meeting, you must stand up now," she said.

The project manager had discussed the possibility of such an occurrence with Martin beforehand.

"Martin, do I really have to stand if I am late for a meeting?" he had asked.

"That's up to you," Martin said. "You don't have to. But I'll say one thing. If he does stand you there and point you out like that, and you take it like everyone else does, you'll earn so much respect from him."

So Martin's project manager got up from his seat and stood there at the conference for the remaining ninety minutes of the meeting.

A couple weeks later, the project manager's driver was delayed and he arrived late for the meeting once again. This time, as he walked in behind the Chairman, the project manager just said, "I know. I know. I've got to stand up."

The group emitted a rare collective chuckle.

"The Chairman would like to know why you were late," the translator said.

The project manager explained about the driver.

"Okay, the Chairman said you can sit down," the translator said.

"No, I was late. I'll stand."

The two, via the translator, went back and forth like that for a while.

"Part of it is a game, you know," Martin said. "Part of it is you're trying to figure out someone's personality. I know what the Chairman's like. I'm not going to challenge him. And I'm not going to argue with him. If you go in there and say, 'Fuck you, I'm not going to stand over there,' or something like that, I mean, you're done. You're done forever. But if you stand up and you make him look good in front of all his staff, like, 'I made the foreigners look bad,' he'll love you. That'll last so long."

The Chairman has been known to take his executives on impromptu extreme-team-building exercises, including eight-hour hikes in the mountains. "Some people pass out," Martin said. "And when it's all done, he thinks it brings all of them closer together."

The Chairman was a small man, but he lived large. Among his fleet of automobiles was a one-million-dollar luxury sedan the size of a Hong Kong studio apartment. It featured fully reclining rear seats and multiple flatscreen TVs. Front to back, the car measured a titanic 6.2 yards; so long, in fact, that it qualified as a truck in several Chinese cities. Officially, it was required to display the yellow license plate usually reserved for trucks and buses, but the Chairman had no intention of having his luxury car lumped in with working class vehicles, so he chose to go without a license plate at all.

"I don't think anyone stops him," Martin said.

The same could be said of the Chairman's accountant. "He goes all out," Martin said. "He's a big spender." When his celebrity course designer is visiting and the Chairman takes his team out to dinner, it's nothing for him to drop seventy thousand dollars on a table of twelve. It's abalone. It's the finest wines. It's a different world.

Martin recalled a conversation he had with the course designer's No. 2 man, not long after such a meal.

"You know that meal we had last week?" the man said.

"Yeah," Martin replied. "It was pretty good."

"It was sixty-five thousand dollars. Those bottles of wine we drank? They were twenty-eight hundred dollars apiece. We had fourteen of them."

When VIPs came to visit, the Chairman was known to splash out on lavish gifts, items worth ten thousand dollars or more, like jade golf balls or gold swords.

But the Chairman was modest in comparison to some of China's tycoons. Another golf course owner was "richer than all of them," said Martin. His company's website boasted about a $57 million private jet and a thirty-five-foot yacht, purchased from a celebrity athlete for $20 million.

Meetings with this owner were also an experience. They required a meeting about the meeting, the evening before the meeting, to discuss "what's going to be talked about, what we can say, what we can't say." It was common for the owner's staff to go without sleep during the twenty-four hours leading up to a meeting, regardless of its significance or urgency – every meeting the owner attended was significant and urgent. Everything needed to be perfect.

One time, a meeting was scheduled for 9 a.m., but it was made clear to Martin that arriving after 8 a.m. was unacceptable. The morning of the meeting, he realized why. While there were only sixteen participants, there were probably a couple dozen additional people scurrying around the place, adjusting this, fixing that. There were two men assigned to placing the attendees around the table. Like persnickety wedding planners, they told Martin and the others not just where to sit, but how.

"You," they'd say. "Move your chair two inches to the right."

"You. Move that laptop three inches to the left."

"You. No iPads allowed."

Everyone was told that if they planned to take notes during the meeting, they were only permitted to do so on paper featuring the name and logo of the owner's company, using similarly branded pencils and pens. All these items, Martin noticed, were laid out neatly on the table in front of him. So much activity, and the meeting hadn't even started yet.

This was an introductory meeting, the kickoff to the construction project, and the owner wasted no time dressing down his staff, who had worked so hard to make the meeting a success. He mentioned Martin's experience at Spring City, and discussed the impressive resumé of the foreign management team the owner had hired to oversee things. "My team is bad," the owner said to the room filled with many members of his team. "They have failed in the past. So now we're bringing in a whole new team." Then he addressed his staff specifically, "I suggest you all watch and learn."

When he wasn't talking, the owner puffed on a clunky Sherlock Holmes-style calabash pipe incessantly for the duration of the three-hour meeting. He came prepared for the long haul, too. He had a rotation of three pipes, tended by two young women whose sole role at the meeting was to see that the owner's pipe was always full and firing. Several times during the meeting, the owner would abruptly hold his pipe above his head. Instantly, one of the minders would appear, take the spent pipe from the owner's hand and replace it with a freshly packed one. She'd hold a flame to the new pipe as the owner took his first puffs. Then she'd disappear again.

People unfamiliar with the way China works often express confusion as to how a country can experience a golf course boom during a moratorium on golf course construction. Those who've spent more than five minutes in China do not suffer from such confusion. In fact, the Chinese have several sayings for the disconnect that often exists between Beijing's best intentions and how they're interpreted – or simply ignored – out in the provinces:

上有政策，下有对策 *(Shang you zheng ce, xia you dui ce)*
Where there are policies from above, there are counter-policies from below.

政令不出中南海 *(Zheng ling bu chu zhong nan hai)*
Policies and commands stop at the gate of Zhongnanhai.

山高皇帝远 *(Shan gao huang di yuan)*
The mountain is high and the emperor is far away.

Simply put, golf courses can't be built in China without major government involvement, but that involvement is always at the local level. Indeed, local officials will often seek out golf-based real estate developments, believing them to be magnets for high-end businesses and a well-to-do clientele, not to mention major generators of tax revenues. That's because golf isn't taxed like a sport in China; it's taxed as an entertainment venue, similar to a karaoke club, at a hefty 23.5 percent rate. In recent years, some local governments have begun offering special deals or incentives that bring this down to a more manageable rate, around 10 percent. One developer likened golf in China to prostitution. "That's illegal, too," he said. "But there are still prostitutes everywhere in this country."

But, perhaps most importantly, local governments welcome land-hungry developments, such as those that involve golf, because they own the land. Ministry of Land Resources data and Chinese media reports in recent years suggest that anywhere between 20 to 50 percent of annual revenues enjoyed by local governments in China come from the sale of land. That doesn't take into account the amount officials pocket on the sly, of course. "These local governments, they want money," a contractor working in Hainan explained. "All the chiefs, all the mayors, they're making tons of money on this stuff. Why are they not going to let it happen?"

Another golf industry professional noted that the term limits set for local government officials encouraged a sort of "race" mentality – "I've got three years to make as much money as I can" is common thinking among bureaucrats.

Local governments are typically willing to "fudge things" in an effort to, literally and figuratively, get the ball rolling on lucrative land development. The benefits, most reckon, outweigh the risks, even the risk that Beijing might crack down on a project that is technically illegal. But the governments are also sly. The first rule when planning a golf course in China: Don't use the word "golf."

"It didn't go away – the moratorium is still there," one industry pro reported. "People just figure out other ways to do it. No one calls it a 'golf course' now. It's green space, it's equestrian, it's an exercise field. They are creative. But the government knows. It's just all about loop holes."

The government office tasked with attracting investment to a district on the outskirts of Haikou, not far from the Mission Hills site in Hainan, had learned the tricks.

One official said that, while most of the prime shoreline properties on the island had already been snatched up, they still had "plenty" of plots dominated by volcanic rock, which is useless for growing crops. Farmland and forest were off-limits to investors, but this land was available.

What if an American company wanted to build a golf course on it?

"Foreign companies can't build golf courses," he said. "In China, there is a restriction on golf."

What about Mission Hills?

"They are a domestic company, and they are not doing golf."

What were they doing then?

"Leisure!" he said with a wink. "Just don't mention golf."

To get around the restrictions, savvy developers would label their projects as "resorts." The official explained: "Plant some flowers and trees, no problem. And maybe some people grab a club and hit a ball. That's just leisure." The official, tall and tanned with a relaxed demeanor, mentioned that he played golf a couple times a month.

The agreement between Mission Hills and Hainan's Xiuying District, which administered much of the land in question for Project 791, never once used the word "golf." The document, according to one of the first investigative stories about it, which appeared in the *China Youth Daily* newspaper, described a "land consolidation" project that would feature "sports and leisure," "health facilities," "culture and entertainment," "leisure and business," "international competitions," "conferences and exhibitions," "creative industries" and "suitable living." The agreement suggested the project would create a "new type of tourism," which would "improve the production and living standards of the local farmers and promote the building of a new socialist countryside." The contract went so far as to label Project 791 as "ecological restoration." The development, the document argued, would "improve the ecological environment" of the area, which ranged from north of Volcano Crater National Park to far south of Wang Libo's village, Meiqiu.

Wang was aware of the tenuous grip he had on his family's land. It had been theirs for decades – centuries, in the case of some plots. But he saw the writing on the wall.

And so, despite concerns about the legacy he'd leave for his children, despite his suspicion he wasn't getting a fair price for his land, and despite his reluctance to say goodbye to the money-earning lychee trees that grew on some of his acreage, he did what he could to speed up the land sale process, not long after the meeting under the phoenix tree.

"The developers and the government negotiated this deal without any discussions with the villagers," he said. "And the land payouts were set by the government. How can I bargain with them? How can I protest and fight against the government and the rich people? They are too powerful to be challenged. What is best for me is go with the trend. So I never protested. I invited the land-measuring team from the town government. Also I invited the town-level official to verify the measuring process on the spot. After they finished, I signed my name and got the money. It's best to go with the government, and figure out a new way to make a living."

Not everyone took Wang's approach. In late March 2008, riots broke out in the village of Yongdong, four miles northeast of Meiqiu. Hundreds of villagers, some wielding machetes and other farming tools, took to Changqiao Hill in an attempt to stop the Mission Hills construction crew from working on their land. The villagers were enraged by rumors that the per-*mu* prices presented to them by the local government were nowhere near the amount Mission Hills had paid. Indeed, a public document on the website of the Haikou city government listed the benchmark land prices for business development in the Yongdong area as 135,000 to 150,000 yuan per *mu* – about $19,000 to $22,000. For Meiqiu it was higher still: 145,000 to 185,000 yuan per *mu*. No one knows for sure what Mission Hills actually paid, but with villagers only getting 12,500 to 29,000 per *mu*, a lot of cash was getting caught up somewhere else.

When the local police arrived at Yongdong, protesters smashed and overturned some of their cars. Then the military police showed up and dispersed the crowd with tear gas. Several villagers were arrested, fined and sentenced to lengthy prison terms for inciting a crowd to disturb social order, and willful destruction of public property. Years after the incident, a slogan remained emblazoned on the side of a prominent building in the village: "Yongdong Must Be United Together!"

News of the Yongdong protest spread quickly to Meiqiu, where villagers were angry about many of the same issues. Those who didn't agree to sell their land, or those who were holding out in the hope of getting more money, were often among the first to find their land had been bulldozed. "You have to sell, because they force you," one villager said. "Without your agreement, they bulldoze the lands then give you your money. Otherwise, the police will trouble you."

In fact, this had happened to one of Wang's friends. His land was full of lychee trees that were still weeks away from being ready to harvest. Yet the bulldozers were called in. In less than an hour, his fruit trees were gone, as was his potential income for the summer. That left him with no option but to accept the government's price. What good was his land to him now?

"Why couldn't they negotiate with him?" Wang asked. "Why couldn't they wait two months and let him reap his fruit? What made it worse was that after they bulldozed his land, they didn't touch it again for several months. It was such a pity."

Meiqiu was quite a bit smaller than Yongdong and couldn't muster a demonstration of comparable size. There were a few dustups here and there, but a couple dozen farmers usually proved no match for men in bulldozers and the Mission Hills security force.

Several of these small protests took place not far from a piece of land that Wang owned the rights to. It was an odd, triangle-shaped property originally intended to be part of the Mission Hills project, until the villagers successfully made a last-minute push to move the Red Line ever so slightly away from Meiqiu before the deal was finalized in late 2007. Wang wasn't sure what to do with the land. It was right next to the cement road, and full of weeds and wild fruit trees too young to be reaped, with a construction site directly behind it. Wang didn't know much about golf, but he was pretty sure that what he saw going on behind his property wasn't golf. A concrete foundation was being laid. He had some construction experience, and he could tell that whatever was going up was going to be huge. Wang knew what he had to do: build a wall.

Usually in China, golf course developers built walls to keep the riffraff out. This time it was the villager trying to keep the golf course at bay. *They've already taken enough of my land*, Wang thought as he laid brick on top of brick, just as he had so many thousands of times before. *They're not going to take any more.* As Wang built his wall, he watched as another mini protest broke out in a contested clearing nearby. It was peaceful, like most of them had been. But, Wang thought, it was also hopeless, like all the others had been. Why yell at the bulldozer driver? Why yell at the security guards? They were probably just villagers, too.

Wang felt for the protestors, and he agreed with them in many ways. But he also believed they were just prolonging the inevitable.

7

SCRAPE THE BONES, DRY THE GLASS

Almost every Chinese pro golfer will complain about the low prize money at tournaments, about how it's difficult to simply break even trying to live from tournament to tournament. But Zhou Xunshu could occasionally step back and take a look at the big picture, and what he saw made him more depressed.

"People say companies, especially Chinese companies, should invest in the game and become sponsors," Zhou said. "But if they invest, they want to make money, right? Without any audience, who will invest? Sponsors are very practical. Who will give you money for no reason?"

When the Omega China Tour had launched back in 2005, many players, including Zhou, were optimistic that it would finally bring some stability to their lives. That first year there'd been four events and the promise of an extra two tournaments added to the tour each year. And the promise had come true: in 2007 Zhou competed in all eight events, traveling from Nanjing to Qingdao to Guangzhou to Yanji to Shanghai to Kunming to Xiamen, and then to Beijing. The tournaments were first-rate operations, too. The tour organizers even ensured the Chinese media, mostly golf specialty magazines and websites, turned out to cover the tournaments, paying their travel and accommodation costs, and plying them with gift bags once they got there, so they would stay until the last day of play. Only one thing was missing: spectators.

The tour organizers discovered their most successful events enticed fans with prizes – people were more likely to show up if they knew there was a chance they could win a home appliance or a laptop computer. Getting them to actually watch the golf was another issue. To get them to stay, they were coming up with a variety of new schemes. One year, spectators who got their ticket stamped after every three holes would go home with a free hat.

It was almost comical that the China Tour organizers hadn't approached a cigarette company about becoming a sponsor, since so many of the players smoked during rounds. Some would sneak a drag during holes, while others seemed to keep a cigarette lit the entire round, only handing it off to a caddie when it was time to take a swing. Zhou was not a smoker, although he'd sometimes light one up if he was "depressed" or needed to "clear his head." If you saw Zhou holding a cigarette during a round, that usually meant things weren't going well. Perhaps another sponsor would, in fact, be better.

Zhou said he knew golf was still a young game in China, but he couldn't help but compare the situation to other countries, where the game was more established, and where being a professional golfer wasn't such an oddity. "When Padraig Harrington won the British Open, the whole country paraded in the streets and took days off to celebrate," Zhou remembered. "I read a report online, and all Irish people went crazy because of the win. They treated him as a hero. Can you see this happening in China?"

He brought up the success of Korean golfers, men and women, overseas. "In Korea, golf is a game for everybody," he said. "Everyone plays golf and the country supports the sport. In China, when people talk about golf it is always about corrupt government officials using public money to play. No one talks about how we can get more people interested in playing the game or how we can make golf more affordable. But this is the situation in China, and there's nothing we can do about it."

He pointed out that the overall prize money per tournament, 800,000 yuan, didn't change between 2006 to 2007, but the number of players who were expected to split the prize money had increased from fifty to sixty. "And the prize money for first, second, third and fourth remained the same," Zhou said. "This is what we call scraping the fat from chicken's feet. How can a chicken foot have any fat? How can you scrape fat from bones?"

He was angry. "In foreign tournaments those who make the cut won't lose money," he said. "Here, sixty people make the cut and the last one's prize money is 3,500 yuan." About five hundred dollars. "After 20 percent tax, that might be enough to pay for the round-trip flight."

Zhou concluded, "The CGA does not care how many tournaments there are for us every year. They just care how much money they've made."

Zhou hadn't practiced all winter. The decorating of their new apartment in Chongqing was still not done, and Liu Yan was still living with her parents. Zhou was at least living in their new place, but the hot water wasn't working yet, and the water pressure was low, so he'd been taking his showers back at the driving range.

Worse, the China Tour was starting earlier than ever in 2008, in an effort to front-load the schedule before the start of the Beijing Olympic Games, an event so big it was expected to bring much of the country to a grinding halt. The first tournament was just a few weeks away, at Dragon Lake Golf Club in Guangzhou, the very spot where Zhou and Liu Yan had met. Zhou had begun to hit some balls in earnest at his driving range, but he was unable to practice any putting there. "The putting green here is unplayable," Zhou said. "It's a mess. No one maintains it. My putting is not very good."

He still considered Dragon Lake to be his home course, and he wished the season opener was somewhere else. He wanted time to get his form back before he played in front of people who knew him. He also wanted time to get his finances in order.

Zhou's house was almost empty. He had a bed, a washing machine, kitchen appliances, but nothing more. "I don't have money for anything else," Zhou said. "I spent it all. I don't even have money for the tournaments yet."

He wasn't getting much sleep either. Zhou's entire building reverberated with the sounds of drills and saws. All his neighbors were going through the same process – buying a new place in the city and trying to make it a home. The air was thick with plaster dust. The insides of the elevators were covered in plywood, on which were scribbled names and phone numbers, hundreds of contractors and handymen peddling their trades.

Perhaps it was all the time alone, but Zhou was in a contemplative mood. He said although he hadn't been able to exercise his body, he'd been thinking a lot about his game. He'd been playing on the tour for two seasons now, and knew what his shortcomings were. Most of them were in his head. "Sometimes I am impatient for success," Zhou said. "For example, last year in Kunming, that ball in the tree." Being so close to the lead affected the way he'd approached that hole. He was trying to play conservatively, to play it safe, and that was not his style. "I should have just played without thinking anything. Sometimes golf is just like this. Your mind says one thing. Your body says another."

Zhou knew he needed to work on managing his temper, to be able to focus on his next shot instead of his last shot. "The littlest thing can affect my mood. Like trying to land a taxi cab, or having to wait for an elevator."

He thought he must have inherited this trait from his father, who was "always strict" and "has a very bad temper." Over the years, he'd avoided talking to his father, who he said treated him like a child and too often preached "antiquated ideas," like doctrines from the days of Mao. "How can people living in the new era still follow those old-fashioned ideas?" Zhou asked, his blood clearly beginning to boil. "For example, right now he will tell you it is not necessary to make lots of money. 'Just make enough to get by,' he'll say. Do you think this mindset will work in this world?"

And if it wasn't quotations from one book, it was another.

"He believes in Jesus, but why won't he take medicine or go to the hospital when he is sick?" Zhou continued. "They believe Jesus will bless them and they will recover without taking any medicine or going to hospital. And this is total bullshit! What the hell does he know? He just believes what other people say."

Zhou rarely went back to Qixin these days. He insisted the reason for his infrequent visits home had been due mostly to the arduous journey it involved. Guangzhou to Guiyang by train was already a twenty-four-hour trip, and then, from Guiyang to Bijie, the closest city to the village, could be as much as another half day. In the 1990s, before National Highway 321 was complete, buses snaked along the treacherous mountain roads and inched across old bridges suspended precariously above deep river gorges. One bridge in particular always made Zhou's heart stop. "It crossed the Wu River, and was held up by iron chains," he said. "There were armed policemen standing on each side of the bridge. Only one car could go at a time." He'd actually prayed for fog sometimes, because he didn't want to be able to see what was outside his window.

On the handful of rare visits since he'd left Qixin for police school, Zhou always brought his father some clothing or food, but beyond that, their interactions were minimal. "I really am afraid to talk to him because every time I did, he would start to talk about those things," Zhou said, referring once again to Mao quotations and the Bible. "And once he does that, I just turn around and leave. No other way. It is impossible to communicate with him, and if I try he would get mad. So the only way to solve this problem is to move him in with me and get him out of that environment."

His mother was "honest and simple," like all people from the countryside, he said. But he didn't talk with her often, either. "What is there to talk about? When I go back, we just talk about the current situations, and I ask her about her health. Just like that. There is nothing to talk about."

Yet he planned to bring his parents to Chongqing after Liu Yan returned with their baby. Zhou didn't think his parents wanted to move, but that made no difference. "Even if they don't want to come, I will still bring them by force. I don't want them to be doing the hard labor at home any more. I want to bring them here, and during the daytime they can just wander around."

It was winter. Zhou's father wore a thigh-length black jacket that covered at least four other layers of clothing. His unhemmed suit pants were long and rolled hastily at the bottom, and he wore black loafers without any socks. On his head was a tall, black Soviet-style *ushanka* hat, perhaps most associated in China with the historical (some might say mythical) figure Lei Feng, a People's Liberation Army soldier canonized by the government as a model socialist shortly after his untimely death in the early 1960s. Zhou's father wore this bulky headpiece with the earflaps buttoned up, displaying just a hint of his salt-and-pepper hair. His face was dotted with liver spots – it was clear he'd spent many long days in the elements – but his skin was taut and smooth, the only wrinkles forming around the corners of his eyes. When he smiled, which he did often, he revealed a full set of badly stained teeth.

Zhou may have been the most successful person to come out of Qixin village, but for some, including his father, he was still the member of his family who was supposed to become a police officer and had failed. "Police officer" was a concept Zhou's family, especially his parents, could understand. It's a concept they knew their neighbors would understand. Golf was different. It was strange. It was foreign. It was completely new. How can you impress your friends with your son's job when you don't understand what he does?

"I just leave him alone and let him mature," Zhou's father said by way of explanation. "We are from the countryside, and we spent about four thousand to five thousand yuan for him to study and live at the armed police school in Zunyi. He did not stay in that school for very long – less than half a year – and then he got the job at the golf course."

The first time Zhou brought golf balls back to the village, it had caused a sensation. "Not only my father, even I felt it was very weird, very strange," First Brother said. "I never saw these things before. There were so many tiny craters on the ball – I was wondering how to play this game. Other people all thought it was very strange, too."

Now, Zhou was ranked in the top twenty of golfers in China. Things must have changed by now. "I didn't know what golf was," Zhou's father said. "Today, I do not really understand what it is. I was just happy he found a job."

Wasn't the family proud of Zhou's accomplishments?

"We all know he is playing golf," First Brother said.

But were they *proud* of him?

"We are in different places. If he can go to every country in this world, if he can go and travel to every one of them, I will be like this," First Brother said, pounding his fist on his heart. "Very proud."

First Brother, born in 1963, was Zhou's only sibling still living in Qixin. He had not seen Zhou – who the family called Fourth Brother – in more than a year. But like Zhou the professional golfer, First Brother spent much of his time on the road, as a migrant worker. He had once worked in the zinc factories in the mountains for thirty yuan a day, but when a friend told him he could earn twice that outside Guizhou, he jumped at the chance. Since 1999 he had been traveling the country working in tunnel construction as a slurry sprayer, one of the unfortunate souls who sprays concrete onto the rough walls of a freshly drilled tunnel. The tunnels were dark, humid, noisy, poorly ventilated and frequently dangerous. Often, pieces of rock would fall; sometimes tunnels would collapse. Projects could range from 100 to 350 yards long, and a job could last anywhere from one to eight months. First Brother had missed Zhou's wedding because of a tunnel job in Hubei province.

"The people living in this village are lucky to earn two thousand yuan per year," First Brother said. "My family – me, my wife and my two sons – at best we'd make thirty thousand yuan per year. And if it is a bad year, we could make nothing at all. If we were not migrant workers, it's probably hard to even earn five hundred yuan per person per year." He took a long drag on his cigarette. At the brick factory down in the valley, things were better. "Their average income per person per year is fifty thousand yuan. They are all bosses."

For his part, Zhou's father had simple aspirations for his sons. "Every time they call and tell us they do not have any problems, we are very happy," he said. "Because now there are many disasters out there, and the world is very complicated. We are very worried they might steal things and go to jail. We are worried they might do illegal things. In our family, before they left the village, we taught them not to do bad things, otherwise it would humiliate us, the elders."

Zhou's nephew, Xiao Hu, or Little Tiger, emerged from the house. "Let's go eat," he said. "We can chat more later."

Zhou's mother was hard at work in the kitchen. She looked strong, and her pleasant face was hard to read, an exercise in stoicism and seriousness. Her husband chatted away while she prepared the evening's meal, picking the stems off of a clutch of wild mushrooms, barely saying a word. For warmth, she wore a charcoal gray men's suit over her other clothing. Her silver hair was tucked inside a light gray stocking cap emblazoned with the word PING, an American brand of golf equipment.

Little Tiger led the way to the *huolu* (literally "fire oven"), a coal-burning stove common in the mountainous regions of southwest China, that serves three purposes: space heater, hot plate and dinner table. Atop a single pedestal sat a square metal table top, with a hole in the middle filled with burning coals. The opening was the perfect size for heating a teakettle or a pot of soup. An exhaust pipe attached to one corner of the table sent the fumes – some of them, at least – out the window.

Like the kitchen table in Western culture, the *huolu* is the heart of the village home. All meals, card games, dramas – and family drinking fests, when First Brother is around – play out around the *huolu*.

On this day, the *huolu*'s only job was to hold the dishes that had been prepared for dinner, and it was failing. Today, though Zhou had declined to make the trip – he was too busy, he said – the village was hosting his American friend, its first foreigner, and there was far too much food, despite the fact that food was hard to come by. There is no refrigeration in Qixin village, and after that year's brutal winter, there was almost no fresh produce, either. When it snows heavily, as it did in the winter of 2008, no vehicles can access Qixin, and the simplest items are a luxury. Villagers must lug heavy bags of rice up the mountain on foot. The cook of the family must get creative with the handful of non-perishable ingredients available. The colorful array of dishes laid out on the *huolu* belied the forced culinary restrictions of the season. "These are fried potato slices. That is tofu. That is fried wheat gluten. Those are rice noodles. Those are pig's ears. That is *larou*. That is also *larou*. And that one, too." Preserved pork, three ways.

In a Chinese village, guests have to pace their consumption cannily, because each time a visitor finishes a bowl of food, someone immediately fills it up. "Eat more," they say. "Eat more pig's ears!"

Nearly everyone seated around the table remembered when there was barely enough to eat. And Zhou's parents remembered when people were starving. In today's relative plenty, it's important to prove you have enough. *"Ni chi fan le ma?"* – "Have you eaten?" – is still often used as a greeting. Guizhou was among the provinces hardest hit by China's great famine, in which anywhere between twenty million and fifty million people died of starvation, the result of Mao's disastrous Great Leap Forward campaign in the late 1950s and early '60s. Some estimates say Guizhou experienced close to one million famine-related deaths – some 5 percent of its total population. Some remote towns and villages saw losses as high as 10 and 20 percent. Widespread reports suggest people resorted to eating tree bark and mud. Evidence suggests many turned to various forms of cannibalism, as well.

Zhou's father spoke of the hard times matter-of-factly, with little emotion. It was as though he was reciting from a timeline in the back of a book. His wife, as usual, didn't say a word.

"The tougher times were before 1949 and around 1960," Zhou's father said. "Life before 1949 was really hard."

"That time, every three households could only share one pig!" First Brother interjected.

"China was under Kuomintang control at that time," Zhou's father continued. "This area was liberated in 1949, but the land-change policy didn't come until 1952 and it took another several years after that to have any effect. In 1956 and 1957 we all joined the cooperatives, and from 1956 to 1958 they started the Great Leap Forward – people did not grow crops and focused on steelmaking. Then, in 1959 and 1960 – starting from September 1959 – the supply of the crops became very tight."

"The whole village shared a certain amount of food," First Brother added.

"Each production team had one cafeteria," Zhou's father went on. "The first two months, the food supply was pretty good, but later on it became worse – just two servings of rice. You could only get a little bit. The rest was things made from corn gruel and wild plants in the mountains, like grass and tree leaves and tree roots. By the second half of 1961 the shared cafeteria was canceled, and you could start to cook on your own. Life got a little bit better. But the 1970s were also pretty bad, a bare living."

"Just barely enough to eat!" First Brother said.

"Probably not one tenth of what we have today," Zhou's father continued. "The farmers' life started to get better in the 1980s, after the land was distributed to each household. You see, we two people raised two pigs these past two years and sold one for over a thousand yuan!"

"It is all because of Uncle Deng," First Brother said. "He started the 'opening-up' policy and the common people's life got better. And in recent years, it is even better, since Hu Jintao is in charge. The farmers do not need to hand in crops any more – just grow and eat their own crops. And for kids going to school, you do not need to pay tuition fees. This is the best policy for the common people."

Sometime between serving six and seven, the faint warble of recorded music could be heard coming from somewhere in the darkness beyond the house. "Ah, the electricity is back. Good," First Brother said. "You see, it is a tradition for this family on the other side of the village to play music through a loudspeaker so everyone in the village can hear it and know the electricity is back."

This was not a very old tradition, since Qixin only got electricity in the mid-'90s. "Right now the countryside has the best conditions ever," First Brother said. "Before, only when celebrating festivals or having friends visiting could we eat meat. Nowadays, we can eat meat any time, every day. Before, drinking beers – no way. Drinking rice wine – no way."

And that was certainly no longer the case.

"Before we did not know each other, and now we do," First Brother said, raising his glass of beer in a toast to me, his first foreign guest. "So we are friends. *Ganbei!*"

This was the first of many toasts First Brother would make that evening. And the toasts continued at breakfast and at lunch. He insisted on drinking alcohol with every meal, saying he could "hardly walk" without sticking to such a regimen. "In Guizhou, good friends just drink together," First Brother explained. "I do not like other forms of communication. For me, no matter whether at home or outside, if someone is not drinking with me, I cannot get along with him. I like drinking the most."

First Brother's toasts got more flowery and dramatic the longer the drinking went on. The intensity of the alcohol increased, as well. He started with beer, a rather forgettable lager from Henan province, purchased at the market at the bottom of the mountain, 180 five-hundred-milliliter (half-quart) bottles at a time. He then graduated to a dubious local moonshine made from corn sold at the market for just three yuan per liquid pound. Finally, First Brother would bring out a bottle he received from his wife's brother-in-law. It was filled with a pinkish-brown substance and hundreds of tiny flecks. It was called *yaojiu*, or "medicine alcohol," and First Brother claimed it contained twenty-five different medicinal herbs that could cure problems with your "lung, liver, kidney, spleen and bones."

He never sipped. It was always *ganbei*, "dry the glass."

"From our grandparents' generation until our next generation, it is impossible to have the chance to have a foreigner come to visit us," he toasted.

Ganbei!

"In our hometown, this is probably a chance every thousand years that you come to our home. We are very happy. So drink more. This is our Guizhou people's custom. You are our friend coming from far away."

Ganbei!

"Our place, although in the mountains of poor Guizhou province, has beautiful views in the spring. Cheers. Three cups, good friend. Three cups for my good friend from far away."

Ganbei!
Ganbei!
Ganbei!

"Today, you came to visit our home and I am very excited. This is something not even money can buy."

Ganbei!

"*Gan* three cups. You are my best friend. You are the best friend in my heart."

Ganbei!

"In my heart, you are my best, best friend."

Ganbei!

"You are my best friend, and it is not easy for you to come all the way here to be friends with us."

Ganbei!

"Okay, my friend. Finish this corn wine and I promise I won't give you any more."

Ganbei!

Zhou's father would drink a glass or two of beer with meals, but showed little interest in keeping up with his first-born son.

Zhou Xunshu's childhood bedroom was being used as a storage shed. Initially, it had been the old *tangwu* – or south-facing, central room – of the original brick structure on the property, and Zhou had shared the room with all five of his siblings; he'd shared a bed with at least one, often two, of his brothers, as well. It had a dusty concrete floor and a rustic wood-and-bamboo ceiling strengthened by two simple floor-to-ceiling posts, bare logs worn smooth. Two of its walls were built with brick, the other two with mud partially covered by newspaper, the dates on which provide the only evidence it existed not in the nineteenth century, but in the twenty-first.

The room was now home to corn, potatoes, fertilizer and coal, although there was little evidence of any of those items at this point of the year, late winter. Up against a brick wall were some mismatched end tables that looked like they once served as a crude kitchen. Two iron woks lay askew on the floor in front of a shadowy corner of the room piled high with wicker baskets and a hand-powered wooden grain thresher, still used today, that looked like it belonged in a museum.

Zhou's parents slept in a cave-like room that had once been the ox pen. Behind the current *tangwu*, it had been their bedroom for more than twenty years. "We always liked this room," Zhou's father explained. "And after the children moved out, we just started to live here. It's quiet and cool." The single tungsten light bulb dangling from the ceiling illuminated the room's hand-laid, irregular stone walls. An unfinished twin-sized wooden bed frame was topped with an area rug instead of a mattress. The rest was clutter – old fruit boxes, and plastic bags full of clothing and other personal items. More clothing was strewn over a wooden branch suspended from the ceiling by two pieces of rope. Plastic tubs stored lard and cornmeal. Large sections of smoked pig carcass hung from the top of one wall like crown molding. A bowl of homemade white tofu rested at the foot of the bed.

In fact, food was on display in every room of the house. Cured pig parts swayed from nearly every ceiling, and almost every room contained a large vat of ground corn, clusters of dried chili peppers and sacks of garlic bulbs. There was no artwork or photographs adorning the walls. Instead, there were constant reminders no one was starving these days.

First Brother and his wife made their home in a newer cinder-block structure attached to the old house. There was a door in the back of one of the rooms that opened onto nothing – no steps, just a drop-off to the forest and fields below. The door's primary purpose, it appeared, was trash receptacle. Family members regularly opened the door and tossed their waste into the darkness.

"People just throw garbage to a certain place," Little Tiger explained. "We throw ours in back of our house. No one comes to get it. The garbage will just rot."

What about plastic?

"For plastic bottles, there will be people who collect them to sell."

What about plastic bags?

"They will be buried in the dirt and rot."

This was the countryside. "It's not like in the city where there are people to sweep that garbage away," he said. "There's nothing we can do."

Qixin in the winter is absent of color. The ground is brown, the sky is gray, the trees are bare and the houses are covered in dust. The only splashes of color come from the villagers' clothing, but even that is muted – it's hard to keep anything clean here for long. When Zhou was a child, he used to bathe in a nearby river. That river had since run dry. Now, the villagers washed themselves in large basins at home. First Brother said most people bathed about once every ten days.

But the village was bustling with activity. Walk through the village and you'd see schoolgirls braiding palm leaves for binding dried grass; women washing clothes by hand, a little boy walking on stilts someone fashioned from branches of a tree; a small old man, hunched over, inching up the trail with a load of dried corn stalks ten times his size strapped to his back. Chickens, dogs and geese roamed freely. And every ten minutes or so, a villager walked by with his or her back weighed down by a tall, funnel-shaped wicker basket filled with a heavy load of coal, fertilizer or corn lugged three miles from the bottom of the mountain. Children carried some of the baskets.

This work was what Zhou blamed for his aching back.

On the China Tour, Zhou occasionally popped a painkiller or two before rounds. Back in Chongqing, he saw a traditional Chinese medicine practitioner regularly for rigorous massage treatments. Some blamed the unorthodox swing Zhou employed during his formative golf years for his back problems. But Zhou blamed his village.

In his hotel room one evening, while talking to a fellow golfer he worked with back at Guangzhou International, Zhou had recalled emotionally the hardships of his youth. He stood up and acted out the words coming from his mouth, a sad game of charades where every answer was the word *ku* – "bitter." He talked about malnutrition not allowing his bones to form properly. And he talked about his mid-teens, when he was the one carrying heavy loads of coal, fertilizer and corn on his back up and down the mountain.

"But that is why your legs are so strong and powerful," the other golfer said. Indeed, Zhou's calves were hulking, and he had the thick thighs of an NFL running back. But it was his back that Zhou wanted to talk about. If it wasn't the burdensome loads he carried upon it that did the damage, surely it was the unwieldy cement poles he had helped to haul and install when Qixin first got electricity.

Zhou's years in the village haunted him. But he seemed to enjoy letting people know how much of a struggle his early years had been, perhaps so they'd realize just how far he'd come. His aching back would often lead to a more general tale of rural Guizhou in the 1970s, of people not having enough to eat ("If a family ate rice twice a week you thought they were rich"), or of nearly tumbling to his death down a cliffside while cutting grass with a sickle (because he was overworked and tired). In Qixin they had only one month of rest per year – the remainder was hard labor.

Zhou also wasn't shy about saying who he blamed for this life, and it wasn't his parents. "If Mao would have lived ten more years, China would have gone backward ten more years," he always said, emphatically.

Little Tiger's brother, Xiao Long, or Little Dragon, walked past the old tobacco smokehouse, past the terraced fields that would first produce potatoes and then corn, past a tall evergreen tree the family used for pine oil. His father had planted it two decades ago. "Down the hill, there is a big walnut tree," Little Dragon said. "It's so big it takes seven or eight people holding hands to circle its trunk." He was going to a landing overlooking the valley, which was still partially obscured by fog. The terrain was dry and brittle: tall yellow grass, white rocks, naked trees. As a child, Zhou would take the family oxen to graze on this spot. This was where he once played the golf-like game with a wad of paper and a long-handled sickle.

On this day, four village boys were taking part in a much more primitive pastime. One would hold a lighter to the land until something caught fire. They'd wait a few moments for orange flames to appear. And when the blaze got to about knee high, they attacked, pounding the fire with tree branches until all that was left was a patch of black grass and smoke in the air. This activity kept them occupied for quite some time.

The boys, who ranged in age from seven to eleven, looked like a gang of Chinese Huckleberry Finns, "fluttering with rags," long blades of grass held between their teeth. They all recognized the name of the village's famous son – Zhou Xunshu – but none of them had heard of golf. Nor had they heard of soccer, basketball, Yao Ming or the Olympics. The only sport they really knew was the calisthenics they performed at school each morning.

So, what do you want to do when you are older?

The boy who appeared to be the leader of the little group thought for a moment, and then, straight-faced, recited the Mao-era slogan, "*Wei renmin fuwu*" – "Serve the people."

The other boys were uninterested and started playing leapfrog in the meadow.

What did they want to do in the future?

They didn't stop their game to answer, "Learn jumping from the frog!" They all laughed.

At home, First Brother was preparing a chicken for slaughter. This was a special gesture, to honor the visiting American guest. Normally, the family would only kill a chicken for Spring Festival. Meat was even more of a luxury when Zhou was growing up. If the family did not slaughter a pig for the new year, there would be no meat until the next year. Mostly, Zhou's family lived on vegetables, cornmeal and rice – which was also a scarce commodity in the village. Families traded two pounds of corn for one pound of rice. And while Zhou's family raised chickens that laid eggs, they rarely ate either, because they needed to barter the eggs for salt. No family would kill a chicken for meat, because no chickens meant no salt. Only when chickens could no longer lay eggs, would they be killed and eaten.

A cigarette heavy with ash dangling from his mouth, First Brother held open the beak of the chicken while his wife poured a clear liquid into its mouth from a white bowl.

"Rice wine," he explained. "That will make the chicken taste better."

Over dinner, with the family crowded around the *huolu*, it was time to turn to the subject of Zhou.

"Yes, I miss him," Zhou's father said. "All of these clothes I am wearing were bought by Zhou Xunshu and Liu Yan." But it was true Zhou Xunshu was the son to visit home the least. "He rarely comes back."

"When he comes back, he still helps the family doing some work. Like plow the field," said First Brother.

"Not in the past several years," First Brother's wife mumbled as she placed some dishes on the table.

"He can also still use the bamboo to make some baskets," First Brother added, as compensation.

And Zhou was well liked. "Every time he comes back, people will ask him to play cards or do farm work with them," First Brother said. "Also, drinking and chatting. But he can't drink too much and he does not gamble."

By the reckoning of his family, what made Fourth Brother the most successful person to come from the village, was that he had a "real profession." That was something.

"For us, going out to work, we may have a job, but not a real career," said Little Tiger.

First Brother agreed with his son. "And my Fourth Brother is not working for money, he is pursuing something he wants. If he was only working for money, he'd already have millions by now."

First Brother was among the family members who hadn't made the journey to attend Zhou and Liu Yan's wedding in November. Second Brother, too, was absent, as was their little-discussed sister, who had married a man from the northeast and moved there. And what of Zhou's parents? First Brother said that they were "too old, and it was too far" for them to make the journey for the wedding, though they had wanted to. "It's because of my leg," Zhou's father explained. "I suffer from hyperostosis and rheumatism." He said he planned to visit the young couple in April or May. "When it gets warmer, my leg will feel better."

Of course, Zhou hoped the visit to Chongqing might persuade his parents to leave the hard life in Qixin. "Zhou Xunshu has called me before and asked us to go to Chongqing," his father acknowledged. "But we can't go. If we were young, we could go.

"Living here now, the conditions, I can't say they are good – just normal," he went on. "Before, my sons tried to help me improve my living conditions, but I did not let them. I just tried to lighten their burden. That is what I am thinking. They asked me if I needed any money, and I just told them you just live your life, take care of yourself."

He was afraid that life in Chongqing would be too new, too strange. "But I am not thinking about this now. We will visit when the weather is warmer and Zhou Xunshu's personal and financial situations are more stable. I'll wait and see after I stay there for a while."

Zhou's father wanted to make it clear he wasn't a stranger to the city. He had been to Chongqing once before. In the late 1960s, he was in Chongqing for ten minutes. He spent the time changing cars on his way to "learn from Dazhai," in Shiyang county, Shanxi province, 1,200 miles northeast of Qixin.

For the generation that came of age after the Great Leap Forward, Shiyang county had become a holy land of sorts. It was home to the fabled Dazhai Production Team, which Chairman Mao held up to the nation as a model farming community, built on hard work, self-reliance and a passion for proletarian politics. Like Qixin, Dazhai was desperately poor and situated in a steep mountain valley prone to drought and soil erosion; China's Loess Plateau, on which Dazhai sits, has many of the same traits as the "Dust Bowl" of the American Midwest. But by the mid-1960s, thanks largely to the backbreaking efforts of its residents, the eighty-family commune at Dazhai had transformed itself into a production phenomenon. The people of Dazhai, with their famously callused hands, literally moved mountains. They carved hillsides into terraces, built dams and reservoirs and erected aqueducts that carried water for miles. Their grain yields were astounding.

"In agriculture, learn from Dazhai!" Mao proclaimed in 1964. The slogan became a common sight in rural China, plastered across walls and riverbanks. There were others, too: "Move hills, fill gullies and create plains!" "Destroy forests, open wastelands!" "Change the sky, alter the land!" The propaganda campaign sparked a pilgrimage. Village leaders from across the country trekked to Dazhai by the thousands to study its ways. Some estimates say Dazhai saw fifteen million guests between 1964 and the late '70s.

In the 1980s, a government campaign (some called it a smear campaign) discredited the Dazhai way, as Deng Xiaoping moved to privatize farm production. State media ran stories saying Dazhai had falsified harvest reports and was less than self-reliant, receiving outside labor from the People's Liberation Army (PLA). Some of the reports claimed the PLA had brought in heavy machinery to move the earth. Later, environmentalists suggested some of Dazhai's techniques actually exacerbated the region's problems with soil erosion.

Still, traveling across the country to Dazhai was a proud moment for Zhou's father, who was one of very few villagers at the time to venture beyond the mountains of Guizhou. "From Shanxi, I went to Shijiazhuang and bought a train ticket for six yuan to go to Beijing," he recalled. "We stayed in Beijing for three days and four nights. Then from Beijing to Wuhan, then back to Guizhou. We also went by Hunan and other places: Guiyang, Zunyi, Chongqing, Chengdu – I was in Chengdu for three days – Baotou, Zhengzhou. I cannot remember all of them now. Now, the route is much better than at that time. When we were in Beijing, we visited the Forbidden City. It was December 1969. I was gone for twenty-eight days."

Back then, Zhou's father was the leading cadre of a production brigade that oversaw six production teams. In modern terms, he was the village leader. And when he returned from his travels, his teams began the arduous – and dangerous – task of carving up the mountainside just as the villagers of Dazhai had done.

"It was very hard," Zhou's father said. "All we used were explosives, sledgehammers and spades. We carried all of the stone with our bare hands."

Zhou's father stepped down as village leader in the early '70s after some villagers suggested he was unfit for the job. He didn't put up a fight. The salary was low – around fifty kilos of crops and 180 yuan (around 1,000 yuan by today's standards, he said) per year – and there were too many mouths to feed at home. Zhou had just been born and Fifth Brother was on the way. Zhou's father figured he'd be of more use working in the family fields anyway.

This was not the expected trajectory for a man who once seemed set to become a city-level government official in Bijie. In his mid-twenties, Zhou's father sold cloth at the city's Supply and Marketing Cooperative. It wasn't a glamorous role by any measure, but it was a steady job with a government agency, and he felt lucky to have it. Back in the village, however, things were far from stable. Zhou's father's father was prone to fighting. They were the only Zhous living in a village full of Zhes and that added to the bullying. It didn't help that Zhou's grandfather had a temper and often drank too much corn wine.

Tired of making trips to the hospital and worried about his father's well-being, Zhou's father left his job at the cooperative abruptly and headed back to the village to look after his dad. By failing to go through his employer's proper exit procedures, Zhou's father forfeited his right to a government pension. Years later, after the Cultural Revolution, Zhou's father returned to the Supply and Marketing Cooperative and asked to be rehabilitated, but he was denied – they said they had no record he ever worked there.

"If I didn't quit the job I probably would have become some big official, too," Zhou's father said. "The people I worked with in the Supply and Marketing Cooperative, who are not as capable as I was, all became some kind of leader later on."

This was one of the many chips weighing down the collective shoulder of Zhou's family, and Zhou's own ambitions in Qixin and beyond. "If he didn't quit that job, we would be much better off now," Zhou said later. "And we probably would've already left that place, the village. According to my dad's level at the time, he would have been promoted to a position in the city. It was just a bad decision made at the spur of the moment."

His father's stories from the old days had gone on too long. First Brother tried to shift the conversation around the *huolu*.

"Eat more," he insisted. "This is our local chicken."

"It didn't even lay eggs yet!" added Zhou's father, as a boast.

Zhou's family had answered so many questions about their history. And Zhou hadn't explained to his family why such questions were being asked of them by their American guest.

"No, Zhou Xunshu did not tell us why you were visiting the village. I never thought about it," First Brother said, raising his glass of beer in a toast. "*Ganbei!*"

"It was my fifth uncle who called and said someone is coming to visit, but he did not say who," Little Tiger said. "He called my uncle in Bijie and my uncle in Bijie called the village."

"We are friends now. I do not care if my youngest brother called or not," First Brother said. "As long as you are my friend I will treat you the same way. We welcome friends, no matter whether from China or abroad."

Later that year, on the Shanghai leg of the China Tour, Zhou was acting the way any proud father would, displaying photos of his newborn son on his mobile phone to anyone within eyeshot. Zhou's pride was genuine, but the photos also gave him an excuse to talk about something other than the awful round of golf he had just played.

"The doctor said he is taller than the average baby his age," Zhou said, beaming. "If he can grow to be 1.9 meters tall [six foot three], I'll let him play basketball."

But if the child wanted to play golf like his father, Zhou said he'd send his son somewhere else, some place other than China. "I won't let him be like the current domestic players," Zhou said. "If I have the financial ability, I will have him study golf in America." He figured he'd need to save around five million yuan to be able to afford that.

These were lofty goals for a man who just shot an 80 and was in a seven-way tie for seventy-fourth place in the Shanghai championship. It was mid-May, and Zhou's mind seemed to be off in Hunan province, where he had recently left his wife and baby boy. Or perhaps, like so many others, he was distracted by the devastating news of an 8.0-magnitude earthquake that had struck Sichuan province just three days before the tournament's opening round. Or it could have just been the wind. Whatever the cause, it was not the kind of effort Zhou had come to expect.

Despite starting the season feeling ill-prepared and unfit, 2008 was shaping up to be Zhou's best year on tour. He had placed sixth, the top performance of his career, at Dragon Lake, and followed this with an eighth-place effort in Xiamen. Two weeks later, he placed twenty-second in Kunming. He was three events into the year and ranked ninth on the China Tour's money list. It seemed this could be the year Zhou finally earned his pro player credentials.

These days, there was a new Chinese star Zhou could look to for inspiration. The hero of the previous year had been Liang Wenchong. He was the son of a peasant farmer, just like Zhou, had won the Asian Tour's Order of Merit, and had been the first Chinese golfer to crack the top one hundred in the world golf rankings. The only reason Liang, six years younger than Zhou, started playing golf was because he happened to grow up near modern China's first course, Zhongshan Hot Spring Golf Club. Liang was fifteen when the golf club, then not a decade old, decided it wanted to start a golf team. Club officials visited local schools, Liang's included, and asked curious students, most of whom had never heard of the game before, to line up and swing a golf club. Those who showed promise were offered a spot. Liang was one of the lucky ones, and he accepted. Playing golf, he thought, must be better than helping his father in the peanut fields. Many of Liang's teammates, unable to handle the club's strict training regimen, quit. But Liang persevered, turning pro just six years after his first swing. Players like Liang, and Zhang Lianwei before him, gave Zhou hope. A humble boy could make it, not just in China, but beyond its borders, as well.

Zhou, too, was beginning to catch people's attention. The media, both local and international, were taking an interest in his story, and on the Guangzhou leg he had signed his first sponsorship. There was no money involved, but Titleist and FootJoy agreed to outfit him with shoes, gloves, hats, balls and clubs free of charge. It was a big shift in his fortunes. Then, a golf course in Chongqing had made noises that they might be interested in sponsoring him on the tour, paying his travel expenses for as many as ten events per year.

"All the groundwork for life and work are finally starting to pay off," Zhou said. "Before I was married, I wanted to find a wife. This was one goal. After getting married, I wanted to buy a house. After buying a house, I wanted to build a perfect family. So we had to have a baby. We planned it, and had a baby this year. Once I had a child, suddenly the pressure was much greater. I'm no longer doing it just for my own happiness. I'm doing it for my family." He told the reporters asking for interviews that his mental game had got stronger after he got married, which meant he had to be more responsible, more mature. He said becoming a father had made him more confident.

But Zhou still wasn't satisfied. "Of course things are better than before, but my ideal life is not like this," he said. "Now that I have a house, I also want a car and some savings." He also wanted to win a tournament or, at the very least, finish in the top three. He wanted more sponsors. He wanted to give up teaching and just focus on playing. But he knew he'd have to shoot much better than an 80 if he wanted to accomplish any of that.

The evening after his poor opening round performance at Shanghai, Zhou lay on his hotel bed watching news reports from the earthquake recovery efforts in Sichuan. He shook his head and sighed. "Every night I watch these reports and cry," Zhou said. "Too sad! But I don't want to donate to any of those official relief organizations. I'd rather give money, even two thousand yuan, if I could directly give the money to the people."

He decided he needed to go out.

"I never thought I would be in such terrible form today," he confessed at a restaurant across the street from his hotel. He wanted to get something to eat, and drink some beers, so he could relax. He was drinking with more vigor than usual.

He explained that his son's name, Hanhan, was chosen because, according to his birthdate, he was lacking in two of the five elements from *wu xing*, the traditional Chinese philosophy used to explain the cosmos: metal (associated with ambition and determination) and wood (associated with flexibility and growth). He had consulted with a university professor, the father of one of his golf students, to help come up with the appropriate name.

"My wife said my son has a big temper like me," Zhou said. "He cries really loud."

The dishes on the table were empty. So too were the beers. But Zhou didn't seem interested in calling it a night. On his way out, he spotted a table full of fellow golfers and decided to pull up a chair. Based on the number of bottles sitting before them, they too had had a rough day on the course. More beers were ordered. Some *huangjiu*, a local alcohol, too. And cigarettes were passed out like so many toothpicks.

Zhou began to get tipsy, and talkative. "I miss my son," he announced to everyone. "I've only spent several days with him so far. The first two days I went back, I couldn't even sleep. I kept getting up to check on him. Too excited!"

More beers were ordered, and the men drank to Zhou's son. *Ganbei*! But soon the festivities came to a close – it was the first day of the tournament, after all. Zhou, however, now more than tipsy, did not follow the others back to the hotel.

"Let's get a massage!" he barked. "My neck is sore." It was late, and he was drunk, but Zhou called his wife as he lightly stumbled to the massage parlor.

"I am very annoyed… I played golf for so long, and I've never had no birdies at all in a round. Never happened… I just felt very annoyed out there," he told Liu Yan.

"There was a film crew following me these past two days. And this morning a golf magazine shot photos of me. I don't know if these things affected me – I was just very annoyed. The photo shoot took an hour. I drank a lot tonight…"

He stopped for a moment, then started up again.

"I called you because I wanted to talk to you. I don't need you to tell me what to do. I want you to trust me, and believe in me.

I can play well… I am in very good form, and I still played like this… I am so annoyed. Fuck… I have been competing for such a long time and today I was annoyed more than ever… I am so annoyed. I do not care what you think…"

Another pause, and then he decided to end the call.

"You treat our son better than you treat me… Just take good care of my son. I shouldn't have called you tonight."

Zhou had been to this massage parlor once before, earlier in the week. Then, the masseuse inspected his rough hands. She seemed concerned.

"What are those bumps?" she asked.

"Calluses," he said. "I'm a construction worker."

The girl said, "Ah, no wonder." She added that it also explained why Zhou was so tanned. She told Zhou that the earthquake in Sichuan could be good for people in his line of work – they're going to need people to help rebuild.

Zhou explained why he hadn't just told the girl the truth. "If I tell them I am a golfer, they will judge me," he said. "They are going to say, 'Oh, you play golf, that is a rich people's sport.' It makes me angry hearing that. What rich people's sport? For rich people that is just entertainment. For us it is a job."

He would not be exposed as a golfer this time, either. The moment he hit the massage chair, he was asleep. His snoring was so loud it drowned out the TV.

An hour went by. Zhou's name was yelled repeatedly in an attempt to wake him, but he couldn't be stirred. A second hour of massage followed, after which Zhou's phone was called repeatedly in hopes the familiar noise might finally rouse the slumbering giant – whose second round tee time was just eight hours away.

First one eye opened, and then the other. Zhou groggily took in his surroundings. Helped to his feet, he slurred, "Am I like John Daly?"

There's a statistic in golf called the "bounce back." Normally, it measures a golfer's ability to score a birdie or better on holes that immediately follow a bogey or worse. But perhaps there should be another gauge for how well a golfer can bounce back from a bender the night before. Zhou would have scored well in that regard. So much so that Michael Dickie had no idea that anything might be amiss.

Dickie, a Scot based in Shanghai, was the head instructor at the city's David Leadbetter Golf Academy at the time (later he would be named coach to the Chinese women's national team). He'd never met Zhou before, but agreed to follow him around the course that Friday, and he largely liked what he saw: an aggressive, modern-looking golf swing and a lot of brute force. Sure, maybe his swing was too short, maybe he stood too low, but he agreed with Jim Johnson, who had assessed Zhou on the China Tour in 2007: the tools were there. "I'm really impressed with his swing," Dickie said. "He's just pure muscle, isn't he?"

Sure, Dickie had his criticisms, too. Zhou's putting and course management skills needed work, as did his distance control. And at times Zhou appeared rushed, unfocused. But none of these faults seemed too surprising for a man who taught himself how to play and who had never had a coach.

As the round wore on, however, and Dickie witnessed how Zhou handled adversity – usually, with a long string of expletives – the instructor's observations grew more perceptive, more personal.

"What's going on in his life?" Dickie asked after one of Zhou's eruptions. "Is there something missing? He doesn't look at peace with himself. All that swearing and the attitude. Not necessarily a chip on his shoulder, but maybe something to do with his upbringing – a sense of inferiority, perhaps. Usually, when everything around a golfer's life is calm, when they start feeling good on the inside, that is when they start playing well."

Dickie's assessment: "He needs to get some Zen about himself."

Zhou didn't find any Zen that weekend in Shanghai. Although he made the cut with an even-par 72 on Friday, he finished the tournament tied for fifty-first, after rounds of 77 and 78 on Saturday and Sunday. It was one of the worst China Tour finishes of his career.

Unfortunately, he didn't find Zen anywhere else, either. Over the rest of the season Zhou placed in the top twenty just once, and finished the 2008 China Tour ranked sixteenth on the Order of Merit. He'd earned 86,525 yuan in before-tax prize money. It was the best total from his four years on tour, but it still didn't cover his travel expenses.

8

TIME TO MAKE CLAIMS

The man wearing a tank top and surfing shorts would normally have been busy shaping a golf hole, but on this day, with a bag of golf clubs slung over one shoulder, he had decided to spend the afternoon playing some of his recent creations. He didn't have the day off; he just had nothing else to do. "Dozer is down again," he said with a shrug.

Nearly three years into his first golf course in China, this veteran American shaper had come to expect delays. The broken bulldozer was just the start. Progress on the course had been stalled by everything from typhoons to temples. And lingering land disputes continued to render five holes off-limits to the construction team. "We were originally going to be here a year," the shaper said. "That was a while ago."

He chuckled, however, as he was complaining. There were worse places than Hainan to while away time. Even after the island's elevation to provincial status in 1988, the same year it had become China's largest special economic zone, Hainan maintained its reputation as an outlaw state, where corruption was king. For years, its economy had arguably been built on smuggling, prostitution and unchecked property speculation.

As China's middle class grew sharply over the past decade, officials on Hainan and in Beijing decided the island needed to reinvent itself as a tourist destination. Golf, they realized, would need to be part of the equation. Never mind the fact that building a golf course was technically illegal. They'd find a way around that. In 2005, Hainan Vice Governor Chen Cheng had famously said the province strived to have as many as three hundred golf courses some day, and they hoped to make golf its *dao qiu*, or "island ball." Hainan was home to eighteen golf courses at the time.

But Hainan was still one of China's poorest provinces, and it was only accessible by boat or plane. Construction delays were common on the more modern mainland. In backward Hainan, slow motion could turn into super-slow motion all too easily. That much was clear to the project manager on the course with the broken-down bulldozer when he arrived in the summer of 2007. An American, he had never heard of Hainan before landing the job, his first in China. "I thought I was going to hit the ground running," he said, laughing at his naivety. Instead, he found himself sitting in an office trying to finalize contract details with potential subcontractors.

The Chinese are famous for haggling, and the process dragged on for nearly five months. That was nothing compared to the year-and-a-half he had to wait for a proper piece of equipment for his head shaper. He finally tracked down the right kind of bulldozer in Hong Kong, but for the first two months it was broken down more than it ran. Breakdowns required a repairman to travel from a dealer more than two hours away to fix the machine with "bubble gum and baling wire" until the proper parts arrived from Japan. "I stopped trying to have a schedule on everything a long time ago," the project manager said. "I have done so many schedules for this golf course. In China, unless you have the Beijing Olympics or the World Expo coming up, a schedule doesn't mean shit."

While specialized equipment might have been hard to come by, laborers were not. A small army of more than three hundred workers, mostly women, were recruited, earning around forty yuan a day to help build the course and perform many tasks a machine would typically take care of, by hand. The extra manpower, no matter how motivated, did not speed things up by much. "I think out of our entire team," the project manager said, "five, maybe ten, of them have even seen golf on TV. So they just don't understand a lot of it."

Most frustrating to the project manager were the complications over the land, the ones far beyond his control. In this way, Hainan was no different than any other rural area of China where officials were embracing development. More than half of the country's 1.4 billion people live in rural areas, and relocating villages had become commonplace. In the last few years, 1.3 million people had been moved in Hubei province alone to make room for the world's largest dam at the Three Gorges site on the Yangtze. Thousands of villagers had to be relocated to make room for the golf course and surrounding developments taking place on this part of Hainan. Not quite the scale of the world's largest dam, but relocation was never a comfortable process, no matter how many people were affected.

In China, land is owned by the government, not the villagers. Developers deal with local officials, who in turn are responsible for compensating the displaced residents. On Hainan, villagers quickly became aware that the amount of money filtered down to them was nowhere near the actual value of their land. Residents of one of the coastal villages said they were paid a one-time sum of around sixty thousand yuan (nine thousand dollars) per person to move. In addition, each family was given a new home – a concrete, two-story townhouse in a specially built relocation community on the outskirts of a town, fifteen minutes from the shore by car.

Hainan is a poor province – according to official government statistics from 2012, the average rural family there earned only 7,408 yuan ($1,176) that year – and some of the coastal villagers were happy to take the offer on their land. Although the new, grid-ded community was a bit soulless compared to their lush and leafy former home, it represented a clear move toward modernity. There was reliable electricity, plumbing, a sewage system and better schools for the children. And the community would stay together.

"We moved because the majority moved," said one elderly man who converted the ground floor of his home in the relocation neighborhood into a small shop. "Life back in the village was not easy. It was unclean. Fishing was hard work and the money was unpredictable. It's a more comfortable life here, but I miss the freedom of the village. I miss the ocean."

Most of those who made the move were skeptical about the future, however. What was going to happen when their compensa-tion money ran out? Nothing had really changed for them, after all. They were still largely a community of uneducated fishermen and farmers. After the development was completed, they would have nowhere to fish or farm. The golf course and new hotels were expected to create thousands of jobs, and the developers held recruitment seminars in the town, where people were given a chance to interview for jobs as caddies, cleaners, landscapers and security guards. Still, most of the local people expressed doubt that such jobs would go to them. "They won't hire dirty villagers like us," one said.

Some villagers chose to express displeasure with their displacement the old-fashioned way – they refused to leave. For the past two years, a small contingent of stubborn souls had lived in makeshift homes on top of the rubble of their former village. They were unsatisfied with the compensation packages they had received, and argued they had never been given a voice in the process and had been removed forcibly from their homes. "Money cannot solve the problem now," said one villager, who claimed to be holding out for either the right to stay or for a stake in the development. "If we move out, the place will never be ours again. Our ancestors left us this piece of land. It can't just be taken like this. If they had properly compensated us, fine. But the government is so unreasonable. Too greedy."

On the construction site, the project's timeline and budget were ballooning while the government tried to persuade the holdouts to move on. "I leave the Chinese politics to the Chinese," a project manager said. "I try to stick to what I know, and that is building a golf course. When they say I can go work a hole, I work a hole." When he finally got the go-ahead, obstacles remained. There was a small temple in the middle of what would become the eleventh fairway. It belonged to an elderly couple, and they started living in it, afraid that the temple would be removed before they were properly compensated. The construction team worked around the structure, and every day the project manager would smile and wave at his neighbors as he drove past in his utility vehicle. It wasn't long before the couple invited him into the temple for dinner.

The job site was also home to hundreds of graves, some centuries old. Mounds of earth occasionally marked by a modest engraved stone, each required careful relocation. Villagers received compensation for each grave removed, and negotiations over the payout for a single tomb had held up work on a hole for half a year. The project manager had picked up only a few words of Chinese, but one of them was *fenmu*, the word for "grave." He had also learned *jiade*, the word for "fake." Because money was involved, some villagers saw this as one of the few chances to get extra cash for their land. Phony graves frequently appeared overnight.

Entire villages, too, had been known to pop up, as opportunistic squatters tried to earn displacement packages. Some cunning villagers tried to double-dip. They'd receive compensation to leave their village one day, and the next day establish residency in another village that had yet to be relocated.

On another project in southern Hainan, aggrieved villagers built cinderblock structures hurriedly along the dirt road leading to the construction site. It was a desperate attempt to claim larger relocation settlements from the local government – since the more property you own, the larger your payout. When the money didn't arrive, they took to blocking the access road. The protests, usually peaceful, shut down construction for three weeks. Such delays were nothing new to this project; various land issues had caused several stoppages since work began.

"We would come to work for a week and then they would shut it down for a week and then we'd work for a week," explained that project manager, who said his team generally had a good relationship with the villagers, even the ones who would occasionally form a human roadblock. "They would come over and say, 'Hey, don't work today.' Nothing real hostile. Some of the other jobs I've known in China, it's been pretty hostile, where it's a safety issue."

The project manager did recall one instance where he felt his safety was at risk. He was visiting the job site with the course architect, and they had been warned when they arrived that villagers were planning to block the access road soon. "Finish up your business and get out of here," they were told. But when they attempted their exit, the road was already blocked.

"The first thing I see is some guy – they are usually pretty drunk – and he came running toward our truck with a big brick," the project manager said.

The project manager and the architect quickly locked their doors and the driver, a local man, attempted to negotiate. Once the protesters learned the car's occupants were not with the Chinese developer or the local government, tempers began to abate. "We heard them say *gweilo*, or foreigner, and then they started easing up," he said. "Near the end they were apologizing. 'Sorry, sorry, sorry.' We said, 'Okay, no problem. We understand.' They just want their money. That's the whole thing."

Not long after, early one morning, several hundred government employees arrived at the site, armed with heavy equipment. They knocked the cinderblock houses down one by one.

"Often, as is the case in China, you just have to take a deep breath and relax," said a Western representative for the developer of the shoreline project. "Things will happen, but in good time. You can't force things. The country is simply run differently."

As it happened, such differences made some aspects of building a golf course easier in China. In the United States, anyone trying to develop on a shoreline would have to jump through a series of complex and time-consuming regulatory hoops, from city to county to state to federal, in an effort to receive proper approvals. There would be issues to negotiate with coastal commissions, community groups and environmental organizations. Most developers agree that it would be almost impossible to build another Pebble Beach in the United States nowadays. But in Hainan? "There are no official environmental challenges here at all," said the developer's representative, noting that rather strict land planning laws exist in China, but are enforced haphazardly. "I don't think China has reached that stage just yet. It's up to the owner if you want to be responsible or not."

That's a scary prospect anywhere in the world, but in this case the developers were determined to do things right. They brought in an environmentally-minded firm to do the master planning, and their initial surveys confirmed what the project manager observed upon arrival: "There was no ecosystem here. Everything was raped and pillaged."

Several decades of development have taken their toll on Hainan's ecology. Some sixty years ago, the major culprit was the conversion of ancient woodlands into "commercial forests," used to produce rubber, timber and, more recently, paper. These had a huge effect on Hainan's biodiversity. Many native plant and animal species came under severe threat, most notably the Hainan gibbon, which today is the most endangered ape in the world according to the Zoological Society of London. In the 1950s, there were about two thousand Hainan gibbons on the island; now, there are between twenty-three and twenty-five, all in the Bawangling Nature Reserve, in western Hainan, established in 1980. Logging was banned in Hainan's natural forests in the 1990s, but enforcement of the law has been erratic. Greed, lack of manpower and oversight get in the way. In more recent decades, hundreds of thousands of acres of virgin forest and natural habitat have been lost thanks to the out-of-control real estate market and the slash-and-burn farming techniques of local villagers.

Environmentalists would likely applaud the efforts this golf course has made to clean up nearby waterways heavily polluted by human waste and scores of tiny fish farms, and restore ecological diversity to the land – the sandy soil had been rendered nearly lifeless after many years of water-intensive watermelon farming. The designers and the construction team were also intent on building a course as natural-looking as possible. They set large areas aside for landscaping, and planted only species native to the island. They created wetlands and reintroduced mangrove forests. Birdlife began to return to the area. Seashore paspalum grass was planted because of its ability to tolerate saltwater and gray water. Fairway runoff was designed to flow back into the course's irrigation ponds and, once the hotels and residences were completed, effluent would be treated and then used as an irrigator, as well. "It's all going to be worth it," the shaper said. "And, actually, I've really learned to like it here. I think we are going to look back at this in five years and say, 'God, too bad it didn't go on another year or two.'"

But for now, no one was allowed to talk about it – on the record, at least. The politics were just too complicated.

★

By late 2008, Wang Libo's new home was almost completed. It was a colossal structure, right on the edge of the cement road, where it couldn't be missed. From the outside, it resembled a fancy jail, with shiny metal bars covering the house's square windows of blue, reflective glass, the kind you might see on one of the brand-new high-rises on the mainland, in Shenzhen or Chongqing. The brick and cement walls of Wang's house were covered in a glossy tan tile. All the lines were clean. Everything was symmetrical. At ground level there were two massive metal front doors, square, just like the windows. They probably measured twelve feet by twelve feet and opened onto a cavernous ground level, with fifteen-foot-tall ceilings and a bare cement floor. It was Wang's garage, and it was large enough to fit dozens of *san lun che*, the type of three-wheeled truck he used for his livelihood. The living quarters on the second floor were basic and spare and totally devoid of character. But the walls were flat and smooth, the floors covered with cold tile. For Meiqiu, it felt like a mansion.

Not ten feet from the back door was the cement home Wang and his wife had built in 2000. It looked ancient by comparison, and was dwarfed by its new neighbor. From the new house's flat roof, Wang could look out and see a timeline of his life. Off in the distance, what to most looked like wild forest, Wang knew to be Cangdao, the now overgrown remains of the village his ancestors had fled at the time of the Japanese invasion in the Second World War. Wang's eyes traced the path his terrified grandparents must have followed to Meiqiu. There, he spotted the phoenix tree and, not far from it, the tile top of his parents' lava stone abode, where he had grown up. Nearby, the lychee trees he had once climbed for both work and play.

To see his most recent history, all Wang had to do was look down. There before him was his first modest cement home, the first place of his own, which just eight years earlier had represented a major leap from old village ways. On the opposite side of his new home, parked next to the cement road, Wang could see his *san lun che*, which provided his new steady source of income not reliant on harvest seasons or the whims of Mother Nature.

On a clear day, Wang could gaze far beyond the cement road and see hints of the Haikou skyline, which had grown in ways his grandfather would have thought unimaginable. In recent months, Wang's view of the city had been partially occluded by a haze of red dust emanating from Project 791, the massive construction site nearby – but that construction site was the only reason Wang could enjoy this lofty perch in the first place.

These days, Wang was looking younger than his thirty-seven years, with his baby face, full lips, big eyes and black hair kept in a crew cut. The worries of the past seemed to no longer play across his brow. Perhaps that was because Wang had been one of the first villagers to sell his land. In the end, he had sold nine *mu*, which netted him around 180,000 yuan, most of which went directly into his new house. Initially, he had, like the others, considered trying to fight the sale of land that featured some of his most prized fruit trees, or trying to negotiate a higher price. But then he considered the parties involved – a powerful Hong Kong developer, an unscrupulous local government, and a poor villager with a three-wheeled truck – and quickly determined his case was hopeless. *People are offering you money for your land*, he thought. *More money than you ever thought anyone would pay for your land. Take the money while it's still there.*

The people of Yangshan district, the volcanic expanse of which Meiqiu was a part, had always felt a special connection to their land. There was a pride of ownership, even though "ownership" hadn't been the appropriate word for decades. The government owns all land in China; the villagers just lease it. Still, many area residents felt they were closer to being landowners than most rural Chinese. "The land in Yangshan is different," Wang said. "It was passed down to us by our ancestors, so you get whatever your parents gave you. And if your grandparents or parents had money, they could buy more land and you get more. It's not like collectively owned rice fields or other farmland. Our land is individually owned."

So, whereas in other parts of rural China, the proceeds from a large land sale would be split up evenly among the villagers, in Meiqiu there were definite haves and have-nots. It all depended on how forward-thinking a person's forebears had been, and where the Red Line happened to fall.

Tucked somewhere safe in every village household was a bundle of old documents, tattered, stained and brown with age. These papers, some more than half a century old, told the story of the land, of Meiqiu and, in some ways, of China. They had the look and feel of old treasure maps, and in some cases had indeed led their owners to previously unimaginable riches. But the bounty came with an uncertain future.

Typically, the oldest document in the bundle was in traditional characters, and read top to bottom and right to left. Titled "Land and Real Estate Ownership Certificate" and dated July 1953, four years after Mao and the Communists came to power, it stated in no uncertain terms that the parties named on the certificate were the sole private owners of the land, and that their rights of ownership cannot be infringed. This was thanks to the Land Reform Law, a mass experiment that took land from feudal landlords and gave it back to the peasants. The law had been formally adopted three years earlier, in 1950. Everything took a little bit longer to reach Hainan.

The documents themselves were beautiful, with carefully handwritten characters in black ink and a square *chop*, or seal, and an ornate calligraphic signature in red to make it all official. Most would say these relics were of little legal value, and might be better off displayed in some kind of museum, but the villagers clung to the papers because they represented the only written proof to their claims. For each parcel of land, the certificate listed the county, the type of land and how many *mu* were included. Then it identified what's known as the "four to's," which took the place of latitude and longitude in specifying the boundaries of the property. For example, one section might read: "East to Shengshu; South to Meixiao; West to Laiji; North to Guoshi." Not exactly scientific, so people built walls, and those lava rock partitions had largely stood the test of time.

The walls remained, even as private ownership soon gave way to collective farming and people's communes in 1958. The walls survived the horrors of the Great Leap Forward and the Cultural

Revolution, and when Deng Xiaoping instituted the Household Responsibility System (HRS) in 1978 as part of his "opening up" reforms, the walls were still there, as well. The HRS marked an end to collective agriculture in rural China, and ushered in a new era of land-use rights, although not ownership, for individual families. And when that happened, the walls helped villagers in Meiqiu go back to using the land that was legally theirs a quarter of a century earlier.

Yet, every paper issued after 1953 also made it plain that the government owned the land and the villagers were simply leasing it, usually for a period of fifty years. One paper said the lessee must give 3.25 yuan to the village and fifty-four kilograms of grain to the nation each year for the right to use the land.

Not everyone in Meiqiu had been as lucky as Wang Libo, who had taken advantage of his bundle of documents to seal a deal with local government officials for the family acreage inside the Red Line. Many people had not yet received any payout, and without that they couldn't build new houses or contemplate the next phase of their lives. In fact, there was two hundred *mu* of contested land still to be settled, and for several villagers, proving they were among the rightful owners of that land was their last chance to cash in on Project 791.

There were three unique claims to the disputed land. Some argued that it was in fact collectively owned, that it hadn't been used until the village reclaimed it at the launch of Mao's Great Leap Forward in 1958. They said the profits from this land should be evenly distributed between the families who were able to present a Meiqiu *hukou*, the official household registration certificate. There was also a small group of Meiqiu villagers, ancestors of residents of Cangdao – the nearby village that had been ransacked by the Japanese during the Second World War – who said a large chunk of this acreage was privately owned, and they had the tattered paperwork to prove it. And finally, there was Wang Puhua, a Meiqiu resident born in 1950 who was a vocal supporter of the group arguing that the land was collectively owned. He also had a distinct assertion of his own: surrounded by the village's land were three *mu* owned by him, and him only.

"My family rented this land before 1958, and I have rented this land since the new land reform in 1978," Wang Puhua said. "If I say this land doesn't belong to me, who else does it belong to? I still have the certificate for this three *mu* of land."

There was a rub, however. Mission Hills had already paid *someone* for the land. Naturally, Mission Hills was arguing that they could do what they wanted with the property; contracts had been signed, money had traded hands and the land was rightfully theirs. But who had the money? Wang Puhua knew he didn't.

The developers had given money to local government officials expecting the cash would reach the proper parties. Everyone, including the villagers, was in agreement about this one fact – it was how things were done in China. But money for more than half of the contested land was unaccounted for. Some thought the Yongxing town government had the money. Some thought Xiuying district government had it. Others thought neighboring Longhua district had it, since it too was claiming ownership of part of the land. How could this happen? One villager summed it up bluntly: "Our government is disorganized."

The money for the other part of the land in question, some ninety to one hundred *mu*, had been tracked down. It had been paid to the Cangdao ancestors, of whom Wang Libo was one. Wang had never really identified as being from Cangdao. He was born in Meiqiu. He lived his whole life in Meiqiu. Almost all of his friends were from Meiqiu. In 1999, his fellow villagers even nominated him to be Meiqiu's governor (an honor he declined). But now he was labeled an outsider, because two groups of people claimed ownership over a rocky and weedy plot of land that no one really cared about until a year earlier, and some of them had been left empty-handed.

Wang Libo believed the contested land belonged to about ten individual farmers, all of whom happened to have ancestors from Cangdao. He said the old documents supported this claim, and that it was those ten farmers who had tended fruit trees on the land over the past several decades. Wang Puhua and others in Meiqiu – many who had yet to see any financial gains from Project 791 – disagreed.

The dispute built another wall, a figurative one, that cut right down the middle of a once tight-knit community. "Wang Libo is divided from us – and he has good *guanxi* with the government," Wang Puhua said, noting that Wang Libo's cousin, Wang Liguo, was a local government official who lived in a nearby town. "He no longer belongs to Meiqiu," Wang Puhua went on. "If the village has a meeting, he says he has no time to attend. If something good happens to him, he won't invite the rest of us to celebrate together. You see, almost all the new cement houses along the cement road are owned by old Cangdao villagers. They sold a lot of land and have enough money to build these big new houses."

Wang Libo didn't feel comfortable discussing the conflict, but he did admit he had stopped going to village meetings because he no longer felt welcome there. "Some villagers act very cold toward me," he said. "Especially some stubborn old men. They never say a word to me anymore."

All this bickering over land and money was somewhat ironic. The residents of Meiqiu had never had money to fight over before, and they never thought anyone would have any interest in their land. The soil was too rocky. They weren't near the water. And this was Hainan – isolated, remote, backward and an afterthought for most mainlanders. Why would anyone want to buy land in this place, where life was so hard?

In the past, if land exchanged hands it was typically from villager to villager. For example, the land Wang Libo had built his new home on was purchased by his father in the 1990s. But, up until the mid-1990s, prices remained quite low. *Huangdi*, or "wasteland," could be snatched up for three thousand yuan per *mu*. For land with fruit trees, you'd be doing quite well if you could attract ten thousand yuan per *mu*, about a third of what villagers received when Mission Hills came to town.

"We never expected such a big company to come and develop our lands," he said.

The former residents of Meiqiu were also split in their opinions about the big company that had arrived on their doorsteps. Their thinking largely depended on one thing, of course: whether the big company had paid for their land or not.

"The development is of no use to us at all," said Wang Puhua. "They took our lands without paying us. How can I say something good about them?"

His daughter-in-law felt the same way. Having Project 791 next door – even if it was destined to be the world's biggest collection of golf courses – was not going to change the quality of her life. "If we just continued to farm the fruit trees and reap the lychee, I think life is still okay," she said. "If we don't farm lands, and do something else, I think it would still be the same. We just have to change our way of making a living. That's all."

Wang Boming, who managed to sell just one *mu* of land to Mission Hills, argued that the development was not going to be the job creator some were suggesting. "They said they would offer jobs for us villagers, but what they really gave us is only the lowest-paid and toughest jobs, like cleaners, lawn mowers, or caddies," he said. "The management jobs are always taken away by the outsiders from other provinces."

A driver from the area – also named Wang, naturally – felt this way of thinking was shortsighted. "The local people are not well educated," he said. "Why should they be put in administrative positions? We have lots of local graduates from Hainan University working for 791. It has nothing to do with discrimination against the locals, what really matters is the education issue. Some local women, they can't read or speak Mandarin, how can we make them do something else beside cleaning?"

He also didn't think villagers should eschew the salaries that Mission Hills was offering – eight hundred to nine hundred yuan a month. "The company pays the insurance and pension," he continued. "If they keep working for fifteen years, they can retire. They need to think long-term. If we add all of this together, their salary can exceed one thousand yuan per month.

"For me, however, I won't do these jobs. I would prefer to buy my own car and drive customers. These jobs are especially good for the illiterate women. In the long run, I am sure this place will become better and better. In the short term, people will feel pity for having lost their land. But we need to look beyond the present day."

Wang Libo, who at first was skeptical about Project 791, was also beginning to adopt a long view of the situation. Perhaps it was easier for him to do so, from the comfort of his new home near the cement road. "In the long run, the development will bring more opportunities to the farmers," he said, "because many areas of wasteland on this island haven't been used for hundreds of years. Now they are being developed, and farmers will receive compensation. Before 791 came, there was no development project, and no chance to make money. Now they have come, and we have good chance to do business. It's better now."

And it was business Wang had on his mind, now that it was spring.

There was yet another small protest taking place adjacent to his walled-off lot, just beyond the border of Mission Hills, but Wang was not interested in the demonstration today. He had seen many of those before. Instead, he focused his attention on the construction taking place on the other side of his brick wall. Buildings were going up fast, and they were huge. Wang knew he'd have to go all the way to Haikou to see anything of a similar size.

"Hey! Friend!" Wang yelled to a shirtless worker wearing an orange hard hat, his skin glistening with sweat and as dark as Wang's used to get when he labored as a brick layer. "What is this place?"

"Workers' dormitory," the young man replied. "Ten thousand people will live here when we're done."

Wang's heart began to race. "Thanks!" he yelled back and hurriedly got back into his three-wheeled truck. He didn't know exactly why he was so excited, but he couldn't wait to tell his wife the news.

Rumors about a Mission Hills project in Hainan had begun to spread among those working in the China golf industry early in

2008. Details were fuzzy, but it was an open secret that the Chu family was up to something on the island, and that it was big – the family didn't know how to do anything small. By April, twelve seemed to be the number most people were whispering. And by that they meant twelve courses.

Then, in August, *Golf Digest* magazine published a series of stories about golf in China, set to coincide with the launch of the Beijing Olympics. In one piece, entitled "Golf in the Year of the Rat," reporter John Barton wrote about some of China's more mind-bogglingly massive golf construction projects – double-digit course layouts, once unheard of, now seemed normal in the country. Barton added, "But even that will be dwarfed by Mission Hills' grand ambitions in Hainan Island, off China's southern coast, where the hope is to build up to 36 golf courses as part of a master plan to turn the island into Asia's Myrtle Beach."

In September, American irrigation systems manufacturer Lindsay Corporation included a boast in the company newsletter:

> Five Watertronics pump stations recently arrived in China. Part of the Mission Hills Hainan project, the pump stations will be used on Hainan Island, off the coast of Southern China.
>
> Mission Hills Hainan consists of 36 18-hole golf courses being developed during a three-year period. Watertronics revenue for this project will exceed $8,000,000...
>
> When completed, the project will be the world's largest golfing complex, catering not only to the Asian market, but to "must play" golfing enthusiasts throughout the globe.
>
> The same developer recently completed Mission Hills Golfing Resort Complex in Shenzhen, China, across from Hong Kong. It consists of ten eighteen-hole courses and is currently the world's largest golf course.
>
> Watertronics has provided pumping systems worth more than $1 million.

There was no more conspicuous a golf project on the planet, but Ken Chu still insisted all those involved treated it as "top secret." The Chinese have a saying about unwanted attention: "Man should fear fame like pigs fear getting fat." No developer wanted their golf course to become the fat pig – the project that drew the eye, and the ire, of Beijing – and was put up for slaughter. One member of the design team tried to explain this "if you don't talk about it, it doesn't exist" mentality. "They don't want to create any more stir," he said. "The last thing they want is Beijing saying, 'What are you doing, building this many golf courses down here?' It's like, 'You might already know, but I'm never going to tell you.' That's what they have to do. That's the game in China."

As Ken stepped more to the fore, his father, David, became increasingly reclusive. According to Martin, it was hard to "get anywhere near that guy," though he was managing the construction of fifteen courses for the family business. Even back in 2002 and 2003, when Martin was building the five Mission Hills courses in Shenzhen, right in the eldest Chu's backyard, it was always an adventure going to see him. Usually, Ken would summon Martin for an audience. "My father would like to talk to you," he'd say, and what would follow would be like something out of a James Bond film. David's office was hidden in a high-security compound, protected by a seemingly endless series of gates and checkpoints. Martin recalled being escorted through "dungeon doors" that weighed "about ten thousand pounds each." Then he'd be asked to wait in a holding room until the patriarch was ready to see him. During the Haikou job, Martin saw and shook hands with David just once.

There were stories about David Chu using an elaborate series of decoys and car switches before boarding flights out of Hong Kong. No one knew whether these stories were accurate, of course, but such tales and others like them flourished, adding to the mystique surrounding the family. Call it extreme caution, or call it paranoia, some of it seemed to have been passed down to Ken. Like father, like son.

Mission Hills was now renowned for its formidable security staff – hundreds of highly trained young men, each a physical specimen, the equivalent of a small army. Early each morning you could hear them running through a workout regimen and tackling obstacle courses. A few times each year, at staff parties, the security team would wow the crowd with demonstrations of combat techniques and gymnastics that were at once thrilling and intimidating. The Mission Hills security detail was also famous for its canine contingent, a hundred or so police-trained purebred German Shepherd dogs imported from the United States. "When they say 'attack,' they attack," Martin said. "My staff used to complain that those dogs lived better than they did."

Workers at the Mission Hills project in Hainan said Ken would fly down to visit the site twice a month. His visits would rarely last more than a day, but always made an impression. He would be driven around the complex in a black car with tinted windows, a sizable entourage in tow. The full motorcade typically counted four cars flanked at each corner by a security guard on a motorbike. "It was like you'd see for the president of the United States," one observer said. At tournaments, Ken would be surrounded by a "fleet of golf buggies" – anywhere from six to twelve carts carrying a variety of security, public relations and other random personnel – tasked with following his every move. "It was excessive, kind of comical, actually," one worker recalled, saying the commotion was all part of "the image." This Mission Hills insider also felt the Chus' "unnecessary secrecy" and the over-the-top security helped to stew impressions that "maybe there is more that we don't know."

The worker wasn't alone. A journalist working on a routine story about the Chu family was delayed for months because Mission Hills went silent during the fact-checking process, stalling on basic details regarding the company's timeline, even the birth dates of key figures. "It was insane," the reporter said. "It was just a mystery what happened. They just wouldn't talk about anything." The impression the reporter was left with, valid or not, was that Mission Hills had something to hide, thus casting a shadow on the rest of the company's story, much of which seemed positive and a true embodiment of the Chinese Dream. "They really bring it on themselves," the journalist said. "There's a difference between secretive and cautious. Acting like everything is so secret is just a mistake."

Some secrets are harder to keep than others, especially if they occupy thirty-nine square miles of land – just shy of 25,000 acres. That was the size of the original Hainan plot Mission Hills was attached to, when David Chu settled on thirty-six courses, seemingly at random, according to those who worked on the project from the beginning. "Good *feng shui*, I don't know," offered one baffled member of the design team. "And they were looking to get more land. Basically it was, 'How much can you give me?'"

And Mission Hills was not alone. All sorts of conglomerates, both state-owned and private, including the China Poly Group and Hainan Airlines Group, were bolstering their real estate portfolios, snatching up large patches of land left and right, with a special focus on Hainan. "It's all about the land grab right now," acknowledged one golf design professional.

It would be difficult for local government officials to feign ignorance of the world's largest golf construction project happening on their island. In addition to negotiating the land purchases from the villages, Hainan government had a monopoly on the sale of sand on the island, and golf courses use a lot of sand. "You ain't getting it unless you go through the government," Martin explained. "They've claimed all rights to it. If you're going to pull your truck down there and set up operations and pull out of there, the government's going to be involved."

The master plan for Mission Hills Haikou called for twenty-two courses on the northern part of the property, close to the airport, and fourteen down south. But from early on, it was clear some courses were a higher priority than others. The original plan to start all of the courses simultaneously evaporated, and Martin's crew was told to focus on the northern tract while Chinese laborers toiled in the south.

Before long, some of the planned courses quietly evaporated, too. Twenty-two, not thirty-six, became the number the crew discussed internally. Dust-ups over land put the entire southern part of the project on hold, even though irrigation was laid for a number of courses there, and parts of two courses were completely grassed. Workers were told to let those two courses grow over.

That a project originally intended to cover such a huge acreage encountered problems related to land disputes surprised hardly anyone. It made sense that a monster undertaking like Mission Hills Haikou, at roughly fifty times the size of the average residential golf course project, had at least fifty times the amount of border disputes. Workers said protesters appeared on the construction site "countless times."

"They always come out with their machetes," one American staffer said. "There'll be thirty little women and they'll all start screaming Hainanese and shaking their machetes and yelling at you. It's always about money. It's always about getting paid. They're never violent. They never do anything. They know that that would just be tragic. They'd probably get shot or something. But anytime that happens, we'll just leave that area."

The worker said it was shocking to come from the United States, where land deals are so "cut and dry," to China, where everything is "muddled." He said the property lines of the Mission Hills project had changed "hundreds" of times.

Sometimes boundaries changed as the result of ongoing government negotiations with the villagers, and other times due to certain pieces of land, seemingly at random, being designated farmland, and therefore off-limits for development. "They wouldn't even let anyone farm there, and anyway it was nothing but lava rock," Martin said, perplexed. "Just some imaginary line the government came up with."

Mission Hills' marquee championship course was affected by such a designation. All eighteen holes of what's now known as the Blackstone Course were completely finished and playable, and then it was determined that parts of three holes – Nos. 16, 17 and 18 – were built on land that was suddenly considered farmland. Ken Chu negotiated with the local government for close to three months, and then one day, after talks broke down, he came to the site and told Martin's team to completely re-route the holes to accommodate the new property line. He demanded a new design be ready by the following day.

"They were great holes, with a lake," Martin said. "The next day we had thirty-two excavators in there completely ripping it all up, irrigation and everything."

A group of high-level local government officials came out that day, as well. They urged the workers to stop, saying they were so close to striking a deal. But Ken wasn't interested in waiting any longer. And he didn't want to make a deal now only to have it blow up on him in a year or two. That was smart. Farmland – or at least land that was being called "farmland" by the government on this particular day – was off-limits, and he didn't want any part of it.

"We ripped up many, many courses," Martin said. He estimates they built two entire courses' worth of extra holes just trying to keep up with the property's protean borders. "This new farmland concept is definitely coming into play," Martin said. "Every time a new plan comes out with new farmland boundaries, we're moving holes left and right."

Other alterations had nothing to do with villagers or government officials. They were more about knowing your audience. One of the courses at Mission Hills Haikou was inspired by the classic American courses of the early 1900s, known by some as the "golden age" of golf course design. An architectural feature common during that era was artificial mounds of earth, often many of them, known as "chocolate drops." Designer Brian Curley had positioned several of these chocolate drops throughout the vintage course, and when Ken Chu first laid eyes on the mounds he loved them, and ordered more. For the next three months, Martin's team added "loads of dirt" to the fairways, adorning the course with the humps and bumps their boss had requested.

One month after the course started receiving visitors, Ken updated his request.

"Take every one of those mounds out," he ordered. "Take them all out!"

Apparently, 90 percent of the Chinese who saw the course thought the mounds looked like graves.

But the delays and dust-ups were mere sideshows to the main event – the largest golf course construction project in history.

"The Mission Hills one on Hainan still kind of amazes me – boggles my mind," said a project manager for a different course under construction on the island. "The scope of the project is larger than the city of Haikou. One guy I know who lives there at the complex has to drive an hour and a half just to get to the part of the site where he works."

By the spring of 2009 there were a dozen golf courses under construction simultaneously. There were more than five hundred pieces of heavy machinery on site. From a distance, it looked a bit like *Jurassic Park*, but instead of dinosaurs roaming the earth, it was giant excavators and rock hammers. And because the entire complex was being built on thick volcanic rock, drilling rigs and dynamite teams were always on call. "This much equipment on a golf site is not normal – not remotely normal," one American worker said, noting that a typical eighteen-hole project would have about 1 percent the amount of machinery. To keep up with the demands of construction, the Chus built their own concrete factory on site, with fifteen cement mixing trucks working exclusively for them.

More than 350 million cubic feet of topsoil, enough to fill London's Wembley Stadium nine times, was brought in from an offsite location by a caravan of more than six hundred dump trucks running twenty hours a day. "They bought a mountain… and they basically cut it thirty meters down and turned it into a lake," an American worker at the site said.

While certain species of trees and shrubs thrived on the volcanic landscape, the rocky earth was not suitable for most forms of farming, nor was it suitable for building and shaping golf courses, which require a couple meters of moldable topsoil. Mission Hills bought a mountain, a small one about five miles from the construction site, and started digging – until the mountain was a hole in the ground. Those six hundred dump trucks ping-ponged between the two sites, transporting the mountain's red earth to the construction site, where it was stored in a huge flat pile that looked like an Arizona plateau.

9

HOMECOMINGS

Zhou Xunshu was watching television, and he was crying, moved to tears by a show called *National Models of Virtue*, which, according to an AFP write-up, honored "53 people who were selected by a pool of 21 million voters for their superiority in the five categories of altruism, bravery for a just cause, honesty and confidence, hard work and filial piety."

The show, Zhou said, made him think about his parents. "I really need to get them out of the village," he said at the time. "Some day, I am going to move them to Chongqing."

When that day came, it was the eve of the Beijing Summer Olympics – and his parents did not yet know that they were about to be relocated.

Salaxi was the last town before the ascent to Qixin. There, Zhou and Fifth Brother and Fifth Brother's girlfriend, who also lived in Chongqing, had made plans to meet Third Brother. At an outdoor market, they each bought a pair of canvas "liberation shoes." Cheap and sturdy, with reinforced rubber toes and cleated soles, they are the footwear of choice – or perhaps lack of choice – for blue-collar workers in China. That they were wearing them could mean only one thing: they were walking up the mountain to Qixin. Recent rains had made the road to the village impassable.

"We need to hurry," Zhou said. "It's getting dark, and the route is slippery."

Zhou did not carry any bags, no change of clothes. As a child he had hiked this route every day, his back either loaded with schoolbooks or a delivery of coal. He thought it would take about two hours.

The mountain had been transformed by the summer. What was once brown and barren now felt like a rainforest, green and overgrown. Lush terraces overflowed with corn stalks that towered over their tenders. Every person along the route was burdened with a heavy load of some kind of crop, be it potatoes, garlic, walnuts or corn.

"There's going to be a good harvest this year," Zhou observed. "Good weather, enough rain. The crops are growing so well now."

A steep incline through a bamboo forest led to an opening in the side of a tall, gray rock face. It was a proper tunnel, albeit slightly small, and with no lighting. The brothers pulled out flashlights and mobile phones to illuminate the path. There was no light at the end of the tunnel – it was more than half a mile long – and the further you walked, the smaller it got. Walls, once smooth and expertly arched, were now irregular and riddled with chisel marks.

"Nothing gets finished around here," Zhou sighed, as he emerged from the tunnel into a stunning verdant valley. Dark silhouettes of jagged hills loomed like shadow puppets in the distance.

It started to rain. The group walked alongside a stream, and then, as the water flowed higher, in the stream. The liberation shoes were soon soaked and struggling to find traction.

"It's a tough journey!" Third Brother yelled from the darkness.

And then, a light played like a firefly in the distance; then two, three, four. The faint barking of a dog came next. With each step, the village slowly took shape out of the night.

Zhou's father was waiting for them in front of the house. "Such a hard and tough journey," he said of the hike he no doubt had made a thousand times himself. "Come and sit. Drink some tea. Dinner is almost ready." Everyone gathered around the *huolu*, and watched the tea kettle boil.

Several minutes later, Zhou's mother emerged from a back room. She shuffled delicately and awkwardly, leaning heavily on a bamboo walking stick. She was in obvious pain, but smiled at the sight of her family filling the room. Zhou watched his mom struggle to take her seat. He shook his head. He held back tears. *This is why we are taking them back to Chongqing*, he thought.

Zhou brushed a fly off his shirt, but two more took its place. They were swarming. A couple dozen of them, little winged magnets, clung to the exhaust pipe extending from the *huolu*, and the insects seemed especially attracted to their guests from Chongqing. It was the shirts – they were the brightest things in all of Qixin. Zhou wore a white Nike quick-dry shirt, and Fifth Brother a white-and-red-striped Nike golf shirt with a red collar to go with his white golf trousers. His girlfriend's ladies golf top was hot pink with a deep neckline. Aside from a few specks of mud, their shirts looked clean and new – three brilliant lights in the monochrome room. Zhou brushed off fly after fly from the front of his shirt, unaware of the colony that was forming on his back. His parents, by contrast, wore drab suits, the same as they had been wearing back in the winter. They melted into the room's gray interior. When a fly landed on them, they simply waited for it to fly away.

"Let's eat!" Zhou said abruptly.

"Let's drink!" Fifth Brother said with a nervous chuckle. First Brother would have usually been the one to get the drinking started, but he was off building a tunnel.

Zhou, his parents, Third Brother, Fifth Brother, Fifth Brother's girlfriend and two neighbor boys who helped out the family in the fields walked to the cinderblock structure adjacent to Zhou's parents' house and crowded around a rectangular table. First Brother's wife served the food. The dishes looked familiar: Various combinations of local tofu, potatoes, pickled cabbage and preserved pork. Corn also made its way to the table, in the form of *mijiu*, a wine that Fifth Brother distributed and consumed liberally.

Zhou had made the decision to return to Qixin only a couple days before. "I always make decisions suddenly. Especially about coming back home," he explained. "It's just not something I can plan. But, you see, my mother fell down while working in the fields several days ago and is using a cane now. So I thought I should come back."

Zhou was smoking a cigarette. He took a long drag and stared at the ceiling.

"You know," he continued. "All I have wanted was to be able to buy a large apartment so my parents could live with us in the city. Now I have done that. But they don't want to move."

The plan had been to wait until after dinner to start persuading the parents to leave the village. But Fifth Brother, perhaps emboldened by the corn wine, couldn't wait.

"Mom and Dad," he began, "last night, I taught two students to golf, and I charged them 2,500 yuan. It's very easy for me to make money. We can hire an *ayi* to do the household chores for you two. You can just enjoy the city life."

"I know you love your parents," Zhou's father replied softly, "but we are rural people since birth. We have lived in the village for decades. We can't get used to the city life. And we will cost you a lot of money."

Zhou groaned. He'd heard all of this a dozen times before. "I don't want to talk about this right now," he said.

But Fifth Brother continued, loudly. "How much money could the two of you possibly spend per month?" he asked. "To be honest, if every month I buy one less item of clothing, that's enough for your monthly expenses."

Third Brother spoke up, in a more measured tone than his youngest brother. "Dad, you are getting old," he said. "Who knows how many years you have left? You have five sons, and you and Mom are still working in the fields? Don't you think the other villagers will think that we don't support you? Don't you think that will humiliate us?"

"But what about our corn?" his father replied with concern.

"You calculate how much money the corn is worth and I will give you the money," Fifth Brother shot back.

"Let's talk about it after dinner," Zhou said. "Let's eat and drink first. After dinner I'll make the arrangements."

But the conversation droned on, different versions of the same arguments that had been made hundreds of times before. Sons tell parents they are old and deserve a better life away from the backwards village; they no longer need to work; they raised successful sons who are able to care for them. Parents tell sons they don't know what they'd do in the city; they don't want to be a financial burden to their sons; they fear for their farmland and crops in the village. Again and again, often with multiple people speaking at once.

Zhou's father looked confused at times, shifting the rice in his bowl with a wooden chopstick. At other times he looked pensive, painfully so, as though the calculations taking place inside his head were physically hurting his brain. His wife, on the other hand, seemed amused by the proceedings. She leaned on her cane and smiled, happy that three of her sons were seated around her dinner table – together – for the first time in years. She was willing to put up with a little shouting in *cuohango* for that, and she knew the loudness was born out of love. When he wasn't shouting, Fifth Brother was feeding her *larou* with his chopsticks.

Zhou was surprisingly quiet for most of the discussion. But once the dishes were cleared and the neighbors were gone, he began to take a more aggressive approach. This was an intervention. And he wasn't leaving until he got the result he had come for.

"You two have already had decades of the tough life in this village in the countryside," he said to his parents. "What if something were to happen to you? You know that saying, 'A slow remedy cannot meet an emergency'? What if something happened to you and the weather is like it is today? How could we get you to the hospital?

"You know, when I was looking for a wife, I didn't care whether she was ugly or not. Filial piety is the most important thing. And if I can't find a woman who will treat my parents well, I would have gone to a temple and become a monk.

"Dad, you started working at the age of twelve, and you have worked hard for almost sixty years. You and Mom had six children, and when Grandpa was still alive, you took care of him, too. The whole family was raised by you two, by your four hands working in the fields.

"Now I am raising my own son, and I understand what you went through to bring us up. You two need to listen to us. The past thirty or forty years we listened to you – from now on, you need to listen to us.

"You must come live with us in Chongqing. We will take you to see the experts in the hospital. You both have leg problems now. You know, for a person without legs, life won't be interesting at all."

There was silence. For a moment it seemed that Zhou's speech had put an end to the back and forth. Then his father responded.

"What about our corn? Our potatoes?"

"We already arranged for the crops!" Fifth Brother said, drunk, tired, exasperated. It was past midnight. He leaned against the *huolu* and held his head in his hands.

"What's the arrangement?" Zhou's mother asked.

"Third brother will come back for the harvest," Zhou said.

"And what about after the harvest?" she asked.

"We will store it for you," Zhou said. "And if you come back, you can eat it."

"If I cannot do it all on my own, I can ask other people for help," said Third Brother.

"Mom, you need to see where I am living now," Zhou insisted. "After you live with me for a while you won't want to come back here. You can eat better in Chongqing, too. You can have more nutritious foods – I can give you fresh fruits and vegetables every day."

"No, that costs too much money," Zhou's mother said.

"We don't want you to waste your savings on us," his father added.

Zhou looked like he was going to explode. Third Brother doled out another round of cigarettes. Fifth Brother poured another glass of corn wine.

"Why are you drinking so much tonight?" his mother asked. "Wine is money, too. In Chongqing, you must drink every day."

"How could I drink every day?" Fifth Brother shouted. "I need to work to make money to support you two and my girlfriend. Tonight, I came back to my hometown, to remove my elderly parents from the poor village. I am very excited, so I drink more than usual."

"Father, you need to go to Chongqing," Third Brother said. "Growing potatoes is too tiring, too tough for you two. You work the whole year, from the planting to harvest, but you still don't make any money."

"Father, several days ago a friend gave me a bottle of rice wine worth two thousand yuan," Zhou said. "I was waiting until you got to Chongqing before I opened it. I want to drink it with you."

"How could you buy rice wine that expensive?" his father asked. "Such a waste of money."

"My friend gave it to me," Zhou said. "If you don't come to Chongqing, I will throw it away."

"No, no," his father said. "Don't do that."

While the brothers smoked cigarettes, Zhou's father puffed on a tiny pipe that had an inch of local tobacco stuffed into its bowl. He sat next to a glass of *yaojiu*, a local medicinal wine, and occasionally dipped his fingers into the liquid and rubbed it onto his aching knees and ankles.

"So, this place – this dirty, poor place – you still like it?" Zhou asked. "You want to stay here for the rest of your life? Don't you get tired of such a remote life? Mom fell down and hurt her leg. No doctors available. Don't you know to call me?"

First Brother's wife joined the conversation. "That's not the problem," she said. "This is just the place they are used to. I wanted to call you, but Mother said she is okay. She said, 'Don't interrupt their life. Don't waste their money.'"

"I am okay now," Zhou's mother added quickly. "I just don't want you to worry about me. Going to the hospital costs a lot of money."

"Health is more important than money!" Fifth Brother shouted.

"You need your money in the city," she replied. "You need it to start your family and raise your children."

"Can't we just stop quarreling?" Zhou pleaded. "Please, let's just stop. There are important things we need to do. You should be packing."

"But what about our corn?" his father said again.

"Aren't you listening to us?" Zhou screamed. "I'll have people harvest them. I'll have people put the crops here. If you want them to be sold, they will be sold. If you want to keep them, you can keep them. Okay? I told you I already arranged everything. Do you not trust me?"

Zhou's father squinted his eyes. He pursed his lips. He massaged his temples. He tapped the stem of his pipe against his forehead. He made a clicking noise with his tongue and teeth. The wheels were spinning.

"Listen to me," his father finally said. "If you have arranged for everything well, I will listen to you and go to Chongqing. We know you want us to have better life and we are very happy that you think about us. But, you know, the corn in the field, and the potatoes. You know, the corn grows very well this year, and the potatoes can fetch three yuan per kilogram…"

Zhou's father went on for close to ten minutes about the crops, the harvest. Zhou did not interrupt. Instead, Zhou stared blankly toward the darkness beyond the window and shook off a couple flies. His father still talking, Zhou walked to the door, opened it and spat. He sat back down. His father was still talking. Zhou just stared. He must remain a national model of virtue.

"Living in the city is already difficult enough," his father finally said. "I don't want to be a burden. I just want you to save money. If I could harvest enough food, you wouldn't have to pay a monthly allowance for my expenses."

It was now past 1 a.m. The three brothers were standing. They had their parents surrounded. They pleaded them to leave the village.

"But what about the corn?" Zhou's father said, again.

"Second Brother and Third Brother will sell the corn," Zhou said. "Don't talk anymore about your reluctance to go to Chongqing. You must go there. Third Brother, Fifth Brother and I have been talking about this for a long time, and it takes us much time and pain to persuade the two of you.

"Think about this," Zhou continued. "Three generations will be living together. Is that not like paradise? Why don't you want that? Money is not important – what matters most is that the family is all together. Right? We can pay for your food, your hospital fees. You should see the outside world now. It's quite different than years ago."

"Don't let us go back with a broken heart," Fifth Brother added. "It's time for you to enjoy a better life. Hard times are over."

"But the crops…"

"Father, don't you want to meet your grandson?" Zhou asked.

It was 2 a.m. The room reeked of tobacco and corn wine. Everybody was exhausted, like prizefighters struggling to stand in the final round of a title bout. Then, suddenly, seemingly prompted by nothing, Zhou's father threw in the towel.

"Okay," he said. "We will go."

Nothing more was said. The lights were turned off. And three grown brothers shared a bed for the first time in twenty-five years.

The next morning, it was raining lightly. Zhou donned his liberation shoes, still wet from the night before, and walked down to the spot where his primary school used to be. Next to it was a piece of flat earth that once served as the village basketball court. It, too, was a thing of the past.

A woman was feeding pigs near the old basketball court. She smiled at Zhou and invited him to her house for tea.

"I can't," Zhou replied. "This morning I have something to do."

He walked on, past the village tobacco kiln, past piles of spent zinc retorts, toward the farmland carved into the mountainside. Another woman recognized Zhou and invited him into her stone home. "Do you want to stop and have a rest?" she asked.

"No, I have something to do this morning," Zhou replied.

He walked on, toward some leafy farmland glistening with the morning rain. It was part of the five or so acres, scattered around the mountainside, that Zhou's family owned. Zhou came alive. "So many memories," he said.

His pace quickened. He spoke like an enthusiastic tour guide. *Look! That's tobacco. Have you seen it in the field before?*
Look! Hot peppers. They will soon turn red.
Look! Jicama. The meat is underground – I ate it as a child.
Look! A chestnut tree. The spikes protect the nut inside.
Look! Sunflowers. Have you seen them grow so tall?

Zhou spun around and took it all in. "This year is going to be a productive harvest," he said. "That is why my father is reluctant to leave."

He had finally arrived at a landing overlooking the overgrown valley. Tall blades of grass filled in the gaps between gray boulders. "This is the place I would graze the cows," Zhou said simply.

A mist hovered over the hollow, but he could just make out the white cliff face, which now wore a beard of green, on the opposite side of the valley – where the stone man resided. "Some villagers think the stone man can make their wishes come true," Zhou said. "They burn papers near him and pray. Maybe I should ask him to help me win a tournament?" He rolled his eyes.

Some of Zhou's fondest memories of Qixin took place on this swath of land. The cows were content to feed, leaving their young minders free to play, explore and roast potatoes on an open fire. They played the golf-like game involving bound-up balls of papers, sticks and scythes. Another game, Zhou called it "village bowling," saw the boys hurling sickles at bundles of tied-up grass. Knock down a grass "pin" and it's yours; fail to do so, and a day's worth of reaping goes home with someone else. Zhou and his friends would also scamper up trees and try to catch adult birds. But he had never managed to catch one. "They are so clever!" Zhou said, shaking his head.

He squatted on a boulder, his back to the valley, and took a piece of grass in his hands. He began to tear it into tiny pieces and stared at nothing in particular.

"I have a feeling of sadness," he said after a lengthy silence. "I don't know how to describe it. This place is so remote, so wild. Look at this muddy and broken road. We have so many villagers here, but they never unite to maintain this road. They are so lazy that they would rather stay at home doing nothing than go out to maintain the road. Once a road is built, cars can drive in easily, and it can fuel the local economy. But there is nobody in charge here. People just live life for themselves.

"I think the quality of life in the village has actually deteriorated. More than twenty years ago, we could grow anything we want and have enough to eat – vegetables and meat. Now, it's just the same, but in the city, life has improved dramatically. We are still stuck in the same place. Everyone else is marching ahead, and we are lagging behind.

"If I ever have lots of money, first I want to build a nice new house here. Then I'd invest some money to maintain this road in winter. I'd like to give the poor villagers some money. But they need to work for it. I think fifty villagers could fix the road in just two months. If you pay every worker one thousand yuan a month, that's fifty thousand yuan per month. Maybe someday.

"This is where my roots are, and I won't forget this place completely," Zhou said. "I may return here again when time allows. During Qingming Festival, I will return to sweep the tombs of my ancestors." Qingming Festival, or Tomb-Sweeping Day, took place each year around early April, when the village road was a bit more passable than during the new year celebration.

He took the muddy path back to the village. Along the way, he bent down and pulled a handful of garlic chives out of the earth. "These will go well with lunch," he said. "My stomach is calling me home. I am hungry."

Third Brother was waiting for him in the courtyard. "Have you decided to leave today or tomorrow?" he asked Zhou. There was unease in his voice.

"I thought it might be better to leave tomorrow," Zhou responded.

"It needs to be today," Third Brother said. "I suggest you leave in a hurry."

Third Brother was obviously concerned that Zhou's parents' early morning surrender had all the permanence of sidewalk water calligraphy on a summer's day. He made it clear: the brothers' mission was not complete until their parents were sipping tea while sitting on Zhou's sofa in Chongqing.

His pronouncement set off a flurry of activity. First, the brothers must host an early lunch, a last supper of sorts, that included the five village men who would be responsible for tending to the family farmland in their parents' absence. As the dishes arrived at the table, Zhou addressed the guests.

"I know I left the village several years ago," Zhou said, "and I wanted to express my thanks to all of you for helping look after my family. I wanted to deliver my thanks to you individually, but because time is very tight on this trip, I didn't have time to walk around and say thank you one by one. In the future, if I have enough time, I hope to catch up with all of my old neighbors."

He closed with some abstract words of encouragement: "I think we people have the ability to do things well. But we need people to guide us in our work. If we have the chance to follow a leader, we can do things well, and make money. Solidarity makes things easier – those who fight alone are idiots.

"Let's eat!"

After the lunch everything became a blur – part farewell party, part forced evacuation. Imagine trying to pack up a life in an hour. Then imagine trying to do it with half of a village looking on with curiosity. This was a major event in Qixin. Village elders rarely left. They rarely had anywhere to go.

Zhou's parents took the dizzying pace of their departure in their stride. They smiled and laughed as they stuffed their most important belongings into plastic rice sacks and cardboard fruit boxes. They didn't pack photos or family heirlooms – they had none of these. They packed sugar, preserved pork, heads of garlic, soybeans, dried chili peppers, fresh eggs, white radishes, tobacco and corn wine. These were the possessions they could not leave behind.

"Should we pack their beds?" a neighbor asked.

"No," Zhou said. "We have those in Chongqing."

They did pack clothing. Two suits each for Zhou's mother and father. Zhou felt the rest were "too ragged," and announced they would be left behind. For about fifteen minutes, his parents' home took on the feel of a charity giveaway. Villagers lined up to rummage through dusty piles of shirts, trousers and jackets – there were no dressers or closets in the house. They tried on items they liked over what they were already wearing. Almost everyone took home a memento of their departing friends.

By now, Zhou and his father were rifling through the contents of the bedroom. It was a small, cluttered, windowless room with stone and brick walls and a single light bulb hanging from the ceiling. Plastic bags were scattered across the bed. They had been stashed inside pockets, under mattresses, and, like mortar, between the stones in the wall. The bags were where Zhou's parents stored important documents, like identification cards and bank books. There was an old ledger from his father's time working in the Supply and Marketing Cooperative. No one knew exactly how many plastic bags had been hidden or what they contained.

"Oh!" Zhou exclaimed, jokingly. "I found a treasure!"

He pulled a wad of pink one-hundred yuan bills out of one of the plastic bags. He counted the money.

"All together 2,100," he told his father. "This is hard-earned money. Bring your ID cards to Chongqing and I will have this put into a bank account for you."

Zhou was inspecting the bounty – sack upon sack upon sack – that had accumulated in the courtyard, and wondering how he was going to get it all back to Chongqing. He had borrowed a Honda CRV from one of his golf students for the journey, assuming the SUV would accommodate five people and his parents' meager possessions easily. But what he saw before him looked like a wholesale farmers' market.

"Don't forget the roosters!" his mother shouted from inside the house.

Of course. Roosters.

Zhou and his brothers chased down five of them, but the brown-feathered birds put up quite a fight. Clearly these country chickens had no interest in moving to the big city. As Third Brother held the roosters by their wings, Zhou tied their legs together with twine. The brothers stuffed the birds into red boxes adorned with pictures of oranges and the word "grapefruit" in English. One rooster was especially reluctant to leave. Push his head into the box, and he'd pop it back out through an opening in the top moments later. This happened several times, until Zhou eventually gave up and let the old bird have its way.

A procession of family and friends – each man carrying at least one heavy sack on his shoulder – walked Zhou's parents away from their village home, down the muddy path to where a truck was waiting to take them to the bottom of the mountain. The morning fog had lifted, and visibility was good.

Everybody was filthy. Shoes, slippers and pant cuffs covered in mud, all articles of clothing speckled in brown. The road was a mess. The driver squatted in a mucky puddle, struggling to affix chains to his truck's balding tires. On a normal day, the road would have been considered impassable. But this was not a normal day. Zhou's elderly parents were not going to leave the village on foot.

The chains were not working, however. The old truck squealed. Tires spun in place. Mud flew. Were they going to leave at all?

"Get some rocks!" Zhou ordered, determined.

Large stones were removed from a nearby terrace wall and wedged under the truck's tires for traction.

"Come, help me push!" Zhou barked.

Zhou, his brothers, and other men from the village leaned into the back of the truck. The engine howled.

"Push with all your strength!"

The rickety truck rocked forward, then back, before finally hurtling ahead to somewhat drier land.

"Hurry. Load the truck!"

With the most precious cargo – Zhou's mother and father – safely up front with the driver, the rest of the passengers took their places in the truck bed alongside the roosters and preserved pork.

"Wait!" Zhou's mother yelled out the window. "We forgot the cooking oil. Can somebody go back and get it?"

The mountains were luxuriant and otherworldly, moss-covered dragon's teeth protruding from the loam. The view was a nice compensation for what was otherwise a loud and jarring ride. At times, the road was a river. It took an hour, but they eventually got to the bottom of the mountain, where Zhou and his brothers could transfer their parents, along with their garlic, tobacco and five crowing roosters, to the SUV.

As they pulled away, Zhou's father popped his head out of the backseat window and looked back toward the road that leads to Qixin. It was difficult to tell if he was smiling.

The following day, Zhou's apartment in Chongqing smelled and sounded a bit like Qixin. Fifth Brother killed a rooster out on the kitchen balcony, covering the outdoor sink in chicken blood. On the living room balcony, Zhou's father puffed on a pipe stuffed full of village tobacco. He was wearing Fifth Brother's white-and-red-striped Nike golf shirt. His head was freshly shaven and, for the first time in years, not adorned by his trademark Lei Feng hat. (Fifth Brother had tossed that in the trash the moment they arrived in the city.)

Zhou's father sat out on the balcony for hours, silent, staring at the view from his son's ninth-floor apartment. From his perch he could see a highway, a strip mall of restaurants, a driving range and several parking lots. But mostly he saw new high-rise apartment buildings, each nearly identical to another. He was surrounded.

"At night," Zhou's father said, "they look like mountains."

Zhou's home was still very much a work in progress. Furnishings were sparse. Walls were bare, save for one children's poster covered in pictures of fruit, the name of each labeled in both English and Chinese. The living room, like most of the apartment, had white walls and white tiled floors. There was a glass coffee table, an oversized mauve sofa and, although the walls came wired for a flatscreen television, a small, boxy tube TV Zhou had received from a friend. This being the home of a baby – two, in fact, as Zhou's mother-in-law was visiting with Liu Yan's nephew, Yang Yang, who was only one year old – part of the floor was covered with soft foam tiles decorated with the letters of the English alphabet. Zhou's parents slept upon straw mats on the floor of what used to be the office, just off the dining room.

The kitchen was nearly spotless. The white tiles on the walls shone like mirrors, and the cabinets were fluorescent yellow. There was a gas stove with two burners, and an extra electric burner that sat atop a new microwave oven. The stainless steel range hood and refrigerator still had the clear protective plastic covers they shipped with. Near the sink, things began to fall apart. A line of crude sacks containing crops from the village was slouching down the wall. Atop the new refrigerator, a tub of pig lard. There were dead chickens in the sink, their clawed feet pointing at the white ceiling.

Zhou's mother, who cooked every day back in the village, looked lost in the kitchen. Too different. Too new. Give her some coal and a wok and she'd be fine. "I don't know how to cook with the gas," she said, frustrated. She looked right at home, however, feeding her grandson on the balcony. She had brought six children into the world. This is something she knew how to do anywhere. When asked what she thought of the high-rises, she responded with single words like "good" and "beautiful" before adding, "But I don't dare look downward." This was her first time in a multi-story building.

There were a lot of firsts during Zhou's parents' initial twenty-four hours in Chongqing. First skyscraper, first elevator, first modern shower and toilet. Zhou taught his parents how to flush, and how to mix hot water with cold. Alas, he neglected to give a tutorial on the balcony's glass sliding door, which his father discovered by walking right into it. But not everything was new. On their second day, while dining at a spicy hotpot establishment not too far from Zhou's home, his father announced this was not his and his wife's first time at a restaurant. It was their second. "The other time was nineteen years ago," he said. "It was for First Brother's wedding."

There were plenty of smiles, but there were also signs the assimilation process wouldn't be simple. You can't move an elderly couple out of one of China's poorest villages, into one of the world's fastest-growing megacities and not expect some difficulty – Zhou must have expected that. Sure, there were familiarities of family and culture, but for Zhou's parents, Chongqing was an intimidating new world, both foreign and futuristic. They were like time travelers who, because of their backwoods dialect and broken Mandarin, didn't even speak Chongqing's language.

Zhou's father didn't like having to use the elevator every time he wanted to step outside, and he worried about getting lost. He said he was having trouble figuring out the shower and that his wife wasn't comfortable in the modern kitchen. They weren't sleeping well, either. They missed their crops, and felt guilty knowing they would be away from the village during harvest time. Zhou's mother was afraid the belongings she left behind in Qixin would be stolen. And both were anxious about making friends in the big city, about finding ways to spend their time.

"I don't want to feel like a bird in a cage," Zhou's mother said. "I hope I can talk to the other old people in the neighborhood. I hope I can have fun with them."

Zhou had never doubted this was the right thing for him to do. He felt it was his duty. His parents were living a primitive existence in the village. He now had the means to offer them a better quality of life in the city. End of story.

"You know, I cried that night when I was persuading them to leave the village," Zhou said. "My mom fell in the field and hurt her leg, but she still wanted to cook rice for us. How can I tolerate my mom living in such a bad situation? I wanted them to live with us with all my heart.

"My parents are part of my life. There will be only one change: We'll make more rice for every meal."

And on Zhou's parents' first full night in Chongqing, the rice bowls were indeed overflowing. Soon, Zhou would take his parents to the hospital for treatment, and to the city's famous Jiefangbei shopping area to buy new clothes. There were many things to do in the days and weeks ahead, many challenges to overcome, but today Zhou chose to focus on what lay immediately before him. It was a feast – dishes of beef, pork, fish, chicken, eggs, potatoes and fresh vegetables – and he was the provider. He was seated at a glass dining room table he had bought, in a new apartment he owned. He was surrounded by his family: his beautiful new wife and their healthy baby boy; Fifth Brother and his girlfriend; his mother-in-law; his sister's teenage son visiting from Shandong; and, of course, his parents.

Zhou, the peasant farmer-turned-security-guard-turned-golf-pro from Guizhou, had made all of this happen. He sat back in his chair, took a large mouthful of Shancheng beer and watched as Liu Yan used chopsticks to feed rice to their son. She sang to Hanhan:

> *In Disneyland, there is a Donald Duck.*
> *He quacks at people every day.*
> *Quack, quack, quack, quack!*
> *Donald Duck, my Donald Duck.*
> *Quack, quack, quack, quack!*

On the final "quack," Hanhan reached into the bowl and grabbed a handful of white rice, most of which ended up stuck to his cheek instead of inside his mouth. Zhou's mother laughed. Then his father laughed. Soon, everyone around the table was laughing.

Zhou's parents had only been living in Chongqing for one week when Zhou had to leave for two tournaments in South Korea. Zhou boarded the plane with unease. The week had gone well enough – his parents had thanked him for the new sets of clothing and their medical treatment, and they seemed to enjoy spending time with their grandson – but Zhou was now unsure how well his parents were adjusting to life in the city.

Even on the initial car ride from the village to Chongqing, Zhou's parents kept muttering about wanting to go back home, about their crops, their livestock. These mutterings continued throughout that initial first week, as well. Zhou thought this was probably natural, and hoped his parents' feelings of homesickness would wane over time.

Plus, Liu Yan enjoyed having her in-laws around, and that should help to get them settled, he thought. Communication was often difficult – Liu Yan's knowledge of the village dialect was limited – but her new houseguests would help stave off some of the loneliness she felt when Zhou was gone for long stretches of time. And she knew how much it meant to Zhou to have his parents in Chongqing.

But Liu Yan also worried that Zhou's parents weren't adapting well to their new surroundings. Their days were empty. They stayed inside watching TV. They had no activities, no chores and very little contact with other people. On the balcony of Zhou's apartment, Zhou's father sat and looked at the view and sighed. "Just a very boring life here," he observed.

They had become what Zhou's mother had feared – birds in a cage. "They seemed lost," Liu Yan said.

Zhou didn't play well in Korea, missing the cut in the tournaments, and he grew anxious to return home to a full house of friendly faces. He flew from Seoul to Beijing and then to Chongqing. During the trip, every time Zhou would talk to Liu Yan on the phone, he'd ask how his parents were doing. "Fine," she'd always say. ("I didn't want to distract him," Liu Yan later explained.) And when Zhou, en route to Chongqing, called during his short layover in Beijing, the topic of his parents did not come up.

When Zhou returned home, he stepped through the apartment door and put his bags down on the floor. Something didn't feel right. The house was too quiet, too still. The door to the office – where his parents had been sleeping – was open, and the room was empty. Zhou's heart sank.

"Liu Yan!" Zhou yelled. "Where are my parents?"

He already knew the answer to his question. He sat down at the empty dining room table, his face blank. Zhou tried to get a handle on his emotions. This was not anger he was feeling. Not sadness. It was confusion. It was guilt. What had he done wrong? What could he have done differently?

"Before they arrived, I had always thought they would adjust to life here," Zhou said. "That is why I invited them. But after they got here, part of me knew they wouldn't stay for long. But I never thought they would leave when I wasn't home." He sighed and added, "They wouldn't have left if I was here. I wouldn't have let them." And that is exactly why Zhou's parents left when they did.

They had spent two weeks away from the village, and that was all they could stand. At first, Zhou's parents were thrilled to see the bright lights, the wide roads, the tall buildings. But after ten days they were just lights, roads and buildings. They were lonely. They felt they had no one to talk to. Back home, they could walk into any house in the village and chat with their neighbors. In Chongqing, they were afraid to leave the apartment.

Fifth Brother tried to convince his parents not to return to the village, but, still weary from the intense negotiations that got them out of the village in the first place, and with no brothers at his side, he didn't put up much of a fight. Liu Yan, too, attempted to talk Zhou's parents into staying, arguing they hadn't given life in the city enough of a chance. But they wouldn't listen. Instead, they told Liu Yan that she and Zhou should visit Qixin more often.

Zhou's parents called the village. Less than twenty-four hours later, First Brother's son Little Tiger arrived in Chongqing to accompany his grandparents home.

"Homesickness can be dangerous," Zhou reflected. "I guess I didn't understand their way of life before. I didn't understand what makes them happy. Now I know. They don't care if our home in the city is cleaner or more convenient than the one in the village. All they need is clothing on their bodies and food in their stomachs. They are happier in the countryside. City life didn't have any meaning to them. It's a generation gap."

Zhou, who had been trying to get his parents out of the village for years, was done chasing this dream.

"Never again," he said. "I think they believe they are too old to live outside the village. It's Chinese culture. If they die outside their village, they can never go home again."

The day after he returned from Korea, Zhou called his parents. He asked them why they left, and they answered with reasons he already knew: the corn, the tobacco, the chickens and pigs. This all made sense to him now.

"If it makes you happy, you should stay in the countryside," Zhou told them.

When asked if his parents ever said they were sorry, Zhou shot back: "No. How can a Chinese parent apologize to their child?"

10

STRIKING BLACK

Wang Libo began to build his future in May 2009. It was his wife's idea, actually. "When we saw that the developer was building dormitories behind our land, and realized the workers living there would have no place to buy cigarettes and drinks," Wang recalled, "my wife suggested we build a small shop to sell necessities on our land. I said yes, because now that we had rented out our fruit tree land, she was jobless."

He estimated the shop he had in mind would cost around forty thousand yuan – a small fortune – but he didn't hesitate before going ahead with the plan. It was a strange time in the village – never before had so many people been flush with cash. Even though he and his wife had spent all their land compensation money on building their new house, they still had some savings. Some relatives, who had also recently profited from land sales, helped them with the rest. "Before, I would have had to borrow from the rural banks, and there would have been a lot of red tape," he said. "Now, every plan is like this. Everything is possible. If you have money, you can do it without concern."

Over the course of the summer, Wang, his wife and her father built the shop with their own hands, one brick at a time. For Wang, it was like revisiting a former life – the mortar and trowel like long lost acquaintances. He didn't miss the backbreaking work, nor was he pining particularly for more time under Hainan's searing summer sun. But this time around, at least, he was working with his wife by his side, and what they were building was all theirs. They may have lost most of the family land, but they were establishing a new family legacy. With each brick he laid, Wang would think of one of his three children. *This one is for my eldest son, Wang Jiaqiang. This one is for my youngest son, Wang Jiaxing. This one is for my only daughter, Wang Jiazhen.*

By mid-August the last brick had been cemented into place, and the entire structure received a skim coat of mortar. It was a simple building, a one-story rectangle with an open showroom and a small side room barely big enough for a single cot, where Wang often slept to stave off thieves. The ceiling and the top half of the interior walls were the only surfaces to get a coat of white paint. Everything else, including the floor, remained smooth and gray. Three cement steps led to the storefront, which was dominated by three large openings yet to be outfitted with windows and doors. From almost any angle, you could look right through the building, out the back door and window, and see the behemoths being built out back. It was hard to see exactly how many dormitories there were, but by this point they were each already seven stories high and surrounded by green mesh and bamboo scaffolding. The orange hard hats the team of construction workers wore looked like ladybugs scurrying across it.

Wang hoped this army of workers would be his way to cash in on Project 791.

If you were flying into Haikou, approaching from the west, it was big enough that you could see it from the air. Viewed from above, the boundless swath of land didn't look like much – fuzzy textures of green vegetation, shadowy pockets of lava rock, incongruous veins of reddish brown soil – but it was set to make history as the largest collection of golf courses in the world.

The scope of the multi-billion-dollar project was staggering. It occupied some thirty square miles of northeast Hainan, a vast expanse of volcanic forest and shrub land the size of Hong Kong island. It wasn't just a few dormitories being built; thousands of workers had been busy clearing trees, moving soil, building greens, fairways, clubhouses and luxury hotels. But Ken Chu was still denying its existence.

"We, um, it's not so much on the course development," Chu stumbled, when asked about his company's projects on Hainan. "Actually, we haven't even started, we haven't even talked about this project. It's something in the pipeline, in discussion, but it's not purely on golf. It's a tourist destination." They definitely had their eye on Hainan, he said, and the pairing was a natural fit: the island was looking to boost tourism, and Mission Hills was in the tourism business. But it was too early to say anything more than that. "There's nothing to talk about," he said.

But a large chunk of the project was already nearing completion. Six golf courses were shaped and seeded, with little more left to do than wait for the grass to grow. Three more courses – including the showpiece Blackstone Course – were even further along. They looked perfectly playable, lush and green, with a troupe of local women wearing rattan hats the shape of Tiffany lampshades, adding the finishing touches to the white-sand bunkers.

The resonant moans of bullfrogs in the marshland along the course's eighteenth fairway had been replaced by the repetitive *ping ping* of hammers hitting metal. Chain-smoking laborers, their skin brown and weathered by the tropical sun, were plugging away at two structures that would be a dramatic backdrop to the course's closing hole. One, a luxury hotel, was such a beautiful, brilliant white, that its grandeur made it hard to remember you were in rural Hainan, one of the ten poorest provinces in China.

It was all utterly telegenic, and that was by design. It had been widely speculated that in a few years' time the Mission Hills Haikou tournament course would host one of Asia's biggest tournaments. PGA representatives had reportedly toured the Hainan facilities.

Mission Hills was building the world's first and only self-contained golf city. Originally, thirty-six courses had been in the plans, but some of the land deals fell through. Still, twenty-two courses – more than the number on the entire island before Mission Hills broke ground – was enough to represent every style of golf course imaginable, from links to desert, to Augusta-like perfection, as well several decidedly non-traditional designs. Picture yourself playing into a waterfall, through a cave, around a volcano or over a replica of the Great Wall. But there were also multiple "town centers" planned, each featuring luxury homes and condominiums, hotels and spas, shopping malls, and streets lined with restaurants and bars. The Chus were transforming the Hainan countryside into a new-style Chinese suburbia. No doubt it was raising the value of surrounding property, and creating thousands of jobs. But a project that was "repurposing" twenty thousand acres of open land and directly affected the lives of tens of thousands of poor rural families was bound to create some controversy.

But there was always a way.

After decades of missteps and false starts, the provincial government had finally announced official plans to make tourism a "pillar" of the local economy. An all-out effort was underway to create an "international tourism island" to rival popular Southeast Asian destinations like Phuket, Thailand and Bali, Indonesia. Visa restrictions would be loosened, duty-free shops opened, flight offerings expanded. The island once known as "the end of the earth" was repositioning itself as an "oriental paradise holiday resort."

Golf was expected to play a major role in this repositioning. According to the Hainan tourism bureau, golf tourism to the island started to pick up around 2006, after Vice Governor Chen Cheng had announced his ambitions for hundreds of courses on Hainan. Golfers from South Korea and Japan started to arrive by the planeload. Golf in Hainan – even with the travel expenses – was a bargain compared to the rates they'd pay back home. "At that time, in Haikou, you could walk into a hotel after dinner, and the golf bags would all be lined at the hotel door – tens, even a hundred of them," said Long Weidong, chief of Hainan's tourism bureau. "And at the courses, all the people you saw had Asian faces, but you knew they were all Korean or Japanese."

But would a hundred or two hundred golf courses make sense on Hainan? While most of the existing courses were fully booked during the peak winter season, the insufferable heat and relentless rains of the Hainan summer kept away all but the most dedicated or frugal golfers. Greens fees were often heavily discounted during the quiet months, but it didn't make much difference.

The lagging global economy was also taking a toll on business. Visitors from Korea and Japan were no longer traveling to China to play a few rounds, and while Russian tourists continued to crowd the island's beaches, few of them were playing golf. Much of the new golf course development, including the Chus' Mission Hills project, was not in the south, around Sanya, Hainan's most popular resort town, but along the eastern coast, near Haikou. That was where the available land was – near villages like Meiqiu.

Long Weidong acknowledged that the historically large outlay of money had brought "some problems" to the previously impoverished region. "The low-level officials had never seen so much money before," he said. "At first there were no problems, but then some people just got greedy. And because of the unequal distribution of money, the farmers were not happy, so they started appealing, accusing the village officials and the town officials."

Long said there was also concern in the provincial government that villagers who received large payouts for land would not know how to manage the funds, given their low levels of education. "They don't have skills besides working on the farmland – they don't know how to do anything else," he explained. "The government is worried they will spend all the money gambling or buying cars. Maybe they'll spend it all in three or five years. Then what are they going to do?"

Long started golfing in 2007, shortly after he became head of the Hainan tourism bureau. He learned from books and DVDs at first, and then received lessons from some experienced golfers. When he played on the course these days, he always did so wearing long sleeves; even in Hainan, no government official wanted to be seen with a golfer's tan.

He did, however, admit that things on Hainan were a bit more lax than they were on the mainland. "This is a holiday island," he said. "If you go to Beijing or Shanghai and you try to talk with the government officials about golf? Impossible." When he traveled to Beijing, staff members at the China National Tourism Administration had told him not to say anything about playing golf. "Being an official on the mainland is different," he said. "Even if they can play golf, they need to say they can't. You can only admit to playing ping pong. Maybe tennis. Never golf."

Long, like many higher-level officials in Hainan's government, was originally from the mainland. He preferred the political environment on the island. "Here, you play golf, nobody gives you trouble. I don't have to be like a thief. I can just tell you I play golf. No problem."

Golf had long been taboo among the mainland's senior politicians. Zhao Ziyang – the country's premier from 1980 to 1987, and general secretary, the Communist Party's highest-ranking official, from 1987 to 1989 – was the only top-level Party official to be relatively open about his golf habit. Zhao could regularly be found teeing it up at Beijing International Golf Club, near the famous Ming Tombs, where thirteen Chinese emperors were buried. But then, he was also often seen wearing tailored Western suits instead of the "Mao suits" preferred by most Chinese officials at the time. Zhao's detractors branded these an example of the "bourgeois liberalizations" he was allowing to pass through China's once airtight seal. In 1987 the *New York Times* had called Zhao the "dapper heir" to reform-minded Deng Xiaoping. In its article, it even noted a photo distributed by the Xinhua News Agency, China's official government media mouthpiece, that "shows [Zhao] on the golf course wearing a white baseball cap and clutching what knowledgeable observers believe is a three-iron." No wonder he'd been criticized by Party hard-liners. Yet Zhao had been ousted not for his golf, but for his sympathetic stance toward the student demonstrators at Tiananmen Square in 1989. He spent the final fifteen years of his life under house arrest (solitary and security-heavy rounds of golf were among the few things he was permitted to leave his house for).

Ironically, when the Tiananmen protests began, Zhao had been a primary target; he was mocked by the students for his obvious love of golf. At the same time, workers angered by uncontrolled inflation were condemning the privileged lifestyles of high officials. The Beijing City Workers Union called on the Communist Party to inform the public of personal incomes and expenses of high-ranking cadres, as well as the number of real estate properties they owned. "Mr. and Mrs. Zhao Ziyang play golf every weekend," the workers said. "Have they paid the fees? Who paid for their expenses?"

In the quarter century since Zhao's ousting, the world has seen no photos of prominent Chinese government officials playing golf. Today, such a photo remains taboo. When asked what would happen if newspapers were to somehow publish photos of China's president enjoying a round of golf, one course manager predicted there would be one million new golfers in China the following day. "I think the possibility of that ever happening is zero," said Song Liangliang, a spokesman for the China Golf Association. "Photos of Zhao Ziyang caused such public turmoil back then."

Clearly, though, the winds were shifting. Long said President Hu Jintao had visited the province in 2007 and listened to reports from provincial officials, and some of those reports had focused on the island's golf industry. Premier Wen Jiabao and First Vice Premier Li Keqiang had also visited Hainan in recent years, and they too were briefed on the province's golf ambitions. Long said Hu had even invited Kazakhstan president Nursultan Nazarbayev to play golf there. Hu never played golf himself, Long was sure, but he had assigned the provincial general secretary, Wei Liucheng, and Hainan's director of foreign affairs to play golf with the Kazakh leader. "It was public," Long insisted. "There was even media coverage. Nursultan got a hole in one. This generation of government officials, their ideas are changing. The last generation of central government leaders, one of them said, 'If a leading cadre plays golf, it is the same as prostitution.' I can't say who it was. He didn't say it in public. But after he retired, he started to play golf."

Between the uncertain politics and the effects of the global financial crisis, Long sensed that talking too much about golf remained "off-message." "We've dwelled on this topic too long," he said. "What we are doing is tourism, and Hainan's tourism resources are, first, our tropical climate and the sea. Second, our volcano culture and ancient villages. And third, our virgin rain forests."

Golf was conspicuously absent from Long's list. Why, then, so much focus on golf in Hainan? Why all the new courses? Because in

China the number of golf courses built has very little to do with the number of golfers available to play on them. With few exceptions, golf courses were being built not to profit from greens fees, but to help sell luxury villas. Developers were not terribly concerned if a golf course sat empty, as long as the properties along it sold. And in Hainan, selling homes had not been a problem. Wealthy bosses from Beijing, Shanghai, Guangzhou and central China's coal belt were sweeping up villas, sometimes several at a time, often paying in cash. The rich were looking for safe investments, and they felt real estate of this sort fit the bill.

Being able to say you owned a home on a golf course in Hainan was about prestige, about face. "It is all about selling vacation houses and having them full three to four months of the year," explained Richard Mon, then vice president of China operations for Schmidt-Curley Golf Design, the firm behind the Mission Hills project. "Three years ago, everyone you talked to was, 'I want to build the best golf course in China!' Now there are a lot more developers out there saying this golf course is an amenity to my project. It is not my project; it is a part of it. It is as important as the swimming pool. It is as important as the hotel. It just happens to take up a lot more space."

Mission Hills' development primarily occupied acreage that the government had classified as *huangdi*, or wasteland. But the designation didn't take into account the land's ecological merits. "If they only build on true wasteland, then there is no problem," said one conservationist active in Hainan. "To me, the [Mission Hills] area next to Haikou is not a 'wasteland.' In Hong Kong, that would be a country park, a very nice forest or wilderness park. Whenever we fly from Hong Kong we say it almost looks like Botswana or something. It is so nice, just a plain of green with some pools and ponds."

The northern section of Mission Hills was less than thirty minutes by car from downtown Haikou, and just east of the national geological park built around the extinct volcano crater. Nearly three years earlier, a Haikou-based NGO believed it had secured around 825 acres of this land to establish a forest park that would help promote environmental awareness. It had worked for two years toward this goal, getting the support of the government, attracting investors and brokering a land deal with the local villagers. But suddenly, the villagers had cut off communication. And that was when the NGO's organizers first learned about Project 791.

"They didn't even notify us," the head of the NGO remembered over a pot of *pu'er* tea. "The government just told the villagers not to work with us anymore. All the years working, the money, the energy, all wasted. It was a devastating hit. It broke our hearts, and we felt so small and insignificant. We knew we could never defeat them. How can you go against the government?" He paused, then added, "I have been an environmentalist in Hainan for eight years. I am tired. I am exhausted."

The NGO was warned not to do anything that might disrupt the Mission Hills project, and it had to oblige. Throughout China, a domestic NGO is never truly nongovernmental. A good relationship with the government is necessary for survival, and going up against golf – an industry that was lining the pockets of many a local government official – would not be a wise move.

"The government is always on the same side as business guys," the NGO director said. "It would be impossible for us to do anything to try to stop this. It's the government's thing, and they do it in secret. They give the project a code name. They call it ecological restoration. Sure, they might plant a few trees, but they also destroyed a mountain and turned it into a lake. They call this ecological restoration?"

At times, even Martin Moore's construction team couldn't believe the ambition of the project. One employee wrote the following in a company newsletter: "It is hard to imagine that every square meter beneath the growing grass on the current twelve courses under construction, lays a solid layer of volcanic rock. Nothing more, just rock, rock, rock. More than ten million cubic meters of topsoil has been imported from off site. More than one hundred rock breakers, along with dozens of drilling rigs and dynamite teams, face the huge challenge of keeping the project moving forward. Almost all mass excavation requires blasting and rock breaking, all drainage and irrigation trenches have to be excavated with rock breakers, even the cart paths are made of crushed lava rock. The magnitude of this construction process is simply incredible."

Wang Libo and his wife were exhausted from their summer of hard labor, but they were anxious to start the new chapter in their lives. They had decided to open their new business immediately. Windows and doors – not to mention electricity – could wait. So on Tuesday, August 25, 2009, they became shopkeepers. There was no fanfare, no banners, balloons or strings of multicolored triangular pennants. The shop didn't even have a name. They shouted over the wall to the workers on the "secret" construction site next door and told them they were open. Word gradually spread.

Offerings were sparse at first – whatever Wang could fit into his three-wheeled truck during a trip to Yongxing. Five metal shelves in the back of the shop housed most of the necessities: water, soft drinks, canned congee, eggs, instant noodles, soap, shampoo, toothbrushes, toothpaste, laundry detergent, soy sauce, and two brands of beer: Anchor and Pearl River. In front of the shelves, a small wooden desk and a glass display case where Wang kept cigarettes, nuts, seeds and a variety of prepackaged pastries. The only other piece of furniture in the mostly empty room was a large terracotta urn filled with a variety of drinks and ice trucked in from Wang's house further down the road. Regular trips were necessary. It was late August on Hainan; nothing stayed frozen for long.

Wang's little shop was in its second day in business. He shuffled a deck of playing cards from the chair behind his desk. "I am currently building two toilets in the back," he said of his work in progress. "If you come back here after three years, there will be so many changes you won't recognize this place. Even compared to two years ago, there have already been lots of changes here. Two years ago there were no buildings here. It was all mountainous wasteland and fruit trees – nothing like now." In a few years' time, he said, "it will be a different world."

Wang paused from his discussion of the development of Hainan to attend to two weary workers in search of cold water. Once he'd served them, he continued. "In the future, the rich people will come to Hainan for holidays and they will live in villas and enjoy all-inclusive 'eat-drink-and-be-merry' packages, some even including beautiful women," he noted. "The course will be very nice, too. It has a man-made lake and all the green grass and trees. It will be the same as in Shenzhen, but this one is even bigger than the one in Shenzhen, and better too."

He said he'd heard about these grandiose plans from "the bosses" of the construction site. "They said developing this area will benefit us and help us get rich. There will be more people coming here, and we'll be very busy. It's not for the people who come here for holidays, because they'll have their own services. It's for the workers and the employees. They need to eat. The dormitories here will have thousands of workers living here and in the future we want to sell them things."

He felt secure about his future, because he owned this land. The local officials had tried to wave off the protests by telling the villagers they were only renting their land to Mission Hills on a fifty-year contract. When the rental period ended, they or their children could renegotiate the terms for the land, which would be much more valuable. But Wang saw through it – and so did the other villagers. "In name, 'rent', but in reality, 'buy.' The government told us we are renting to them for fifty years, but after fifty years we will never get that land back," he said. The developers, after all, had not signed a contract with the villagers. "They signed the contract with the government not with us farmers. So they say fifty years, who knows, after fifty years we might not even be alive. They won't give the land back even if we are."

He saw no point in all the protests. "As an ordinary citizen, how can you fight against the government officials?" His best bet, he thought, was to find some way to continue to profit from the project.

A car pulled into the dirt patch in front of Wang's store. It looked new. The brand was BYD, or "Build Your Dreams," a plucky Chinese company based in Shenzhen. A man in white shorts, a white golf shirt and flip-flops hopped out. It was Wang's cousin,

Wang Liguo, a district-level government official on the island. He said he was sure Mission Hills Haikou was going to be bigger and better than the one in Shenzhen.

"I have been to the Mission Hills in Shenzhen," Wang Liguo stated proudly. He explained that he and around one hundred other village representatives from the area had traveled there on an all-expenses-paid trip so that they could understand the plans.

"Do you want to have a look inside?" Wang Liguo asked, motioning toward the Mission Hills property.

There seemed no way to get past the security.

"Who can stop me?" he scoffed. "Who can stop the government's car?"

"I feel so gloomy these days," Zhou Xunshu said. "I can't find a job." And then, with one swift twist of his wrist, he brought a fish head to the surface of the pot. Sichuan peppercorns covered its skin like barnacles. A small pool of bright red broth settled in the bottom of the ladle. Zhou dumped the whole thing into his rice bowl and began to pick it apart with his chopsticks. The surroundings matched Zhou's mood. The neighborhood restaurant was tucked into a dark, sooty suburb near Beijing's international airport. The kitchen workers sat shirtless at a corner table smoking cigarettes and playing cards, seemingly oblivious to the occasional cockroach scratching its way up a wall or a customer's leg.

It was early September 2009, and Zhou was in Beijing for the China Unicom Pro-Am, an independent tournament with a large purse – 1.5 million yuan ($215,000) in total prize money – and a wacky format. During the final rounds of the event, when the Chinese professionals should be focused on competing for one of the biggest paydays of the year, they were being forced to play in groups that included inexperienced amateur golfers, usually local business people or clients of the title sponsor. These interlopers often proved to be more interested in socializing and glad-handing than playing a serious round of golf.

"I don't know whose fucking idea this was," Zhou fumed. "The pace is intolerable. They shoot in the hundreds. One round feels like it lasts a week. Sometimes players in the lead will lose their advantage because they are teamed with bad players. It is totally beyond understanding."

Zhou sighed. "Chinese golf really sucks in our generation," he said, "and I doubt we'll see it improve in my lifetime."

Although he may have wanted to, Zhou couldn't skip the event. The lure of the prize money was far too great. This was especially the case in 2009, which was shaping up to be a lean year for professional golfers in China. The pro-am was the first domestic tournament since mid-June, ending a perplexing hiatus during what was supposed to be the heart of the playing season. The China Tour had mysteriously fizzled out. Only four of the planned eight to twelve tournaments had been scheduled, and the tour's organizers had offered little explanation to Zhou or the others as to what was going on. At the Beijing pro-am, some players were still clinging to the hope of a fifth event in Guangzhou, and maybe another in Shanghai. But no one could say exactly when these would take place. It could be next week. It could be never.

The lack of tournaments was getting to Zhou. Emboldened by his performance in 2008 – those two top-ten finishes especially – he was determined he would earn his pro player card in 2009. He had to place third or better in a sanctioned China Golf Association event, or finish in the top twelve of 2009's order of merit, which wouldn't be easy.

Zhou also desperately needed a sponsor. He had a family to support, and this might be his final year on tour if he couldn't find some help to cover the expenses. There was a businessman in Chongqing who owned a golf cart factory and had already offered Zhou a job as a salesman. If Zhou's playing career didn't pick up, he'd have to consider taking it. That prospect didn't excite him.

So in February, Zhou took a risk. He arranged an unpaid break from his job at Haoyun Driving Range, said goodbye to Liu Yan and little Hanhan and left Chongqing for Shanghai's David Leadbetter Golf Academy, more than a thousand miles away. There, he would train with Michael Dickie, the Scottish coach who had been so privately critical of Zhou's attitude in 2008. Dickie had agreed to take Zhou on free of charge. This bit of good fortune had to mean this would be Zhou's big year.

For a solid month, all Zhou did was train. Dickie analyzed every aspect of his game and, as he had suspected, discovered Zhou had all of the physical aspects down. Sure, a little fine-tuning here and there wouldn't hurt, but Zhou's biggest obstacle really was the mental game. Zhou said Dickie had taught him to calm down: "My mind is more peaceful than before." He also got in better shape. He lost nine pounds while he was in Shanghai, and his trousers were all now a bit loose. He was becoming more fit, in every way. "I've never felt like a professional golfer before," Zhou reflected. He'd always been too distracted by his day job, too preoccupied with paying the bills. "But this month, I finally feel like a pro. All you do is think about how to golf well."

But, despite Dickie's generosity, this feeling didn't come for free. Zhou had to make major sacrifices to live like a pro during his month in Shanghai. He had no income, and worried about his job security at the driving range. His bosses there didn't hide their displeasure with his plan. He had to pay for his flight to Shanghai and a room at a two-bit boarding house on the outskirts of the city, and he was convinced the landlord was going through his things while he was gone.

On one of his days off from practicing, Zhou visited a fitness center in the city. The gym was small, but relatively high-end for China, and part of a luxury apartment complex popular with foreigners in Shanghai's French Concession. A long row of cardio machines sat behind a tall wall of windows looking out onto Huaihai Road.

Zhou was probably the strongest person there, but he appeared tentative, unsure. He watched the other people in the gym closely. Several times he hopped on a machine immediately after someone else had finished a set. His movements were hasty and often awkward, but believable enough that his approach could be chalked up to cultural differences in technique – somewhat like his home-grown style of golf. But when Zhou decided to give the treadmill a try, the jig was up: it was clear he had no idea what he was doing.

He straddled the moving belt as if it was a mighty river surging beneath him, and he clutched the grips so tightly his hands turned white. He built up the courage to dive in, but did so in spurts. He'd run a few steps, then straddle, run a few steps, then straddle, as though the belt was burning his feet. "I kept thinking the machine was going to push me backwards and make me fall off it," Zhou later said.

His confusion seemed odd – at least one of the Chinese golf magazines had run photos of him using an elliptical machine as part of a profile. "That was just posed," Zhou explained. "The magazine made me do it. The machine wasn't even turned on."

It turned out that, although he'd seen gyms on television and in movies, he'd never been to one before.

He wasn't a stranger to physical training, however. As a teenager, he said, he would lift weights occasionally – large rocks, really, carved into the shape of a square, with a hole cut into one side to fashion a handle. They were called Chinese stone locks, and they'd been around for thousands of years, a sort of an ancient kettle bell. Zhou had seen the stone locks used as strengthening tools in the *kung fu* dramas he watched as a child, and he had wanted to be big and strong like the stars of those shows. "I did it when my village friends were with me," he said. "We'd always compete to see who could lift the most." Zhou could lift sixty-five pounds (thirty kilograms) five or six times in a row back then. "Today, I wouldn't be able to do that," he said.

Still, Zhou was feeling good about his game. He had finished second at a local event at Shanghai Links Golf & Country Club, and he liked his chances at the two-day Shanghai qualifying tournament that would take place in mid-March before the Volvo China Open in April. Simply joining the field for such a prestigious event, the longest running international tournament in China, would be a major achievement. He needed a top-three finish in Shanghai to earn a spot in the China Open.

Zhou felt confident going into the final round of qualifying not because of his weeks of training with a coach, or his newfound levels of fitness, but because of a dream. The night before, Zhou had dreamed that swift waters had overtaken his hometown. He

was certain this was a good sign. According to Chinese super-
stition, a flood of water in a dream means a flood of wealth in
real life.

At the tournament, Zhou bogeyed two of the final three holes
and finished in fourth place, just one stroke out of third. The Volvo
China Open would have to wait for another year. "The flood didn't
swallow me in the dream," Zhou said later. "Maybe if it did I would
have had better luck."

He didn't have time to dwell on what could have been. He was
on a flight headed for Xiamen just four hours after finishing his
round. The following morning he was scheduled to tee off at 7:30
a.m. in the opening round of the Dell Championship at Orient Golf
Country Club, the official season opener of the 2009 Omega China
Tour. And there was a full schedule of events to come.

Perhaps Zhou needed a flood to wash away all of Guizhou province, because as the China Tour began, things were not going
according to plan. At Xiamen, Zhou placed fifty-eighth, his worst
result since 2006. A month later in Nanjing, he opened with an 80
and had to hustle to finish in the top forty. Finally, in June, things
started to improve for him. He finished under par and cracked
the top twenty at the tournament in Chengdu. And the following
weekend, in Anji, he closed with rounds of 69 and 70 to finish tied
for twenty-fifth at 3-under.

He was starting to play more consistently. But then the tournaments stopped. And Zhou lost his job back in Chongqing.

Over the past year, Chongqing had been caught up in a political crackdown. The crackdown had nothing to do with illegal
golf courses – it was a government attempt to wipe out organized crime. The campaign, called *dahei*, or "striking black", was
the brainchild of Bo Xilai, son of one of the Communist Party's
"eight elders," Bo Yibo, and most recently the country's minister
of commerce. At the Party conference in 2007, Bo Xilai had been
assigned to serve as chief of Chongqing as part of a reshuffling
of the Party's politburo.

Bo seemed intent to use the position to prove himself to the Party leadership. Thousands of people were arrested, including gangsters, businessmen and the former deputy head of Chongqing's Public Security Bureau. "Many former Chongqing leaders had no way to deal with the gangsters," Zhou said. "But Bo Xilai is the son of a powerful ex-official. He can do this. No one can get him into trouble."

Zhou said several of the "bosses" at his driving range were involved, in one way or another, in the types of "black" society activities Bo Xilai had targeted. One was arrested. Others ran away. This exodus at the top, according to Zhou, left all the decision-making power at the driving range to one man – Zhang Yong. "And he's very mean," Zhou said.

When Zhou's contract came up for renewal in July, Zhang refused. There was no "thank you for your four years of service," no farewell party, not even a free box of golf balls. Zhou learned through backchannels that he'd been replaced by a foreign coach, a Canadian who'd been working in Shanghai, in an experiment Zhang hoped would drum up more business. "He doesn't even speak Mandarin," Zhou said of the new coach. "He coaches through a translator. But the translator doesn't know golf terminology. How can that be better than being coached by me?"

Zhou was stupefied. He was insulted. And he was short three months' pay Zhang still owed him. But once the initial sting wore off, Zhou realized what he really was: lost. He'd never really stopped to consider just how integral golf had become to his life – for the past fifteen years or so, it had always been there. Now he lacked both a place to coach and, with the China Tour faltering, an outlet to compete. He thought about his wife, his son, his house. He was jobless and clueless, a dangerous combination.

"What skills do I really have?" Zhou said. "It's not like I can just hit the street and line up to find a job, right? I'm a golfer."

Zhou made some calls inquiring about coaching positions, but he'd never been a very good salesman, especially when selling himself. He had some leads in Guangdong, but he was reluctant to move back there. Guangdong was part of his past, and Zhou was all about moving forward.

Some suggested he move to Beijing. But Zhou said people in the capital were too aloof for his tastes. And he wouldn't be able to put up with the city's traffic and air pollution. Shanghai? Too expensive. Zhou was worried he wouldn't be able to afford a good quality of life for his family there. Indeed, Zhou had reasons against moving to a variety of Chinese cities,

"It's not that easy," he said. "I am not single now. I have Hanhan and Liu Yan." He paused to take a sip of beer. "But I would go to Hainan," he added. "People there are very down-to-earth and leisurely."

He knew he couldn't afford to be picky much longer. He realized it every time he took a look at his dwindling bank account, which he jokingly compared to the Chinese stock market, "becoming less and less." He still had some savings. He could still cover his daily bills. But something had to change.

"I lost my job on July 21," said Zhou, still picking at his fish in the suburban Beijing restaurant. "Now it is early September. I have spent ten thousand yuan this month. I don't know how I have spent that much."

Zhou was paying more than 1,000 yuan a month for an *ayi*, or nanny, to help look after Hanhan. Earlier in the summer he had spent 10,000 yuan trying to help Liu Yan open an ill-fated clothing store. And then there were the more extravagant purchases that only a year or two earlier would have been unthinkable for Zhou. Purchases that, if word of them ever traveled back to Qixin, would give his parents a heart attack. After a job interview in Guangzhou, Zhou crossed the border into Hong Kong and bought a 3,000-yuan necklace for Liu Yan. During a tournament in South Korea, he brought her back 3,000 yuan worth of Lancôme cosmetics. At this dinner in Beijing, he was decked out in a brand-new outfit. Shoes by Adidas: 550 yuan. T-shirt by Nautica: 330 yuan. Jeans by Lee: 700 yuan. "I just want them to see what a good life I am living even without a job," he said.

But it wasn't a good life. Not at all. Later Zhou would admit to being in a state of depression. When he was in Chongqing he slept often, and spent many of his waking hours lying on the sofa, doing nothing. "I didn't know what to do at home," Zhou said. "I couldn't calm down to do anything." He stopped hearing from his students. He stopped reaching out to his friends.

Zhou did buy a membership at a gym a short bus ride from home, and he worked out for a few hours each afternoon, learning how to master the equipment there. He said he used this exercise to "balance his life." After the gym it was time for dinner, followed by an hour or two with Hanhan – rare moments of happiness for Zhou – some TV and then bed. It was the same routine every day.

Yet, for the first time in more than a decade, that routine did not include golf. Pride would not allow Zhou to return to Haoyun, his old driving range. And he had little motivation to find another place to practice. The tournament schedule was nearly empty, save for the annoying pro am that had brought him to Beijing, and a couple other events he had no chance of winning.

"If I had the money, I would emigrate to Hong Kong, Taiwan or Macau," he said, pouring another glass of Yanjing beer. "That way I could attend more tournaments. Many Chinese winners in international sporting events say they feel proud of China, but I don't think so."

The restaurant was empty now. Even the kitchen workers had wrapped up their card game and left.

"I'm very happy to be drinking beer," Zhou said. "I have finished three bottles now. Last night, I drank two bottles of beer, and today I shot 2-under." He ordered another bottle, betting four beers would mean 4-under in round two.

"If I can finish second here, and make a cut in the two tournaments in South Korea, I have great opportunity to be in the top twelve at the end of the year. Finally get my pro card." He sipped his beer. "I know that is impossible, but I still can daydream like that."

He finished his fourth beer and a taxi was called. Outside, everything but the flicker of restaurant neon and the glow of two taxi headlights was black. It was not yet 10 p.m., but that was late for this neighborhood on the outskirts of Beijing, which, aside from the golf courses, comprised farms, small factories and a few villages.

Zhou sighed as he got into the taxi. "After drinking some beer, I will sleep well, I hope," he announced to no one in particular.

"I think you are right," the driver said, and drove off.

Zhou shot 1-over, not 4-under, in the second round at Beijing, but by the end of four rounds he had managed to finish in seventeenth place and earn a 24,000-yuan pre-tax payday, his best haul of the season. But his daydream was not to be realized. Later that month, he missed the cut at both tournaments in South Korea. In October, he finished sixty-first at the Midea China Classic in Guangzhou, earning a measly 1,040 yuan. And the Omega China Tour never started up again. The abbreviated four-tournament schedule marked the end of the tour's five-year run.

China Tour organizers said the tour folded because Omega, the title sponsor, had backed out. Omega said they hadn't backed out and were just as confused about what was going on as the players. One person close to the situation simply blamed the "global economic situation."

"It was a low valley in my life," Zhou later said. "No tournaments, no job. I felt like a failure without any future."

Zhou may have been struggling to find a job, but Martin Moore was overwhelmed with them. According to the National Golf Federation, fewer than fifty new golf courses opened in the United States in 2009, down from a peak of nearly four hundred openings in 2000 and the lowest total the NGF had on record since the early 1980s. Meanwhile, in China, it was estimated that as many as 250 courses were under construction, with some 600 more in various stages of planning. It was unclear exactly what percentage of new courses China accounted for globally, but one leading course designer said the figure was sure to be "staggering."

So too were the sizes of the projects being discussed, one after the other featuring numbers that would have been unheard of before the likes of Mission Hills. "This year alone I have probably heard of ten projects that are ten-course deals," one golf design professional said. "All over China, from Beijing to Kunming to Qingdao to Hainan to Chengdu. Ten-course deals are like the magic number now."

China was propping up the entire industry. Like it or not, if you weren't working in Hainan or somewhere else in China, you probably weren't working at all. And, in 2009, no one was working more than Martin.

Martin had bought out his Flagstick business partners, golf course architects Brian Curley and Lee Schmidt, who by then, with their special focus on Asia, were among the busiest designers in the world. Flagstick had begun as the construction arm of Schmidt-Curley Design, and was intended to focus primarily on building Schmidt-Curley courses. But Martin wanted to get more projects on his plate. More and more designers were looking to China, and Martin wanted Flagstick to build their courses, too. Schmidt and Curley weren't crazy about the idea. They saw it as helping the competition and suggested it would be best if Schmidt-Curley and Flagstick parted ways. "I paid a pretty penny to them," Martin said.

Over the years, he'd realized some people just didn't have the right temperament for China. There was a project manager, someone he would hire in a second in the United States, that Martin felt sure "wouldn't stand a prayer" in China. He wouldn't have the patience for Chinese politics. He wouldn't be able to self-censor. "He'd get in a meeting with the Chinese and tell them all to go fuck themselves," Martin mused. "He'd say, 'You guys are stupid. That's not what I said.' You know, that kind of guy. He'd do that in a meeting in America and get respect from people. But, he'd get killed over it in China."

Martin had put in the hard spadework, and it was time to reap the rewards. After the buyout, he went on what he called a "splurge." "Fuck everybody," he said. "I'm going to sign every job I can get." He spent the majority of his time chasing down new projects, sending out letters to every golf course architect he knew. This hustling paid off. He went from three jobs in China to fifteen.

China, of course, was the only place in the world where numbers like that were even possible. Everyone in the industry was knocking on China's door, and Martin was getting a lot of calls. "Do you need help?" underworked colleagues would inevitably ask. Big firms started coming to him for advice, too. They knew they wanted to be in China, but they had no idea where to start. Would he be willing to give them some pointers? Martin was reluctant to give up his "secrets," but he did tell them what he had long been telling everyone else all these years:

> *It ain't like America.*
> *Getting your money is harder than hell.*
> *They don't know what they're doing.*
> *They don't listen to you.*
> *It's frustrating.*

Some of the conversations Martin had with potential competitors actually reassured him. China was going to eat these executives alive. For example, one person heading to the Beijing Golf Show for the first time had sought out Martin, who prepared himself for the usual "Business in China 101" line of questioning. Instead, he got something like this:

> *So we land at the Beijing airport?*
> *Are there buses that can take us to the hotels?*
> *How do we get around?*
> *How about hotels?*
> *Are there any you can recommend?*
> *How about eating over there?*
> *I've heard you've got to be really careful over there because what you eat can make you sick.*
> *Is that true?*

"It's like, come on," Martin said. "We're talking about flying into Beijing, not Changbaishan or Changsha or someplace like that. We're talking about the biggest city there is, where there's three hundred taxis waiting outside the airport, where there are more five-star hotels than any city you've been, where there are some of the best restaurants in the world. I mean, he better not ever leave Beijing, you know?"

The person who worried about taxis, hotels and food was not the only China rookie at the Beijing Golf Show that year. The number of American golf architects pitching their wares alone had increased fivefold from the previous year. The competition for new jobs was going to be fierce. But Martin felt confident about his track record of building golf courses – and not just any golf courses, but high quality ones – in the challenging environment. "The owners want to know what you've done in China," said Martin. "The owners know how their business works here. And they know the 'green' guy doesn't stand a chance."

At an introductory meeting with a developer, Martin would invariably whip out his map. It was large and printed in color, designed to make a splash. He would fold it out and show the developer all of Flagstick's projects in China, each marked with a flagstick, of course. "That impresses clients," Martin said.

Price was important in these early discussions, but perhaps not in the way most people would expect. Martin often heard that Flagstick was too expensive, and even some of his staff suggested they should start offering a cut-rate package to better compete with local Chinese construction companies. "I'm not doing it," Martin would reply to such proposals. "You know, that's not who I'm competing against. They want to hire them for half the price, let them hire them. That's not the same service we provide."

Just as often, he was being told his prices were too low – especially when he was talking to some of the high-end builders. Golf was still new to many Chinese developers, and they often had no idea how much it should cost to build a golf course. Really, they had no idea what services a golf construction management firm offered. They just knew they needed help. So if one firm came in with a bid of forty thousand dollars a month, and another came in at twenty thousand dollars, the Chinese owner might actually lean toward the more expensive option. "A lot of the Chinese mentality is that they want the best, and they've got the money," Martin said. "They think if they pay them more, they are going to get a lot better service. That might not necessarily be true, but a lot of them think that way. I know we've worked a bunch of jobs where we were the most expensive bidders."

Sometimes, the lack of experience building golf courses inspired Chinese developers to make strange requests. Martin recalled one owner who wanted to build a water-themed golf course. No golf carts. No cart paths. Golfers would travel from hole to hole by boat. Another owner wanted to build a villa right in the middle of a par-3 fairway. And then there was the guy who wanted a hole to be a giant funnel – anyone whose ball landed within thirty feet of the pin on this par-3 hole was guaranteed a hole-in-one. "Mini-golf on a professional golf course," Martin sighed.

To show potential clients the company was established and serious about both golf and China, Martin opened an office in Kunming. He also set up a legal Chinese company, Kunming Flagstick Consulting and Management (unsurprisingly, they were advised not to have "golf" in the name), enabling him to offer contracts in yuan, which gave customers added convenience and allowed him to work with businesses that didn't have large amounts of US dollars at their disposal. He said that being able to sign contracts in yuan "was huge."

An office and a map weren't enough to land a job in China, however. He had to invest a large amount of time and money in pursuing prospects. There was usually a long, drawn-out courting process. Every golf course, he came to realize, was a potential girlfriend who liked to be spoiled, and enjoyed playing hard to get. It wasn't abnormal for Martin to meet with a potential client six or seven times before everyone signed on the dotted line; one client played hard to get for more than a year. At least half of the time they would meet over big dinners that merged into *baijiu*-fueled drinkfests, Martin picking up the tab. He would make sure to come bearing presents, too. Maybe a nice golf club, or a Flagstick shirt, or a hat signed by Jack Nicklaus. If he was getting really deep in the process, he might break out something a bit bigger, like a set of Jack Nicklaus golf clubs.

He had learned that the key to these pre-deal dialogues was simple: he had to be sure he was meeting with the right person. "You can waste a lot of time and effort… if you're talking to the No. 3 or No. 4 man, and you don't know he's the No. 3 or No. 4 man," Martin said. "He'll let you believe he makes the decisions, but all he wants is a piece of the action, and a free meal or two."

Once the job was contracted, Martin would inform his project managers to stay adaptable. Every job, every owner, was different.

There was no how-to for building a golf course in China – and even if there was, it'd have to be written in pencil. "You need to be able to meet that owner, that client, the first time, and you really have to figure out their personality, their way of business," he said. "What they like and what they don't like and all that. And then adapt your management skills to it."

In 1984, when China welcomed its first modern-day golf course, the venerable travel book publisher Fodor's came out with a guidebook to the People's Republic. "You need have no fear about money dealings with the Chinese," the book told its readers confidently. "They are always scrupulously honest, and will follow you out of the shop to return a couple of coins if you happen to leave them on a counter."

Martin's experience during China's golf course boom hadn't been quite so quaint. In fact, he guessed some 95 percent of his industry colleagues would have little nice to say about their money dealings with the Chinese. "From a business standpoint, people say they're liars and they're crooked and all that stuff," Martin said. "But, you know what, that's fine. We're successful here and the others aren't. They don't have the patience for it, and they don't know how to deal with the Chinese way of doing business."

And patience was essential.

Martin said many Western businessmen who arrived in China full of enthusiasm were "blown away" by how things operate. Some would take it personally, get pissed off, and leave. "I think that's one of the keys to our success," he said. "We know there are side deals. We know that the owner's rep, who might be our direct contact, has all kinds of deals and we know that's going on. I always tell my guys that we have to do the best we can to make it right."

For example, if Martin's team discovered that a developer's No. 2 or No. 3 man was getting a side deal from a certain gravel supplier, who happened to be providing the wrong kind of gravel, Martin instructed his project managers to tread very carefully. "If we become an obstacle for that guy," he said, "he's going to get us kicked out of there. He will do it and he will succeed at it. And we won't stand a chance in hell."

Most important, he said, was to stay out of price negotiations over construction materials, because that's where the lucrative side deals occur, and it was a quick way to make an enemy. "Fight for quality all the way," he would tell his guys, don't get tangled up over a yuan here and there. "I just want the quality to be good," he said. But it wasn't enough to fight; you also had to document that fight with memo after memo to the developer. The paper trail was important. "At the end of the day, we can't force the developer's guy to do something. If he does something we know is wrong then our ass will be covered ten times over. If one of the big, big investors comes down and says, 'Why did you let them do that?' – it's going to be documented."

Then there were the "experts" that often came attached to jobs. These people may or may not have tangible experience building golf courses, but for one reason or another they had the ear of the owner (who usually had no experience building golf courses). Often they were the owner's friends or confidants, and they were paid to monitor the construction process. The only way they had of proving their worth was to point out mistakes, real or imagined, or take credit for things they didn't do. "Problem here is we get people who don't know anything about golf, and they get so involved that they just screw up everything," one of Martin's project managers said. "So you've got to keep fighting them and telling them that's not the way you do it. And it's tiring."

Martin said such meddling was representative of a general lack of trust common in business relationships throughout the country, especially when one of the parties in the relationship is foreign. "It's a China thing," he said. "They screw everybody, so they think everybody screws them." This constant air of skepticism created reams of paperwork for Martin's crews. Everything had to be logged and documented. It was a never-ending effort to defend their work and prove their own worth.

Martin often wished he could ask for the same proof of worth from some of the subcontractors he was forced to work with. On one project Martin worked on in Yunnan, he said the cart path contractors were "horrible" and built "the worst cart paths you've seen in your life." Everyone, from Martin's project managers to representatives of the Chinese developer, was out there telling the contractor that his work was unacceptable, that they needed to rip everything out and start over. "Well, they were the local government mafia," Martin said. "And they weren't going to rip out anything. And there's nothing we can do. They're basically going to let them put in a shitty cart path for fifty-four holes, pay them all their money and get them off the job, and then go hire someone else to come rip it out and start all over." But what about those times when a contractor did a good job? "I've been told that I'm not allowed to say that the contractor is doing a great job, even if he is," one of Martin's project managers reported. "Because if I say that, then the owner thinks I'm getting paid under the table!"

Contractors' profit margins were also unusually high in China. In the United States, contractors who won a job were likely to get, at best, a 7 to 10 percent profit. In China, that figure could rise as high as 40 to 50 percent. There were simple reasons for this. First of all, contractors were often obliged to pay commissions to the people who helped them secure the job in the first place. Then they had to issue more payments to the people who helped them perform their work with minimal interference from government regulatory bodies. It was said some people added a line item to all of their budgets: "NEGOTIATE WITH GOVERNMENT AUTHORITIES." That covered all sorts of contingencies (and sounded slightly better than "bribes").

Contractors would also bump up their margins on the front end (and constantly look for ways to cut corners during the job) because they knew they were likely going to get stiffed on the back end by the developer, sometimes by 25 percent or more. "You ask any contractor," Martin Moore said. "If they sign a contract for six million dollars, he'll be the first to tell you that if he gets 75 percent of that money when he's completely done, then he's happy."

So Martin started writing into his contracts that four months' worth of the agreed work must be paid in advance. In return, he wouldn't bill his clients for the last four months of service. The more money up front, the better, as far as Martin was concerned. And few clients tried to renegotiate those terms. "My concern is that I've gotten stiffed a few times over the last three or four years, and I want to always be ahead of these guys," Martin said. "I'm more willing to negotiate my fee down if I can have more up front."

While Martin had become fluent in Chinese contract negotiations, he wasn't fluent in the Chinese language. In fact, it was rare for anyone with any experience overseeing a golf course construction site to have "proficient in Mandarin Chinese" on his resumé. Early on, Martin's project managers would rely on translators provided by the developer for basic communication, but the inherent conflict of interest in that relationship meant Martin's team rarely got the full story. "On one of our early jobs," Martin recalled, "I turned to the translator and said, 'Hey, tell that guy, bullshit. We're not doing that.' And the guy said to me, 'I can't tell him that. I work for him.' And that's when we learned." They would end up having little knowledge of what was going on beyond plain sight. It also made it nearly impossible for Martin to communicate, at times.

Since that experience, Martin had made sure to have a "project coordinator" on the payroll for every job. This person was always local and fluent in Mandarin, English and perhaps a couple other Chinese dialects, but the job description varied from place to place. Often the project coordinator was part translator, part fly-on-the-wall, part *guanxi* envoy. "I wanna say 25 percent of their job is translating," Martin said. "The most important job that they fucking have is listen, hear, understand all the shit that's going on behind the scenes, the politics, and bring that to our project manager's attention." It was an extra six thousand yuan (one thousand dollars) a month per project out of Martin's pocket, but what these project coordinators provided was invaluable. Martin remembered one project coordinator who was "lazy" and "couldn't do anything else worth a crap," but he earned his keep because of his excellent skills at entertaining clients. He was a fantastic karaoke singer, and could hold his liquor. These are skills hard to place a value on in China – especially if his American boss had never managed to acquire a taste for *baijiu*. Martin had learned to strategize his *baijiu* consumption. "I don't mind saying no, but if it's with a client or prospect or something, I'm going to drink it," Martin said. "I'll pay for it the next day." And there was one "trick" he no longer fell for. Often, he said, when he was the only foreigner in the room, each person would approach him individually and offer to do a shot with him. "I stop that right off the bat," Martin said. "I say, 'No, this ain't ten against one here guys.' I say, 'If I'm drinking, we're all drinking.'"

Ninety-five percent of achieving success in China, Martin thought, came down to learning how to navigate the Byzantine world of local Chinese politics. And that was a matter of managing relationships and making smart local hires.

11

THE GOLF POLICE

Wang Libo often wondered what his life would have been like if Project 791's Red Line had not been moved; had he not been able to keep the sliver of land outside the Mission Hills worker dormitories and open up his shop. Leaving Hainan was something he and his wife had never considered. Not even in their wildest dreams. "I don't know the best places to visit," Wang's wife said. "I don't speak Mandarin well, and I wouldn't know the way to go, if I go to other places. Anyway, I have no money or time to travel."

Wang supposed he would have continued driving his *san lun che* back and forth between Yongxing and Xiuying every day. And he figured his wife would have found some other way to earn money. They would have sorted it out somehow, he thought. They were survivors.

Thankfully, they hadn't been forced to make do. While business at Wang's still-nameless convenience store was not brisk, he had a steady stream of customers. Thousands of migrants had taken construction jobs at the world's largest golf complex next door. Wang and his wife weren't getting rich, but they were doing well enough to be able to grow their inventory each week. The once empty showroom, now hooked up to electricity, was filling up.

Their days were filling up, too, so much so that Wang barely had time to lament the loss of his land and his fruit trees. His feelings about the forced land sales appeared to be evolving.

"Farming is tiring and tough," Wang said. "We don't miss it. Before 791, most people went outside to find jobs. Fruit trees bear fruit only once a year and harvests can vary greatly depending on the weather. We had to think about our kids and future grandkids. Our generation and my father's generation had been living a much harder life – not enough food or clothing. Now the developer comes, and we have money to start new businesses and make more money and lead a better life. Someone who sticks to the land and passes the land to future generations will still be living a hard life, while the villagers who sold land have already built their new cement houses."

Of course, only one Meiqiu villager owned the plot of land that just happened to be right outside the entrance to the buildings that would soon house ten thousand people. The fluky nature of this good fortune was not lost on Wang, who admitted his location was "convenient."

"But I am not the only lucky one," Wang protested. "All the villagers along the road are lucky dogs."

Not all of the village's residents were feeling quite so charmed, however. It had been more than a year since Wang Puhua had taken the case over the contested land to the Xinying district court. He had yet to hear a thing. "If I complain, the government doesn't respond to it at all," he said. "They have taken the money and split it up among different levels of officials. They are corrupt."

Things came to a head on November 10, 2009, two years after the land sales began in earnest. The disputed land had largely been left alone, but the bulldozers were approaching. Villagers could see them, orange and yellow, like several fierce suns growing bigger and bigger on the horizon each day. The people of Meiqiu still waiting for their first taste of Mission Hills cash decided they had to protect the land they insisted was collectively owned.

They started with a stakeout. Working in shifts, they made sure one of them was watching the land at all times. They'd act as though they were working in the fields, chopping wood or cutting branches, as they kept up their surveillance surreptitiously.

"How can we tolerate the developer leveling our lands without any payment?" Wang Puhua asked. "We are not stupid."

Then, on the sixth day of their vigil, early in the morning, it happened. Three bulldozers encroached on the contested land. The farmer who saw it happen quickly called the new village governor, who went door to door, rounding everyone up. Some hopped on motorbikes, others chose to run. Before long, some two dozen villagers arrived on the scene – and found they were not alone.

Ten police officers were already there, awaiting their arrival. Soon the number swelled to nearly a hundred, a mixture of armed police, Mission Hills security and a large contingent of *chengguan*, a somewhat thuggish element of China's public security apparatus. "They knew we were coming," Wang Puhua said.

Wang said some villagers came directly from the fields and therefore carried a variety of farming tools with them, some of which looked more threatening than others. They had no intention of using them, of course, and any onlooker to this face-off could tell which side was the underdog. The villagers were a ragtag lot, mostly middle-aged or older, half of them women, but they didn't back down from the bulldozer-backed brigade of young and uniformed men before them. They formed a human shield between their land and the bulldozers. The women stood in front, in an effort to dissuade the security team from using force.

It was uncommonly hot and humid for November, with morning temperatures already approaching ninety degrees Fahrenheit (thirty-two Celsius), and the burning sun made the tense situation even hotter. Reddening faces simmered under beads of sweat, and it seemed things could boil over at any moment.

"We yelled at them, even cursed at them. However, they never listened to us," Wang Puhua said. "We did nothing to them, just persuaded them that this land belongs to us. Any development without payment is wrong. We had to try to stop them."

While the shouting continued, the bulldozer drivers cut their engines and waited – it was clear they had been in situations like this before. "If villagers come to us and want us to stop," explained a driver who had confronted similar village protests, "we just stop and call the developer and ask them to deal with the situation. We just listen for the boss's order. We understand where the villagers are coming from. Their lands were rented with little compensation, sometimes none, and they have the right to defend their lands. It is their job to defend their lands, just like it is our job to follow the boss's order to drive our bulldozers. But at the same time, the developer has already paid for all the land. Why can't they bulldoze it, if that is what they want to do?"

Not everyone at Meiqiu that day was quite so level-headed. One of the *chengguan* spotted a knife in the hand of a farmer, a man in his sixties, and demanded he turn it over. "It's for cutting twigs!" the villagers shouted. "To feed the goats!" The *chengguan* didn't pay them any mind. He tried to grab the knife, slicing his hand in the process. The blood changed everything.

"The security guard beat the old man," said Wang Boming, another villager who was there that day.

The protest escalated quickly. The villagers were incensed, and vowed to stand their ground. But then came the tear gas, and the crowd was forced to scatter. Some *chengguan* used their hands to smear a pepper-spray-like substance on the faces of some of the slower villagers, who were mostly women. They removed the last stragglers from the field by force.

There were no more protests after that. "Our village is so small," lamented Wang Puhua's daughter-in-law, who sustained minor injuries in the scuffle with the security forces. "We don't have enough people. We can't persuade the government, and we can't fight back because we lack people. What can we do? Nothing. Once the government decides to press on you, you have no way out."

Once he was sure everyone had returned to the village, Wang Puhua grabbed his camera and started documenting all of the cuts, bruises and items of ripped clothing they had sustained. He wrote everything down, logging each offense in great detail, and added the papers to his ever-growing pile of documents for the court cases.

The land was bulldozed the following day.

In late November 2009, when various ministries of the Chinese government held a press conference to announce their most recent crackdown on illegal land use, five specific investigations were highlighted as among those that would receive "harsh punishment." Three involved heavy industry: a coking plant, a plastics factory and a rare earth metals mine. The other two alleged offenders were golf courses, and they got all the international headlines. "Golf defies rules to gain ground," proclaimed *China Daily*. The Associated Press followed suit: "China vows crackdown on illegal golf courses."

Martin Moore brushed it off as just another in a series of toothless threats from Beijing. His China business was better than it had ever been. Since 2004, the year the central government had instituted its nationwide moratorium on golf course construction, some four hundred new courses had opened their gates. Almost all the nation's six hundred or so golf courses were technically illegal in some way. Back in October, the International Olympic Committee had announced that golf would be a part of the Summer Games for the first time in more than one hundred years, returning in 2016 at Rio de Janeiro. Many people expected golf's new Olympic status would lead to newfound legitimacy for the sport in medal-crazy China.

But then the government brought out the heavy equipment. Then they started digging up fairways.

The bulldozers arrived at dawn on a Friday in early December. There were more than a dozen of them lined up outside the clocktower gate of the Anji King Valley Country Club, located in Zhejiang province, 140 miles southwest of Shanghai. The convoy drove into the compound, past the fountain and the bronze mounted knight, past the grand Tudor-style clubhouse, to the multi-million-dollar eighteen-hole golf course that had been open for little more than a year and was scheduled to host a Ladies European Tour event the following autumn. For ten days the excavators ate up the fairways, ripping up turf and snapping irrigation pipes buried in the soil. There were no signs of gophers, but it was a demolition that would have made Carl Spackler proud.

On the surface, the government's reasons for the destruction were simple. King Valley, it claimed, was occupying more than a quarter of its picturesque four-hundred-acre plot illegally. Nearly thirty-five acres of the illegal property was farmland, the officials said, and that was an increasingly precious commodity in a country that had to feed 21 percent of the world's population with less than 8 percent of its arable land.

Since 1996, China had lost more than thirty thousand square miles of arable land, and its total of around 470,000 square miles was getting dangerously close to the 463,323-square-mile baseline the government said was necessary for sustaining the country's massive population. While China's ability to feed itself had been improving dramatically – the government was claiming better than 95 percent self-sufficiency in grain, which had experienced record-setting yields in recent years – the United Nations still classified around 100 million Chinese as "undernourished." Land grabs were a plague on the countryside; China reported 42,000 cases of illegal land use in 2009. Even though golf-related construction accounted for a tiny fraction of that total, the "rich man's game" remained an easy target for the authorities in a nation with some 700 million poor farmers.

Ironically, the Chinese government's reluctance to embrace golf, or at least come up with a realistic set of regulations to slow and standardize its inevitable growth, was exactly what had allowed things to get out of control. At this point, Beijing didn't even know how many golf courses existed within the country's borders. At the press conference in November 2009, Ministry of Land and Resources officials said they were using satellite imagery to try to get a handle on the number. Back in 2004, when the moratorium had been announced, state media reported that only ten of China's then 176 known golf courses had received proper approvals from the central government.

"Right now the market is just in chaos," said one golf developer. "This local bureau approves a golf course. Some other local bureau says they can also approve a golf course. Nobody actually has the right to do it, but everybody is doing it."

This was precisely the case in Anji county, home of King Valley Country Club. Anji had always been one of the poorer counties in Zhejiang – its lone claim to fame, and most precious natural resource, was its 150,000 acres of bamboo forest (featured in the climactic fight scenes in *Crouching Tiger, Hidden Dragon*). The area's top government official was fond of telling people he had two dreams for Anji: a university and a golf course. Ask anyone in Jianshan village, where that second dream came to fruition, and they'll tell you the King Valley golf course was a pet project of the local government, designed to attract well-heeled patrons from Hangzhou and Shanghai to the impoverished countryside and stimulate the local economy.

A King Valley membership may have cost upwards of 340,000 yuan ($50,000), but there were many signs of the area's historically simple way of life outside the club's fences. In the creek separating the golf course grounds from Jianshan, local women rinsed their laundry and men herded flocks of ducks upstream using long bamboo poles. The people often still referred to their "production teams," a holdover term from the pre-reform days of China's communal farming system.

In the village, there were also many indications of growth, such as eco-friendly demonstration homes and small factories manufacturing decorative bamboo wall-coverings. Rickety blue trucks rumbled continuously along the road, overloaded with bamboo in various stages of production: bundles of logs, planks, slats and items ready for market. Further down the street, townhouses and apartment complexes were under construction, their brick and concrete frames covered in bamboo scaffolding. Across from one such site were the stone buildings that make up Jianshan Farmhouse, a kitschy, revolution-themed restaurant and lodge with framed portraits of Mao, Stalin, Lenin, Marx and other Communist all-stars displayed outside its guest rooms. All this development had happened after construction on King Valley began in 2005.

"Our village committee got rich by relying on this golf course," said an old man at the brand-new community center next door to Jianshan Farmhouse. "We used to live on the golf course – three production teams have been moved here. More than one hundred new houses. Without the golf development, how could we afford to build these houses?"

At the community center, a mural on a large outdoor wall just beyond a basketball court read, in bold letters:

Three core objectives of creating "beautiful countryside" in Jianshan Village:

- *Accelerate intensive development of the leisure industry*
- *Increase the wage income of farmers*
- *Advance the construction of a peaceful and harmonious society*

The words were printed on an image the size of a movie theater screen – a color photo of King Valley golf course taken when the fairways had been decidedly greener.

Access to the club was closed in early 2010, soon after the "crackdown" press conference, but if you crossed the creek you could find a dirt path winding around the course's southern end, offering several fence-obstructed views of what was once known as the back nine. Nearly a yard of earth was removed in some spots, and most of the fairways looked like freshly plowed fields awaiting the spring planting season. But a closer inspection revealed what could, at best, be called "peculiarities." All the greens and tee boxes in view – the most expensive architectural features on a golf course – were untouched. Many of the cuts around them seemed to follow a neat line. Greens, and what remained of some of the fairways, were being watered and mowed daily. The paved cart paths were still in place. So were all the buildings and most of the landscaping. Some smaller shrubs remained wrapped in white plastic to protect them from the winter cold. Was this the new workers' paradise? A putting green for every production team?

"Don't worry – the course is not going to become farmland," one of the several dozen workers who remained at King Valley said reassuringly. "We are working on repairing the underground pipes that were broken. It's just a matter of time before we open again. Since the greens were not harmed, of course it will take a very short time to rebuild it. The government has certain *guanxi* with our company."

That favorable relationship would seem to be strained these days. When Beijing's focus turned to King Valley, the local officials made a figurative mad dash for the hills. Many of them denied knowing a golf course existed inside the "Anji China Ecotourism and Fitness Center," as King Valley was then officially known. This was, of course, ridiculous: King Valley had been a stop on China's domestic golf tour the year before; it had been the official training center of the Zhejiang provincial golf team; and the large sign the local government installed beside the highway directing people to "King Valley Country Club" included the stylized silhouette of a man swinging a golf club. "Only a ghost would believe their claims," said a shopkeeper in Jianshan. "Government officials go there all the time. How can they not know?"

Despite the workers' assertions at the golf course, sources familiar with the situation said Hangzhou-based Handnice Group – the company behind the project – was in no hurry to pay for the necessary repairs, or to jump back in bed with the local government officials who they felt had betrayed them. Many in Jianshan believed the course's destruction had been a calculated move by the local officials, a grand display intended to shield them from punishment from Beijing. It's noteworthy that the bulldozers were brought in with little public fanfare. The only newspaper report about the drama at King Valley, which appeared in Hangzhou's *Youth Times*, was later expunged from the paper's website. "The local government already turned their back on [Handnice] once, so it's very hard to say they will not do it again," said the source. "The developers will not move forward unless they can be assured the project is now fully legal."

Handnice, to be sure, deserved its share of the blame in this mess. The risks associated with opening a golf course in China, while seemingly benign in recent years, were no secret. And while official land designations in rural China often changed on the latest whims of those in power, no one could miss the fact that villagers were farming – rice and pears, mostly – on a portion of the land that would become King Valley Country Club. In fact, the company had paid close to $1.2 million in fines for illegal land use between 2006 and 2008, so they were well aware of the turbulent political climate. But after each fine, sources said, the local government urged them to carry on with construction. The fines were viewed merely as a cost of doing business.

In this case, it seemed the process of relocating and compensating villagers got too messy, placing King Valley on the central government's shortlist for investigation. Because the state owned all the land, money from the developer had gone directly to the local government, as per usual. Much of the money had got caught in the government filter, and never made it to the villagers who called the land home.

One elderly man in Jianshan said the 100,000-yuan settlement he received was not enough to cover the cost of his new home, and that the 1,000 yuan he was set to receive in "rent" each year from the golf course, which charges up to 800 yuan for a round of golf, was "definitely not enough." He shrugged his shoulders and added, "But what can you do?"

It was unclear what would come next for King Valley's owners. When asked for a status update, a worker at the Anji Land and Resources Bureau said only "that's already been dealt with" before hanging up the phone.

Such stories rang true for Martin Moore, who estimated that 90 percent of his projects encounter land-related "obstacles" of some kind, be they villager relocations, the removal of graves, or disputes over what was or wasn't farmland. The farmland issue, which according to Martin had been cropping up more and more in recent years, was a thorny one, because, as one course designer put it, "it seems like every square inch of China that is not already under a building or a highway is being used to farm something." Such complications should be settled between the local government, the developer and the area's residents long before a construction crew hits a site. But in Martin's experience they rarely were.

Even when things were ironed out, and all the local agencies declared themselves satisfied, the golf course was still technically illegal, after all. You could get permits for construction and permits to move land and permits to plant grass, but you couldn't get a permit to build a golf course. So when government inspectors (the "golf police," Martin and others called them) came knocking, as the owners of King Valley learned, you're only as good as your relationship with the local brass. And if Beijing decided to get involved, that probably wasn't getting you very far.

"These guys get approval from local government, and it's all about how many nights in the karaoke and this and that," Martin said. "They're going to eventually convince the local government to say, 'Yeah, yeah, yeah,' but when the central government comes down on them, those guys aren't going to say, 'I told them they could do it.' It's pretty ugly, and that's the history with the village issues. These owners don't go in there and clear all the villagers. They go in there and negotiate with the local government. 'Okay, we have this many villagers. Here's the compensation.' And how much of that goes from the government to the villagers? It's never enough, and the owners are always digging back into their pockets because you still have villagers who aren't going to move. That's business in China, I guess."

Martin always steered clear of this side of the business. But he found developers rarely did all the necessary legwork before launching into their projects. "I ask the same questions to every one of them when we first meet," Martin said. "Do you own all the land? Do you have any villager problems? Do you have this? Do you have that? Please do your due diligence, do your homework and find that out. We need to know that now rather than later because we mobilize a big crew and if we hit all these walls it just costs them millions of dollars. Obviously some of them have better connections with government than others so even those that do have obstacles can get clear pretty quick."

That developers could move forward with so many question marks hanging over their projects was proof, Martin acknowledged, that some kind of crackdown was probably justified. But he thought it wouldn't make much difference. "They are never going to be able to stop all the golf," he said. Martin reported that most of the "respected" people in the industry agreed with him that the government needed to get "a better handle on things." The real problems were people "who wake up with a dream" to build a golf course and take off on a development project "destroying the world, without anybody knowing about it."

Initially, when Martin read all the "crackdown" headlines – his colleagues had forwarded them around like wildfire – he figured it was just the "government flexing its muscles before Chinese New Year." Martin had been in China long enough to know not to overreact to every story about the government targeting golf course development. The busiest years of his career hadn't come until after China had made his profession illegal! He'd seen probably a dozen stories about a supposed crackdown in the past six months. "The first couple used to scare me a bit, but now for every crackdown announcement, I get twenty-five leads right behind it," he said.

"Maybe I'm just trying to be optimistic, but I see no way in the world China's going to be able to put it to a halt. I've been telling people, if they shut down 50 percent, even 70 percent, of projects, there are still too many of them – a hell of a lot of golf courses are still going to be built. I counted my prospect list this morning because I had a meeting, and I had eighty-seven golf courses on my prospect list and thirty-seven of those are what I call 'hot' and 'new' leads."

In the past few weeks, Martin had heard that several golf projects around Chengdu, the capital of Sichuan province, which had become a hotbed of construction activity, had been put on hold, pending further review. The golf police had been frisking golf courses, both finished and unfinished. An official provincial notice called for local governments in Sichuan to "stop approving and building new golf courses." It cited the 2004 moratorium issued by the State Council and insisted the authorities "immediately clean up and correct" existing golf courses and other "forbidden projects." The province's "limited land resources" were instead supposed to be used to "build important infrastructure." Golf courses currently under construction, the notice said, must be halted, and those in the planning stages were "forbidden to start."

Martin was about to sign a contract for a new twenty-seven-hole layout south of Chengdu called Seasons International Country Club, and he feared it might get caught up in the crackdown. He was soon told the contract would have to wait until after Chinese New Year. Then, just a few days later, he got word that the people behind the project wanted to hurry up and sign the deal before the holiday, with an eye toward "moving dirt by March 1." "That's right in Chengdu, so they must've resolved what problems they had," Martin said. It seemed proof to him that the latest crackdown wasn't "for real."

But after the Chinese New Year, he kept hearing stories about projects in Sichuan. Some were saying all course projects in the province were to be shut down for six months. Worse, he'd been told that a nearly completed course on the outskirts of Chengdu had been forced to reforest its fairways. People talked about the hundreds of new trees sticking out of acres of freshly landscaped lawns, but no one could pinpoint the course where this had supposedly taken place.

There were other examples of government interference that Martin couldn't shake off as hearsay, however, because they were happening on his own sites. The owner of Seasons International had officially extended the construction schedule into the following year, and the scope of the undertaking was starting to resemble the "sports park" it was known as in the official documents – more so than the golf course he'd been contracted to build. They were going to clear trees and move dirt, build lakes and shape the layout. They were going to do everything to it except make it look like a golf course. No greens, no bunkers no tee boxes; just a very expensive park with no public access. "It's basically landscape architecture right now," Martin said. He suspected that the owner had a long-term plan in mind. "It's going to look just like that, and then, when they think it's going to ease up, they'll bring somebody in to cut out the greens and bunkers."

Things were less "funny" at one of Martin's other projects, northeast of Chengdu, where workers had become accustomed to helicopters "and all kinds of shit" flying overhead on a daily basis – the Beijing golf police's not-so-subtle way of letting them know they were being watched. It got to be like working in a war zone. "The owner's comment to my guy was, 'Screw 'em. We'll shoot 'em down,'" Martin said. "There we are, grassing holes and cutting in bunkers and putting in sand. Either the owner is just not listening or they know the right people. Who knows how it works?" And that was coming from someone who had worked in China longer than almost anyone.

Martin had just returned from San Diego, where the annual Golf Industry Show, or at least what he called the "Campbell's condensed soup" version of it, had been held. The industry, like the economy, was hurting, and attendance was down. In the United States, far more golf courses were closing each year than opening. "It's China, China, China," Martin said of the mood at the trade show. "That's all anybody was talking about: China, China, China." Meanwhile, the annual China Golf Show in Beijing was growing every year. Martin recalled when few paid the show any attention. Now, everyone was "whoring for the business."

China may have been a perplexing, and at times infuriating, place to build a golf course, but it also was pretty much the only place building golf courses. One representative of an American golf course design firm compared the goings on in China to the Oklahoma Land Run combined with the California Gold Rush. With so many firms going all-in on China, a helicopter here and a bulldozer there were causes for concern. Just what were the golf police going to do next?

"I'd lose sleep trying to think about what is going to happen, because I surely can't control it," Martin said.

In the midst of all this confusion, China's State Council issued a notice with far less fanfare. It seemed to acknowledge that some forms of golf development were now permitted, but only in one location: Hainan. The document, made public on December 31, 2009, entitled "Several Opinions of the State Council on Promoting the Construction and Development of the Hainan International Tourism Island" discussed openly the government's goal "to sci-entifically plan, limit the total quantity of, rationally distribute and regulate the development of golf tourism under the preconditions that land use planning and urban planning regulations are adhered to, arable land (especially basic farmland) is not occupied, forests and the ecological environment are effectively protected, the legal rights of farmers are safeguarded, and land-use legal procedures are strictly abided by." Section three of the notice was called "Exploiting Hainan's unique advantages, and raising overall service standards in the tourism sector." In it, the State Council outlined an official desire to "encourage the hosting of large-scale cultural performances and festive events, to enrich the performance event market, and to support the hosting of international regattas, international cycling events and professional golf tours in Hainan."

The notice was publicly backed up by a press conference less than a week later. It was a familiar, almost annual, routine: Hainan's government leaders announced their latest plans to turn the island into the next Hawaii or Bali. This time, several stories followed, mostly in the state media. They talked about Hainan's plans to "clean up" tourism and become a "tourist heaven." They mentioned Hainan's plans to promote "red" tourism while at the same time dabbling in games of chance, including, someday perhaps, horse racing. There was also talk of adding facilities for water sports, scuba diving and cruise ships, and offering visa-free travel and tax-free shopping.

Buried in the print coverage was just one line about golf course development: "Asked about expanding golf courses in Hainan, Luo [Baoming] denied the province had violated China's strict rules on building golf courses and had never used subsistence farmland to build golf courses."

The denial had taken place at the press conference, during an exchange between Hainan's governor, Luo Baoming, Hainan's Party chief, Wei Liucheng, and a reporter from Associated Press Television News, David Wivell. Wivell had asked Wei and Luo directly about Project 791:

> DAVID WIVELL: The central government has in recent
> years been urging developers not to build more
> golf courses, but reports say Hainan is completing

a twenty-two-course project – I think it is called the 791 Project. Why is Hainan building so many? And how will that impact the environment?

WEI LIUCHENG: As to golf, you mentioned building twenty-two new golf courses – I'm not really clear about it. The documents from the State Council do have one regulation about Hainan developing golf. That's Article 3, Item 8, and it says, if it conforms to the general plan for the utilization of land, doesn't occupy basic farmland, protects the ecological environment effectively and protects the interests of farmers under the premise of scientific planning, total control and rational distribution, the golf industry may be developed with regulation. Throughout the world, golf is an important factor to tourism, and regulated golf development is probably good for the development of tourism and the development of an economic society. But it needs to be standardized, and we cannot mess this up.

LUO BAOMING: Let me add one point. Although the State Council said in the document that we can develop the golf industry, it has very restrictive conditions. I can say this: Hainan has never developed golf in a way that goes against the general plan for the utilization of land, and golf has never taken one acre of basic farmland. With this as a prerequisite, according to our plan's demands, we will develop the golf industry moderately and orderly and within the parameters of State Council policies. The plan regarding this aspect still needs approval from the State Development and Reform Commission and related government departments.

One would assume that Wei, as the Party's secretary, would be aware of a construction project the size of Hong Kong on his island. In October, ninety holes had been finished and grassed at Mission Hills, and two courses were playable. There had been talk of opening the courses to the public for limited play before Spring Festival in mid-February 2010. Some local government officials had already been spotted hitting balls on sections of the finished courses. In fact, there was one fairway in particular they used so often, workers dubbed it the "government hole."

Perhaps Wei was simply abiding by the gag order on all things Project 791, all things Mission Hills, all things golf. The open secret was still officially top secret. But not for much longer. The grand reveal was coming.

Less than three months later, on March 15, 2010, the International Federation of PGA Tours and the International Golf Association announced, and then the Associated Press followed with news that golf's World Cup was changing homes, and in 2011 would move from Mission Hills in Shenzhen to the new Mission Hills mega-complex on Hainan. It seemed a pretty standard press release, but it was significant for one reason: it represented the first admission in the media that Mission Hills Haikou was more than a myth.

It was unlike Mission Hills to do something so subtly. Hundreds, maybe thousands, of stories had been written about the Chus' massive twelve-course golf club in Guangdong province (course Nos. 11 and 12 had opened in 2007 with a splash). Nearly every television broadcast in Asia of a major golfing event seemed to come "brought to you by Mission Hills." Numerous advertisements would remind viewers of Mission Hills' Guinness World Records-endorsed "World No. 1" status, even though Nanshan International Golf Club in northeastern China had Mission Hills beat by sixty-three holes. Ron Sirak, writing in *Golf Digest* magazine, called Mission Hills' Shenzhen complex "golf's version of Walt Disney World."

Chasing after the superlatives, Mission Hills didn't content itself with golf, either. It boasted of having Asia's largest tennis center (fifty-one courts), Asia's largest spa, the world's largest putting course and the world's biggest clubhouse (Mission Hills' Dongguan Clubhouse checks in at a tidy 78,000 square yards). And Cindy Reid, chief instructor at Mission Hills, was being touted as the "World's No. 1 Female Golf Instructor."

Some who have worked with Mission Hills suggest the Chu family's obsession with big numbers, with being No. 1, can often lead to unnecessary inflation of the statistics related to their projects. They want storylines they can sell to the media and the public, and to get them, sources said, they were willing to fudge the figures. Sometimes the publicized numbers were double the real ones, because Mission Hills wanted to be able to say, for example, that they had moved enough dirt to fill Beijing's Bird's Nest Olympic Stadium thirty-six times, or installed enough electric cable to wrap around Hong Kong Island ten times. A PR staffer at some of Mission Hills' bigger tournament events, including the 2008 World Cup, at which the club claimed 180,000 spectators, said attendance figures were routinely inflated by as much as ten times. "It was weird," the worker said. "The actual figures were impressive enough. They were historic, in fact. No sense in making new numbers up."

Ken Chu had another explanation for the string of superlatives in his company's promotional materials. "We are perfectionists," he said. "I think it runs in the family. You have to be devoted. You have to do it right." Tenniel Chu, Ken's younger brother and the executive director of Mission Hills, also held forth on the subject: "Mission Hills is a huge golfing PR machine. In the world of golf, whatever movement we do or event that we host, certainly we never hold back in terms of any of our golfing publicity."

But, there it was, Mission Hills Haikou, the soon-to-be world's largest golf club, making its public debut by playing a supporting role to a golf tournament decidedly lacking in visibility and significance. One had to wonder whether the press release was sent out too early – there wasn't even a mention of Mission Hills Haikou on the Mission Hills website. But the release referred to "the newly opened Mission Hills Resort Hainan" as if the existence of the once top-secret project was common knowledge. It included a quote from the elusive David Chu, who said, "We are extremely pleased to be bringing the World Cup to our new development in Haikou on Hainan Island. Similar to its role in setting off the golf boom in China when it arrived at Mission Hills for the first time in 1995, the World Cup will undoubtedly play a significant role in establishing Hainan as the world's foremost sports and leisure destination." George O'Grady, chief executive of the European Tour added, "The impressive new Mission Hills complex at Hainan Island will offer a new experience for our players and for fans from around the world."

A couple days later, however, a proper PR offensive took shape, and it was more befitting of Mission Hills' typically grandiose style. After years of secrecy, the Hainan resort made its first appearance on the company website, where it promised travelers to the new destination they would find "limitless play" and "limitless prestige." Then, on March 18, 2010, Mission Hills gathered media in Haikou for a press conference announcing not the club itself – that would have been too simple – but rather a star-studded tournament scheduled to make its debut at the new complex that October: the Mission Hills Star Trophy, billed as "Asia's premier lifestyle event." Reuters reported that the winner-takes-all purse of $1.28 million was "Asia's richest individual prize." On hand for the announcement were golf stars Greg Norman and Zhang Lianwei; Zhu Hansong, vice mayor of Haikou; Andy Pierce from Creative Artists Agency; Fan Xiaojun, vice chairman of the China Golf Association; and Tenniel Chu.

The very same day, in a separate conference hall at Mission Hills Haikou, Du Jiang, deputy head of China's National Tourism Administration, told the crowd for a special session of the 2010 Bo'ao International Tourism Forum, that "China encourages well-planned environment-friendly development of golf tourism, especially in Hainan, the country's only tropical island province." Xinhua, China's state-run news service, ran a story from the forum entitled "Hainan aims to be China's golf capital" and called

Mission Hills Haikou, which had three courses open for play, "the largest collection of golf courses in the world."

This was another of those perfectly timed, expertly orchestrated Mission Hills "fortune teller" moments. China was in the midst of a tense crackdown on golf course development. The entire industry was on edge. And on the same day Mission Hills chooses to go public with its gargantuan Hainan project – at odds with Chinese law for much of its two-plus years of shrouded existence – it's made clear that, thanks to recent changes in local law, the project was not only legal, but also part of an important government initiative.

The following day, March 19, 2010, the *International Herald Tribune*, the global edition of the *New York Times*, ran a 3,300-word advertising supplement paid for by Mission Hills entitled "Golf Tees Off in China." The five-page advertorial, which featured color photos of the clubhouse and the Blackstone Course, called the resort "Asia's premier golfing destination" and mentioned multiple times that Mission Hills Haikou was "central to a government-led initiative to make the island into a sports and leisure capital." A quote from Haikou Vice Mayor Zhu Hansong supported the claim, saying "both Mission Hills Haikou and the Omega Mission Hills World Cup are central features" of the government's plans to "help promote Hainan around the world." The piece mentioned that Mission Hills still had "grand plans" for the resort, but never mentioned more than the three completed courses. Ken Chu crowed happily about the big project: "Our reputation has earned us an early start in Haikou. The Hainan government was aware of the influential role we had played in stimulating investment and job creation in the Shenzhen area, and they were confident that our presence in Haikou would enjoy a similar effect. At the time of our launch, we will be employing forty thousand people in long-term, sustained jobs that will bring a renewed confidence and economic platform to further improve their lives."

Of course, there were superlatives, including the "region's largest aquatic and natural-spring development" featuring "Lava Lake," a twelve-thousand-square-yard pool where one lap might take fifteen minutes. There was mention of "ten-thousand-year-old lava rock" that "greatly inspired" the resort's golf courses and architecture. And Ken Chu himself spoke glowingly about the environs, saying he found Hainan "wonderfully charming," before concluding, "The people are friendly, and life here is very much in harmony with nature." The advertorial went on to call Mission Hills the "leading golf brand in the world" and deemed the one-day-old Hainan complex "one of the world's most memorable golf resorts."

It was like someone had flipped a switch. Just eight months earlier, Mission Hills Haikou was such a sensitive topic that Ken Chu denied its very existence. Now it was clear he and the rest of the family wanted everybody in the world to know about their newest resort. "They are advertising the hell out of that project now," Martin said.

By late summer, billboards announcing the latest jewel in the Mission Hills crown adorned nearly every major airport in China. In Hainan, it was as though Mission Hills had staged a complete takeover of the Haikou airport. A billboard featuring twenty-three celebrity headshots and the upcoming "Star Trophy" tournament event was the first thing passengers saw in the arrivals area. The last thing they saw at baggage claim was a permanent Mission Hills Haikou shop of sorts, a remote lobby where you could book a room or a tee time. It was sharp-looking with glass sliding doors, wood paneling and an illuminated sign announcing that the club had been "unveiled."

Not long after the Mission Hills press conference, Martin said Hainan alone was building more golf courses than anywhere else in the world. "I wouldn't doubt if there are one hundred golf courses under construction within Hainan within a year," he said at the time. He added that the local government's recent announcements had reinvigorated many of his projects, especially Mission Hills Haikou, where twenty-two courses now seemed like a possibility again.

But even something as simple as the number of golf courses at the resort was a moving target. The company line constantly changed. One day Ken Chu would say to go with ten; the next day it would be six. This remained the case long after the grand opening. A Star Trophy tournament staff member was reprimanded for allowing a camera crew from a major international TV station to film from the top floor of the hotel – the true scope of the project was apparently still top secret.

At one point, in an internal Flagstick newsletter, Martin wrote that his team was approaching the finish line on the first ten courses at Mission Hills Haikou.

"Martin, what are you writing that for?" he was asked. Apparently the rest of the world was only supposed to know about six courses. But many outsiders had already heard it was going to be thirty-six courses. And the resort website listed ten.

As they headed into the end of the year, there was talk about finishing those courses and adding two more – and doing it all in three months – for a total of twelve courses. But that never happened. Projects were stalled all over the country, even in Hainan, the future "Hawaii of the East."

Just after Christmas, the *Washington Post* published a story talking about the "12-month frenzy of construction" on the island. As far as golf courses, the paper wrote, "26 are complete, and 70 others are underway." Martin scoffed when he heard those numbers. "No fucking way," he said. "Dream on. I'd be surprised if there were seventeen under construction."

Even the seemingly unstoppable Mission Hills was running into roadblocks – literally. The resort seemed stuck on ten courses, a far cry from the twenty-two that everyone involved with the project thought was still the goal. Late in the year, Ken Chu had spent three days dealing with local government officials, trying to get some movement on the long-dormant southern portion of the property, where courses had been started but left to grow over due to what people close to the situation called "zillions of problems" relating to villager and government land disputes.

Chu was determined to force the government's hand. He requested a fleet of heavy machinery – twenty excavators, several bulldozers and a tractor-trailer or two – to head down to the disputed land to make a statement. But the convoy couldn't even make it through the gate. A large and determined crowd of villagers stood in the road and wouldn't let the construction equipment pass.

Now, some workers who had originally expected to come back to work after the Chinese New Year had been told not to return until future notice.

The past few years under the artificial ban on golf course construction had been bizarrely good for business. But Martin couldn't shake his belief that it would be much better if he and his colleagues had some kind of pathway to stable, long-term legitimacy for their profession in China. If Beijing acknowledged the inevitability of golf's growth, and actually tried to control course development rather than ignore it, many in the industry would applaud the move. Tell them the hoops they need to jump through to build a 100-percent legal golf course in China, and they would jump through them, he said. Everyone was tired of living in limbo, tired of looking over their shoulders wondering when the government bulldozers and helicopters might arrive.

12

THE ROAD IS WIDER

Zhou Xunshu was not prepared for the 2010 competitive season. While there were several reasons for this, two stood out:

1. He was extremely busy.
2. For a long time, he had no idea if there was even going to be a professional golf season in China this year.

The busy part was largely a good thing – it meant Zhou was no longer unemployed. In November 2009 he had landed a job at a driving range. It paid him eight thousand yuan a month and was his first steady flow of income in more than five months.

But the job was in Chengdu, a city two hundred miles away from Liu Yan and Hanhan back in Chongqing, and the work itself was a chore. Zhou was teaching golf, which he enjoyed, but he was also involved in the daily management of the driving range, which he often found tedious. He did not like drama, and being stuck between layers of adolescence (his staff) and dysfunction (his superiors) added much of it to his life. Worst of all, he was working from 8 a.m. to 10 p.m. every day and barely had any time to practice. And practicing was what he enjoyed most.

"It was difficult, but I have to work, right?" Zhou said. "Without a job, the family has no backbone. I needed to find a job to balance my life. I couldn't just stay home all day long – even if the job means I need to be separated from my family."

Zhou liked the driving range itself. It was newer and much bigger than where he previously worked. Its English name was

Seasons International Country Club, and Zhou said his bosses were the richest men in all of Chengdu. One made his fortune from pharmaceuticals, the other from real estate development. He had been told that there would be a tournament-caliber golf course attached to the driving range and clubhouse. "But the government stopped construction," Zhou said matter-of-factly.

Zhou didn't concern himself with the details surrounding this turn of events. He didn't have time to. He had thrown himself into his new job, with barely enough hours to see his family. He worked straight through the first month, and only started making semi-regular trips back home to Chongqing – a day here, a day there – in late December. The one-way trip was four hours by bus, or two hours if his schedule and budget aligned with that of the newly built bullet train. The train cost ninety-seven yuan each way.

Zhou was a hard worker by nature. He was what the Chinese might call a *gongzuo kuang*, a workaholic. But these days Zhou was also motivated by not a small amount of fear. He didn't know when his next tournament might be; he didn't know if there would even be one. The way the Omega China Tour had just vanished, coupled with the fragile state of the global economy, had Zhou wondering if professional golf in China was over. Would he have to stop counting on tournaments as an extra source of income? Would he have to give up on his dream?

Zhou had no answers. So he put everything he had into his new job, and that meant barely playing the game he loved. Over the course of his exhausting fourteen-hour shifts, Zhou was lucky if he had time to hit one hundred balls at the driving range, seven hundred shy of his normal routine. He almost never got an opportunity to play on a course. In fact, in the nine months since he had lost his job at Haoyun Golf Club in Chongqing, Zhou estimated he had played a full round of golf outside competition only three times. He could count on his fingers the number of proper driving range practice sessions he'd completed.

Then, in mid-March, the email came. "Did you hear the news?" a fellow golfer wrote. Zhou clicked the embedded link and watched the 2010 China Golf Association tournament schedule load in his web browser. It was surprisingly full, by Chinese golf standards, and it was starting soon. The first tournament, the Luxehills Open, was only a little over two weeks away. And it was taking place in Chengdu.

Zhou was excited. His dream was still alive. He also was panicked. He had sixteen days to prepare for a tournament at which his new bosses, colleagues and students would have a front-row seat.

"I wanted to golf well to win honor for my club," said Zhou, who wore the Seasons International Country Club logo on his shirt for the tournament.

Truth was, even if Zhou had prepared properly for the tournament, he had little chance of ranking near the top. The Luxehills Open was a stop on the OneAsia Tour, which World Sport Group (the same organization behind the defunct Omega China Tour) had launched the previous year as a potential rival to the already established Asia Tour. OneAsia's goal was to "provide an Asia-Pacific alternative to the PGA Tour and the European Tour," and the total prize money for Luxehills was one million dollars – a purse intended to draw the top pros from the entire Pacific region. The field was dominated by Australian and Korean players competing regularly in international tournaments. Simply advancing beyond the first two rounds would be an incredible accomplishment for a coachless golfer like Zhou.

After a solid first round that saw him birdie three of his first seven holes, Zhou found himself in a strong position to earn some respect. He shot a 2-under-par 70, good enough to be tied for thirty-third place in the 152-man field. There he was, his name up on the top quarter of the leaderboard, surrounded by foreign names and foreign flags. What surprised Zhou most was how comfortable he felt out on the course, even with the extra scrutiny that came with being a "local." He was putting well and his mind was clear. It was as if his lack of preparation and his lack of expectations were turning into positives.

But he still had to play the second round. A quadruple bogey on hole No. 4, a double bogey on No. 6, and Zhou was already 6 over and out of contention. He finished with an 82, twelve strokes worse than the previous day, and was eliminated. He went back to his job at Seasons International in sole possession of 146th place.

"I think my golf club had high expectations for me in that tournament," Zhou said. "And after the first day, when I shot a 70, they were very happy. After my performance in round two, I don't think the club cared too much about it, but I felt very upset. It was my first tournament since I started working for them, and playing poorly made me feel like I had committed a crime."

Zhou didn't have long to feel guilty. In less than a week, he was off to Shenzhen to take part in the first leg of the China PGA Champions Tour, one of two new tournament series geared at China's domestic golfers. The Champions Tour, with $200,000 purses per event – double what had normally been on offer on the Omega China Tour – was organized by DYM International Sports Development, a Hong Kong company owned by the father of China-born and Canada-raised Su Dong.

Su, who had turned pro in 2009 after three top-three finishes on the China Tour the previous year, was only twenty years old, but he represented the future of the game. There was a new generation of players nipping at the heels of homegrown and self-trained older golfers like Zhou. Mostly rich kids, these Chinese players were young enough to have grown up playing the game, and wealthy enough to afford quality coaching.

When Su and the other well-to-do, foreign-educated amateurs found themselves lined up next to their older and more rough-and-tumble counterparts – the Chinese working pros – the contrasts were striking. From their hair, to their clothing, to their meticulously coached and elegant swings.

In post-round interviews at a 2008 China Tour event, eighteen-year-old Hu Mu – who had been saddled with high expectations since someone labeled him "China's Tiger Woods" when he was in his early teens – unwittingly made clear just how stacked the deck was against the self-trained golfers on the tour. Hu credited his fine performance to a call he had placed the night before to his coach, the world-famous swing doctor David Leadbetter. Later in that tournament he thanked Dr. Jim Loehr, a renowned performance psychologist, for the focus he maintained on the course. The reaction of players like Zhou? "What's a performance psychologist?" Hu played one year at the University of Florida before turning pro.

The playing field may have been slightly more level in Shenzhen than at the OneAsia event, but Zhou's rustiness remained. He did not feel good about his chances. But, quite to his surprise, he didn't much care, either. That was good, because he opened with a sloppy round that included five bogeys on the back nine, resulting in a 4-over 76. His strong putting had carried over from Chengdu, but his drives were all over the place. His performance was exactly the opposite of what he had come to expect in years past. Still, even with his poor play, Zhou finished day one tied for thirty-seventh place. He suddenly realized he might not be the only Chinese golfer who hadn't been practicing.

Zhou seemed to have found the Zen that Scottish coach Michael Dickie had said he was lacking back in 2008. His calmness garnered him solid, if not spectacular, rounds of 73, 70 and 72, and somehow this effort was good enough for an eighth place finish, seven strokes back from winner Zhang Lianwei, the legend himself.

"I don't know how I finished in the top ten," Zhou said. "I didn't perform very well. I guess the other players just played worse than me." But any celebrations were necessarily brief. After the tournament, he immediately threw himself back into his job at Seasons International. Though he had about six weeks until his next event, he didn't start practicing in earnest until the final seven days.

This was partially due to time – he had very little, after the demands of his work – but he had not recovered the feeling of motivation that had consumed him in the past. There was no urgency. No drive. No giant chip on his shoulder. No hint, no inkling he was about to enter the most important tournament of his career.

A smaller circuit, called the China Challenge Tour and operated by the state-owned China Sports Travel organization, was also making its debut this year. The prize money for the Challenge Tour was more in line with events in previous years: 800,000 yuan per tournament. The first event had a rather awkward

English name: the Handa Cup Philanthropy in China. (The Chinese name translated directly to the much more manageable "Handa Fraternity Cup.") The cup was a joint venture between the China Golf Association and the International Sports Promotion Society, a Tokyo-based organization founded in 2006 by Dr. Haruhisa Handa, a "golf philanthropist" dedicated to supporting charitable causes through sporting events. Ten percent of the prize money from the tournament was to be donated to charities aiding the disabled in China.

Zhou was fairly certain his mandatory donation to charity, if he was lucky to win anything at all, would be minimal. His confidence was already low, and the course, at the Jinghua Golf Club about twenty-five miles east of downtown Beijing on the banks of the Chaobai River, was known for its difficulty. The course's Korean architect, Tiger Song, had put water into play on more than half of Jinghua's holes. Zhou knew his typically aggressive style of play could prove disastrous on such a tricky course, so he decided to employ a more conservative approach, one that seemed to match his current mindset.

Early on, however, it didn't seem as though any approach was going to work for Zhou. The four-day tournament started on a Sunday, which was unusual, but no Beijing courses were willing to close their doors to business during the prime days of the week, especially for an event featuring mostly domestic players. It was brutally hot – reaching ninety-five degrees Fahrenheit (thirty-five degrees Celsius), with 82 percent humidity – and Zhou slogged his way through the front nine. He was 2 over at the turn, buried in the middle of the pack, and showing no signs, either to himself or anyone else, that he was about to break loose.

Then something happened. It wasn't dramatic. Probably nobody noticed. But Zhou collected himself, like a cat preparing to pounce. A birdie on hole No. 10, a birdie on No. 12, and he was back at even par. Zhou added two more birdies, offset by two more bogeys, and entered the clubhouse with a 72. He was in nineteenth place, four strokes behind the leaders. There was nothing spectacular about his round. He surely hadn't raised any eyebrows. But Zhou, for whatever reason, was feeling good.

Monday was cooler, and it was windy. The course was almost free of spectators, but if you closed your eyes when the wind swirled through the tall trees lining the fairways it sounded like a large gallery of whispering fans was following the action. And if that had actually been the case, they would have been chasing Zhou Xunshu, who was far and away the best player on the course that day.

While the wind wreaked havoc on the field, Zhou occupied his own pocket of calm. The leaderboard was littered with bogeys and double bogeys and the occasional triple or quad. Most players were sliding decidedly downward. Sunday's leaders – Chen Xiaoma and Yang Jinbiao, who both carded 4-under 68s in the first round, were a combined 10 over par for the day. Zhou, meanwhile, was climbing steadily upward. He was even par through the first nine holes, and tallied three birdies on a bogeyless back nine. His 69 put him in a tie for the best round of the day – no one else had shot better than a 73. When the final scores were counted, Zhou Xunshu's name sat alone at the top of the leaderboard.

In years past, Zhou might have cracked under the pressure. This was the first time in his career he'd ever entered the last two rounds of a tournament in the final grouping, let alone with the outright lead. On Tuesday, he didn't wait long to make it clear he was not shying away from his moment in the spotlight – he was seizing it. He birdied two of his first three holes and opened up a convincing lead. After eight straight pars, he added another birdie on the twelfth hole. Two more pars later, his lead over second place was a commanding five strokes. Zhou's goal of finishing in the top three seemed a foregone conclusion. His dream of winning a tournament was well within his reach. Somehow, despite his lack of preparation, Zhou was playing the best golf of his life.

"I'm more relaxed in my mind," Zhou said. "It's not like before, when I would stress over every stroke, because if I didn't play well my family would starve. Before, I was too aggressive, too anxious to win a tournament. Without prize money, I couldn't support my family. So I viewed every stroke as my last chance to succeed."

The break between domestic tournaments, coupled with his own period of extended unemployment, had been "torture," he said. If he had learned anything from the ordeal, it was the value of patience. Exactly what Michael Dickie had tried to counsel little more than a year earlier in Shanghai.

"Yes, Michael told me to be patient, to slow down my pace," Zhou admitted. "He told me to raise my head, to lengthen my stride, and to speak more deliberately. He said all of these things could help calm me down during competition."

It took Zhou a while, but he finally decided to put Dickie's advice into practice. "Before this year, every stroke I took was overly ambitious," Zhou said. "I played with too much urgency. I took too many risks. Now, I want to think and make sure every stroke is steady and secure. If I want to win, I have to put safety first, right? Before, I never understood this cause and effect. Now I do. Now I am beginning to understand what Michael really meant about being patient."

Hole No. 15 at Jinghua was a pretty straightforward 458-yard par-4. It was surrounded by water – the fairway and green occupy a small peninsula that juts out into a lake – but the playable area was wide enough that, for a skilled golfer, the water rarely came into play. The bunkers, on the other hand, were a different story. Four of them framed the green like a pendant necklace, and they had claimed the hopes of more than a few players during the tournament. Statistically, the fifteenth hole was the fifth most difficult on the course, causing fifty-five bogeys, or worse.

But Zhou had managed to birdie the hole in rounds one and two. He had seemingly figured it out. Given his large lead, he felt a conservative approach made the most sense again. So, he held back a bit on his tee shot, going more for accuracy than distance. *The safe move*, he told himself. *The smart move.*

It very well might have been, too, if only he had hit the ball cleanly. Zhou was perhaps too concerned with being careful, and his driver only made contact with the top half of the ball. It skipped forward ungracefully, finally settling around 150 yards away from him in the left rough.

The hole marked the end of conservative, Zen-like Zhou. He was beginning to tire, and he desperately wanted the round to be over. He went for the green with his second stroke, and instead found a bunker. On his first attempt in the sand, the ball didn't budge. On his second, it sailed over the green and into the rough. He managed to get up and down from there, but the damage had been done. The double bogey turned his five-stroke lead into a three-stroke lead. One of the earlier leaders, Chen Xiaoma, birdied the following hole. This shrank Zhou's once insurmountable advantage to two. That's where he remained heading into the final round.

In his post-round interview, Zhou told reporters his plan for the final round was to not think too much. But thinking was all he could do. Zhou had never been this close to winning a tournament before. He'd never been this close to achieving his dream. Every time he tried to empty his mind, a thousand new thoughts forced their way in. They played like a slideshow of images in his head, of what he wanted to do on each hole, each stroke. Images of him winning, raising his arms on the eighteenth green, raising the trophy in front of a wall of flashing cameras. And then negative images fought their way into view – hooking a drive, missing a putt, sailing the ball into the water. He shook his head, trying to reshuffle the pile. But he had lost his sense of control. He was having anxiety dreams before he even fell asleep.

Zhou went out to dinner, like he normally would have, thinking the diversion would help clear his head. He had a couple beers, like he always did, thinking it would help him sleep. Neither seemed to work. He managed about five hours' fitful sleep that night. He couldn't stop thinking about winning, but did he actually think he could win?

"I knew I wanted to win," Zhou would say later. "But I guess I wasn't sure if I could do it. I thought about it too much, about how to win. I was really distracted."

In the final round, Zhou's main competition was Chen Xiaoma and Su Dong. Zhou had often played against Chen on the Omega China Tour, and they came from similar backgrounds – from the family's fields to a job on a driving range in their twenties. They were the old generation, matched up against the new. But Su never really made a run in the final round, and it was clear early on that the Handa Fraternity Cup was going to be a slugfest between the two journeymen, when Zhou bogeyed the second hole and Chen birdied. Just like that, the two were dead even.

Two holes later, Zhou bogeyed again, and Chen took the lead for the first time since early in the second round. Another birdie by Chen on the fifth hole, and it was Zhou who was now staring at a two-stroke deficit. The bad images that bullied their way into Zhou's head the night before appeared to be winning.

But Zhou battled back. He'd been fighting his whole life, and he wasn't going to give up now. By the start of the back nine, Zhou had regained a share of the lead, and he and Chen remained knotted up until the fourteenth hole.

"Even when he had a two-stroke lead, I didn't let it bother me," Zhou said. "I just worried about myself. I never took Chen as a scary competitor. I never thought he could beat me. We both weren't putting well. I missed several birdie chances. We were neck and neck."

Meanwhile, poor Liu Yan was back home in Chongqing following the action in perhaps the most frustrating way possible. There was no TV coverage of the domestic golf tournaments. No radio, either. So fans trying to follow the action remotely – and, to be honest, these were mostly the wives and girlfriends of players – were left with two options: either try to distract yourself for five hours, maybe go shopping or do some housework, and wait for a phone call from the player, or spend the afternoon staring anxiously at a computer screen, pressing "refresh" repeatedly, waiting for the numbers to come, muttering, *Why haven't those idiots posted new numbers yet?*

Liu Yan had chosen the second option.

Obsessing over the online tournament scoreboard was by far the most maddening of the two options, but it was also hard to resist, because it was the most immediate, even if the rate at which the numbers were updated was wildly inconsistent. Often, scores would be updated three holes at a time. There were sudden bursts of excitement or disappointment, followed by long periods of jittery inactivity.

The interpretation of a golf leaderboard in China is quite simple: black numbers are good; red are even better; and blue are bad – very bad. But the computer screen offers no context. There were no explanations, no backstories, just batches of scores magically appearing on her screen. No nuance, just numbers. It's the most one-dimensional way to follow such a complex and multi-layered game. Ahead then, behind now, ahead again. It was all she had. So, as her husband forged ahead toward the most important five holes of his golfing career, she sat in front of her computer, and hit "refresh" again and again.

Hole No. 14 was a 416-yard, dogleg-right par-4. The fairway curved around a lake, with the most direct route to the green sailing the ball over the water. And Zhou decided to take the most direct route. His tee shot was perfect, leaving him eighty-four yards from the green. Then he saw his opportunity: Chen's drive ended up in the rough. Zhou knew he had a chance to get a stroke back. He took out his lob wedge, hoping to place himself in line for a birdie putt. But Zhou hit it shorter than he wanted, and the ball found the edge of the green. Instead of skipping forward, it spun backwards, and settled into the fairway.

Meanwhile, Chen escaped from the rough unscathed. His second shot found the fringe, and he putted to save par. Zhou putted poorly, and his third bogey of the round had him back down by one stroke.

Zhou bogeyed again on the fifteenth hole, after his drive landed in the rough. Another par for Chen, and Chen's lead was back to two strokes.

"I began to be impatient," Zhou said. "I was too aggressive. I wanted to finish the round as soon as possible."

Chen stopped being Zhou's only concern. By now, Su Dong was just a couple shots behind Zhou, too close for comfort. And two players in the group ahead were also closing in on his score. Another mistake and, forget winning a tournament, Zhou could find himself outside of the top three.

But Zhou didn't panic. He knew there were opportunities for him to make up ground on the final three holes. Hole No. 16, a 544-yard par-5, was the easiest of all the holes during the tournament. In fact, it was the only hole on which the entire field was under par on average. Zhou himself had birdied it twice. So when Chen sent his tee shot into the rough, Zhou saw another opportunity. With a solid drive, a birdie was well within Zhou's reach.

The crowd was not large for this final round – it was a Wednesday, and China's domestic tour, after all. Less than thirty people were following the lead group, and Zhou sensed each one of them was rooting against him. No matter, Zhou thought to himself, I've been the underdog my whole life.

Zhou lined up his crucial tee shot, intent on showing the onlookers they had backed the wrong horse. But, as he put it, "something bad happened." As he addressed the ball, he noticed a golf cart – likely containing some VIP members of the club – moving on the path fifty yards away. Zhou stepped back from the ball and waved the cart on. It came to a stop. Zhou stepped to the ball again, taking a deep breath, visualizing sending the ball down… the cart was on the move again. Zhou stepped back, visibly angry now, and waited for the cart to pass. It eventually settled beneath a willow tree. Zhou regrouped, and stood over the ball a third time.

Focus. Focus. Focus. This is the most important shot of your life. Don't think of anything other than…

The cart started moving again. Zhou was enraged. *Are they doing this on purpose?* he wondered. *Are they conspiring against me?* The cart didn't move a fourth time, but he was rattled. His face was warm with rage. And he nearly drove his ball into the water. With an almost impossible lie, his only option was to knock the ball sideways back toward the fairway. His birdie chance, like the VIP cart, was long gone.

Zhou and Chen both ended up with pars on the sixteenth hole, as well as the seventeenth. Zhou found himself walking to the eighteenth tee two strokes down. The odds were not in his favor, but Zhou knew anything could happen on the very tricky hole, a 452-yard par-4 with trees to the left, water to the right, a very narrow fairway and more than a half dozen bunkers.

When Chen sent his tee shot deep into the left rough, Zhou knew he had lucked into one last chance. From the tee box, no one could tell for sure where Chen's ball had landed, but it didn't look good. The trees were tall and the plant life thick to the left of the fairway. Some wondered whether Chen would be able to find his ball, let alone hit it out of there.

Zhou tried not to be too distracted by Chen's plight, because if he didn't focus he could very easily end up in a similar situation. In Zhou's mind he needed to at least birdie; this would force a playoff with Chen. Mistakes were not an option. Zhou closed his eyes and tried again to clear his head. He tried to force out the wind and the trees and the water, and the spectators rooting against him. He tried to forget about his wife and his son and his parents back in the village who were depending on him. He tried not to think about the trophy and the prize money and his dream of winning a tournament, which thus far had eluded him.

He tried to break this moment down to its essentials. A man. A club. A little white ball. No different than it was when he was just a security guard sneaking out onto the course at Guangzhou International Golf Club. No different.

Every golfer remembers that first time they hit a ball perfectly. It almost feels like you didn't hit the ball at all. The body remains relaxed. The club does all the work. Zhou recognized this feeling immediately, and watched as his ball flew straight through the air and landed cleanly on the widest part of the fairway. Zhou knew he could reach the green from there. A birdie was within reach.

Things had just got interesting.

For the moment, that is. Chen not only found his ball in the forest, but it turned out he had a decent lie, as well. He was able to snake the ball through an opening in the trees. It skipped across the fairway, and looked destined for the right fairway rough, or even the water just beyond it. But the ball died just before it reached the long grass. Luck, it seemed, was again on Chen's side. His next shot, his third, landed on the green, not far from the pin.

A birdie for Zhou was now imperative. He needed to find the green on his second stroke, putt it in with his third – and hope that Chen two-putted, at least. Zhou had heard about situations like this. He'd read about them and watched them on videos and on TV. But, aside from the occasional daydream, he'd never been right in the thick of it. He'd never lined up a shot with a tournament hanging in the balance.

But no one watching Zhou would have known this. He approached his second shot in an entirely businesslike manner, as though he was doing something he had done thousands of times before. The moment he made contact with the ball he started walking down the fairway. He knew his ball was headed for the green. It didn't land as close to the hole as Zhou would have preferred – he still had a long way to go – but he had secured his chance for birdie.

Chen could still put the tournament out of reach, however. Despite his close brushes with nature, he could save par. It was a long putt, but doable, and he proved as much by pushing the ball to within inches of the hole.

The stage was set for Zhou. Make the putt and force a playoff. Miss the putt and lose a tournament he had seemed destined to win not twenty-four hours ago. Zhou's ball sat fifteen yards away from the hole. It was a long shot, in every sense of the phrase. But, then again, so was Zhou. Peasant farmer, security guard, golf pro. Wasn't tournament champion the next logical step for this illogical life?

No. Not on this day, at least. Zhou's putt, and his dream, came up just short – four inches from the cup. It was Chen Xiaoma who raised his fist in triumph. Chen Xiaoma who was in the photos, a thick necklace of flowers around his neck, posing with hordes of smiling caddies, hoisting the championship trophy, receiving a giant commemorative check.

There were no photos of Zhou Xunshu that day. After signing his scorecard, he raced off to find a quiet place to call Liu Yan, who had just seen the final disappointing numbers appear on her computer screen.

Zhou was overflowing with conflicting emotions. His goal all along was to finish in the top three of a tournament. Now he had finished second and won 100,000 yuan in the process, more than five times what he had ever won before. But he had been so close to winning. So painfully close. One stroke, just one stroke. His mind was flooded with what-ifs, could haves and should haves from the past four days. So many moments that seemed insignificant at the time – a different bounce here, another inch there – that might have altered the outcome.

"I wasn't sure how to feel," Zhou said. "I was full of happiness and regret. I was excited. I was upset. I was excited that I finished second. But I was upset at the mistakes that I made. I should have been the champion."

Already, Wang Libo's predictions had proved correct. His shop, and the road that led to it, were almost unrecognizable. It took just over a year, not the three he had imagined, for this to happen. By the autumn of 2010, new construction had started sprouting up all along the cement road from the Mission Hills employee dormitories, past Meiqiu village and into Yongxing town. The buildings were growing at an alarming rate. Stay for a week and you might see bare ground become two stories of brick before you leave. Most of the finished products strongly resembled the house Wang had built along the road two years before. They were cavernous, boxy and covered in tile. In rural Hainan, this is what a McMansion looked like.

Wang's once modest shop had also grown considerably, or more to the point, Wang's empire had expanded around it. The shop itself was still the same size, just packed with more shelves and merchandise, but a new building now stood to its left, more than doubling the business's footprint. A corrugated steel awning extended twenty feet beyond all of it, covering two pool tables, a TV, a makeshift outdoor kitchen and dozens of pink and purple plastic chairs. In April 2010, not long after Mission Hills' surprise grand opening, Wang and his wife had opened an outdoor restaurant, which now accounted for the bulk of their income and employed seven family members. None of them had any experience serving food.

Wang's wife said business was "just so-so." There were more potential customers – some of the dormitories behind the shop were now fully occupied – but there was also more competition. No longer was Wang's place the only game in town. Three grocery stores had opened inside the Mission Hills compound, offering a level of convenience Wang could not compete with.

Outside the Mission Hills gates, more budding businessmen had followed Wang's lead. Next door, Wang's brother had opened a small mah-jongg parlor that, not surprisingly, also did a steady trade in drinks and cigarettes. Beyond that, Wang's cousin Wang Liguo, the local government official, was building a large structure along the road, which he planned to turn into a hotel. Another door over, another cousin had opened a karaoke bar that looked very similar to Wang's new home, but for the large illuminated sign advertising Tsingtao beer.

Wang didn't view the new businesses as rivals – "family never competes with family," he said – and seemed content trying to do the best he could with his tiny piece of the pie. Wang was never much for bookkeeping, so he only had a vague knowledge of his expenses and sales, but he felt he was doing "a little better than before." The easiest way for him to gauge growth was to inspect the pile of empty five-hundred-milliliter beer bottles growing along a cinderblock wall at the far end of his yard. There were hundreds, maybe thousands, of them, green glass bottles with white foil around their necks, stacked neatly on their sides, one atop the other. It was beautiful, in its own way, and maybe somewhere else in the world it would have been considered a fine example of found-object art. But Wang was only interested in watching it grow. If in the morning he saw a noticeable difference in the size of the stack, he knew the previous night had been a good one.

Wang was proud to employ several family members – two of his wife's sisters, a brother-in-law and two nephews – and he was happy that, unlike before, when he was off in his three-wheeled truck and she was tending to the fruit trees, he and his wife were involved in this venture together. And, though the hours were long, he relished that he got to spend at least a handful of them with his children nearby.

When they weren't in school, third-grader Wang Jiaxing and his older sister Wang Jiazhen, a fifth grader, were regular fixtures around their parents' businesses. They did inventory at the shop, prep work for the restaurant, and staffed the counter, giving change for orders of cigarettes and beer. The rest of the time they were either honing their billiards skills or glued to the outdoor TV (their favorite cartoons were *GG Bond*, about a naughty pig with super-powers, and *Pleasant Goat and the Big Big Wolf*, about a group of likable goats and the bumbling wolf who wants to eat them). Wang Jiaxing was quite the budding pool shark, even though the sticks were as tall as he was. He had the trash talking down, too. "Don't waste your strength," he'd tell his competition. "You are not going to beat me."

It was becoming obvious just how close Wang's businesses were to the world's largest collection of golf courses. The green netting and bamboo scaffolding had been removed from some of the buildings directly behind Wang's shop, revealing the giant, seven-story white dormitories with more than a hundred windows on a side, a row of uniform flower baskets hanging under every one.

Opposite Wang's lot, the land on the other side of the cement road was also taking shape. This was the site of Meiqiu's biggest land protest less than a year earlier. It had once been labeled *huangdi*, an expanse of lava rock wasteland topped with dense fruit trees and tall grasses. Now it was something altogether different. Two spotless white cement roads weaved their way through a field of freshly turned red earth. From his patio, Wang could watch a continuous parade of bulldozers, backhoes, excavators, cement trucks and the occasional golf cart full of red-uniformed female caddies roll by. Beyond the roads and a row of mature trees, he could just make out a swath of freshly cut bright green grass that strongly resembled a golf fairway.

Closer to Wang's place but still on the other side of the main cement road, wild shrubs and grasses remained, for the time being, and the scene was more familiar. At a certain time of day you might see a brown cow grazing, accompanied by a rail-thin seventy-eight-year-old man wearing shorts and a tank top — Wang's father. Later in the afternoon, he'd be back, riding a bicycle with a five-gallon paint can strapped to either side of the rear wheel. Every day he came to Wang's restaurant to collect the slop from the previous evening and bike it home to feed to his pigs.

"My father has been through a lot, and he hopes these new businesses can be successful," Wang said. "He knows that after losing our land, my wife and I need to have a job to do. Without the restaurant and grocery store, we have nothing to live on."

Wang himself was thankful his livelihood was no longer dependent on his *san lun che*, which hadn't aged gracefully over the past five years. The three-wheeled truck's battered, primitive appearance belied its relatively young age. It looked like it belonged in a museum of automotive history, perhaps in a wing dedicated to failed experiments of the Cold War, with its rudimentary and rusty exposed engine, and its driver's seat falling apart despite dozens of strips of tape trying to hold it together. The truck was also obnoxiously loud. When Wang turned the ignition key, all conversation within a fifty-foot radius was forced to stop.

Making a living from driving this little blue monster was getting increasingly difficult, especially as more and more of the villagers could afford their own modes of transportation. Indeed, the roads were getting more crowded, as Wang saw on an almost daily basis when he took his three-wheeler into Yongxing, or the big Xiuying wet market in the suburbs of Haikou, to pick up fresh produce, meat and seafood for his restaurant. Though it meant little sleep for him (the restaurant often didn't close down until two or three in the morning), Wang insisted on making the early-morning run to the market himself.

"First, I have the time to buy my own products," he explained. "Second, I can guarantee the quality of the products if I buy them myself. And third, I know how much I need to buy. If I pay somebody to buy for me, they may purchase too much and waste money."

There was also a fourth reason. These regular trips to the market traced the same route Wang took when he was driving the *san lun che* for money, and this allowed him to keep in touch with his fellow drivers. He might stop off in Yongxing for a few cups of tea, or have lunch at a greasy spoon popular among drivers, called Ba Gongli, literally "eight kilometers" – roughly the restaurant's distance from the Xiuying wet market. For old time's sake, and a little extra pocket money, Wang would pick up passengers on his way to and from the market, but he was glad he no longer had to rely on these fares to support his family.

"The road has become wider, and there are more private cars than ever before," Wang said. "People have more money now. Chinese people have two dreams, right? A new house and a private car. Most cars here are BYD brand, but you can also see Toyotas, Fords, Hondas, Mazdas, Volkswagens and even BMWs and Mercedes Benzes. Not too long ago it was all three-wheeled trucks like mine, or public buses."

Lately, Wang had noticed owners of private cars becoming increasingly frustrated that they had to share the road with the little three-wheeled trucks. They'd beep their horns and curse at him. Sometimes Wang felt as though some cars were trying to drive him off the road. The area was changing.

Back at the restaurant, once Wang returned with his purchases, the day began for the rest of the family. There were chickens to be butchered, vegetables to be cleaned and chopped, cloves of garlic to be peeled, dumplings to be stuffed and folded – a seemingly endless list of tasks to take care of before the first Mission Hills shift ended at 5:30 p.m. and the dinner crowd began to arrive. A few times a week, Wang would bring back a large sack of sea snails and spill the contents onto the cement patio. The tip of each spiral-shaped shell had to be broken off with a hammer. There were hundreds of them, and Wang's wife attacked the bag one shell at a time.

"We are farmers," she said. "We're used to being busy. Life before was tend the trees, look after the kids, chop the twigs to feed the goats. Now, it's still busy, just different work."

Did she miss anything about the old life?

"Let the past be the past," she said. "Why should I miss it?"

While his extended family prepared the food, Wang would often try to grab a midday nap in a room just off the kitchen. After he awoke, his wife would try to do the same. But the naps never lasted long enough. There was always work to be done. The clock was always ticking down to the evening rush, which was preceded by a flurry of activity: Wang's wife sorting and cleaning the vegetables, his brother-in-law frying eggs and chopping garlic, both sisters-in-law placing the barbecue items on their wooden skewers, his nephews arranging the chairs and tables. Wang's job was to fix any new rips in the felt of the pool tables with some clear plastic tape.

Once the sun landed just above the tree line and the shadows grew longer, their customers – Mission Hills caddies, hotel workers, cooks, cleaners and security guards – arrived mostly on foot, from the dormitories on the other side of the gates. They were young, and they came from all over China. For many of them, this was their first time living beyond their hometown or province. They had come to Hainan to pursue their own versions of the Chinese Dream.

"We want to make them feel at home," Wang said, noting they added boiled dumplings, not common in Hainan, to their menu to cater to clientele from northern China. "They are mostly from other provinces. If we offer our best service to them, they will come to our shop more often. We want to treat them well, which can also help us expand in the future."

One demographic that wasn't queuing up for a seat at one of Wang's tables was his fellow villagers, especially those who were still, all these months later, waiting to receive a land payment. They were stewing in their resentment of Wang and the other Cangdao ancestors who had made their deals and then built new houses and opened new businesses in prime locations along the cement road. "We have our own rice," scoffed Wang Puhua, who remained one of the more vocal Meiqiu villagers. "We can cook by ourselves. Why would we go to his restaurant?"

Visitors to Wang's restaurant were never given a menu, and though the items on offer rarely changed from day to day, a menu never existed. This was common in rural Hainan. Asked how customers knew what to order, Wang's wife looked puzzled. "You just write down things you want. And you don't write down things you don't want."

The outdoor kitchen was simple: a gas-powered wok, three large pots cooking on open flames and a long rectangular barbecue pit filled with burning coals. That, and a small cutting space, were all Wang and his family needed to produce a rather diverse offering of dishes. The most expensive was stir-fried pork with green vegetables – only fifteen yuan ($2.25) and well within the budgets of the golf course workers. Those who were saving money to send back to their families on the mainland opted for cheaper items – grilled chives on a stick (one yuan); grilled beef on a stick (1.5 yuan); grilled chicken wings on a stick (3.5 yuan); grilled squid on a stick (seven yuan); or boiled dumplings, fried rice noodles or stir-fried sea snails (each five yuan).

Bottles of Anchor, Yanjing and Tsingtao beer sold for four to five yuan. There was also a considerable selection of harder alcohols – rice wine and *huangjiu,* or "yellow wine," mostly – ranging from four to sixteen yuan, and you could get a pack of Lotus cigarettes for 2.2 yuan. For those craving something a little bit healthier, Wang kept a pile of young coconuts next to the TV, the water from which he'd serve up for two yuan.

The games Wang had installed proved to be a good investment. The mah-jongg table, tucked off in a side room of the shop, was twenty yuan for a morning or afternoon of play. Mission Hills security guards came early each day to take their places at the table. The pool tables, which ran three yuan an hour, attracted a different sort; young men with spiky hair and blue jeans who arrived on motorbikes. There were plenty of ways to while away the hours at Wang's restaurant, and many customers did. Sitting at one of Wang's tables in the dark, you could look across the road and see lights from the Mission Hills dump trucks and cement trucks working into the night.

These were long days for Wang and his family, too. But as the orders raced in, as the hours drew later and later, they were always smiling and laughing. They seemed happy. Could that be? "No, we are not happy at all," Wang's wife said with a chuckle. "But just because we are tired doesn't mean we can't laugh. We are too busy for any rest, but we can still laugh. We tell jokes to each other."

It was 2 a.m. on a Wednesday and Wang looked exhausted. He was sprawled out across two pink plastic chairs, his arms resting across his stomach, his legs up in the air. It was monsoon season, and the rain sounded like a hundred hammers banging on the steel roof. "This job is tough," he said. "The money is better than before, but all at the expense of our health and time."

Wang's wife nodded her head. "He started to lose weight the moment we opened the restaurant. He was a little bit fat when driving his truck. Now, he can't have regular meals."

Regardless, Wang's brother-in-law knew this was better than the life he'd had before. "One thing we are happy about is that we get to work together. If I was working as a bricklayer, I'd be alone and unhappy."

Later that morning, Wang was out on the patio, preparing for the day's trip to the wet market. He took a look at the pile of beer bottles to see how much it had grown and thought to himself, *Not bad*. Then he turned his attention to the commotion in the clearing on the other side of the cement road. Mission Hills workers were using an excavator and a tall hydraulic crane to plant a long line of fully-grown palm trees. Wang had never seen anything quite like it.

"There were already trees there before they bulldozed the land," he said, shaking his head. "They were old and tall. Some were probably hundreds of years old. Now they are planting new ones that look old?"

He shook his head again and got back to work. He had another long day ahead of him.

There was still one section of Wang's land yet to be developed. It was a small but lush gully between his brother's property and his own. Wang wanted to fill it in and build on it. For what, he hadn't figured out yet. "I will build it first, and then decide," he said. "I can rent it to others who want to do business."

He sounded like one of the big bosses over on the construction site. But becoming "Boss Wang" wasn't part of his plans. "I am just a self-made man," he said.

Still, he was concerned whether everything he had worked so hard to build might be taken away at any moment. What if Mission Hills decided they wanted to expand? If he had learned anything over the past few years, it was that nothing could be guaranteed, that what you thought was rightfully yours could be taken away with very little warning.

"If they want to rent our land by force, we have no way out," Wang's wife admitted. "That land over there" – she pointed to acreage that Wang Puhua and other Meiqiu villagers were contesting, on the other side of the cement road – "was bulldozed without compensation or measuring. Instead, they built a road to the course on that land. They said that it was owned by the public, and that they could take it at any time."

There used to be more butterflies in Meiqiu. Not long ago you could see them nearly anywhere in the village. They seemed especially fond of a clearing near a small temple not far from where Wang Libo built his restaurant. Until recently, trees surrounded the temple and its garden, and the butterflies would flutter around and drink the nectar from the thousands of wild flowers that dotted the yard.

"The butterflies are becoming fewer and fewer," Wang's wife said. "In the past, we had more trees. When they bulldozed the trees, many of the butterflies went away."

The temple, like so much of Meiqiu, was now neighbor with the massive Mission Hills golf complex. Where there were once trees on one side of the garden, there was now a short wall and a wide-open view of overturned earth, new roads and freshly planted palm trees. The tall white employee dormitories loomed on the horizon. Not far from the temple, there was an old stone tablet, etched with the names of villagers who had passed away – the character for "Wang" is everywhere. An archway of lava rock sheltered the tablet, but it had once been protected by so much more: trees, shrubs and isolation. Now it was right out in the open, just a few feet from a new thoroughfare leading to one of the biggest developments in modern China, a small monument to the old way of life and a stark reminder that, in this new China, everything and everyone must be prepared to adapt and change, whether they want to or not.

In the years since Mission Hills had broken ground in Hainan, Wang had been inside the compound many times. When he worked as a *san lun che* driver, he'd often taxi workers in and out of the site. Security guards came to know him and allowed him to pass freely. Occasionally Wang would forget he was now driving on private land. To him, it still felt like home.

Now that Mission Hills was open to the public, there was no way a villager on a *san lun che* would make it past the gate. Thankfully, Wang's cousin, Wang Liguo, the local government official, had an official pass to get through security, and he was more than happy to flaunt it. He had stuck it to his dashboard, for everyone to see. Beneath a large Mission Hills logo, it read, "Yangshan District Land Consolidation and Ecological Restoration Project."

Life had been good to Wang Liguo since Mission Hills had arrived. He wore a diamond ring on his pinkie finger. He'd opened a restaurant in Yongxing, and he was building a hotel along the cement road. He'd given his BYD car to a younger brother and bought a new Honda Civic for himself. That was the car with his official pass, the one he drove when he gave his cousin Wang Libo a tour of the grounds around the Mission Hills clubhouse.

They took the road right around the corner from Wang's restaurant, and they didn't have to drive far to realize they were no longer in Meiqiu. As soon as they passed through the gates, it was obvious they had left the randomness of nature behind them. There were trees and shrubs and even lava rock walls intended to keep the local flavor, but everything had its own place; everything appeared planned and polished. Off to the left was a collection of cookie-cutter mansions, the garages for which probably cost more than Wang Libo's entire new home. It was amazing what a difference a two-minute drive made.

"Many stars will come here. I don't know their names," Wang Liguo said, referring to the upcoming celebrity tournament, the Mission Hills Star Trophy.

His cousin knew the names, as did many of the people on the other side of the gates, in Meiqiu. "Jet Li, the *kung fu* star, will come," Wang Libo said. "And Eric Tsang, the Hong Kong comedian, will come, too. Many people in the village know this."

To discover the rest of the names, all they had to do was read the banners attached to the light posts lining the road. Wang Libo didn't recognize many of the faces, a sign that he perhaps wasn't the target audience. In typical Mission Hills fashion, the first public event at their new resort was destined to be the biggest celebrity golf event ever held in China. Dozens of famous faces greeted visitors as they approached the clubhouse. There were professional golfers, such as Greg Norman, Nick Faldo, Colin Montgomerie, Lorena Ochoa, Annika Sörenstam, Se Ri Pak and Zhang Lianwei. And there were celebrities, like Catherine Zeta-Jones, Michael Phelps, Hugh Grant, Matthew McConaughey, Christian Slater, Li Ning and Sammo Hung. Another banner appeared regularly along the road. It was red and let people know they were arriving at "The World's Golf Club."

"Mission Hills has given me tickets to see the Star Trophy," Wang Liguo noted proudly. "I have been to Shenzhen to learn to play golf. I went there twice and I played golf. I have also been to Beijing and Shanghai to play golf. Project 791 has asked me several times to return to Mission Hills in Shenzhen, but I refused. Because soon I'll be able to play near my house."

The Blackstone Course, on which the celebrities would soon be playing, was stunning. With its irregular lines and eroded sand traps, it managed to appear rugged and natural, even though there was very little natural about it. Incorporated into the design were old, overgrown lava rock walls and archways left over from the land's previous occupants, along with some mature lychee, ficus and acacia trees that managed to elude the clear-cutter. The result was a landscape that seemed as though it had occupied the earth for decades, maybe centuries – not months. A drive along the cart path made of crushed lava rock gave the impression of a Jurassic-era safari – that is, until the massive hotel and clubhouse came into view. Fashioned in a "Mediterranean Revival" style, white with red and black tile roofs, they were unlike anything else in Haikou.

Wang Libo didn't say much as he walked through the lobby of the Mission Hills luxury hotel. It was a lot for him to take in. The decor was immaculate, everything shiny and new. There was plush furniture, marble floors and art hanging on the walls. He'd never seen anything quite like it before. He followed his cousin out to the big balcony, which looked out onto a swimming pool the size of a football field. The pool was surrounded by dozens of red-and-white umbrellas and lounge chairs, and for each one there were two palm trees. Behind it all were two towering man-made volcanoes. Kitschy nods to the region's actual volcanoes, the two mounds looked like giant primary-school science projects, poised to spew vinegar-and-baking-soda "lava" at any moment. Mission Hills was trying hard to impress. And largely, it succeeded.

Wang Libo stood at the railing and stared at the scene in silence. "There used to be a mountain here," he said. "I think this looks better."

On the drive back to the village, Wang Liguo explained why he thought the Mission Hills development was good for the area. "If the lands are not rented out, the farmers have very little chance to make money," he said. "Even if they grow lots of fruit trees in their fields, they'll never make enough money for a new house. Building materials are much more expensive than before, but the fruit still costs the same as years before. The 791 project gives us land compensation with which we can start our own businesses; also they can provide us with jobs. People may lose land in the short term, and their quality of life may not immediately improve. But their children will have better opportunities."

Back in the village, Wang Libo took a seat underneath the phoenix tree where he and the rest of the village had first heard about "land compensation," Project 791 and Mission Hills – before anyone had ever questioned whether he was a true Meiqiu villager or not. The setting was undeniably different from the five-star resort he had just returned from. The old volleyball court was full of weeds, its net sagging sadly in the middle. The stone top to the Chinese chess table was broken in half and lying on the ground. It all put Wang Libo into a reflective mood.

"Quality of life is getting better and better," he said. "More and more people are building new houses. But the thing is, more and more traditions that were once available under this phoenix tree are disappearing. We always played volleyball or chess or talked about the news right here. Today, all of our attention is focused on how to make money. Interaction between villagers is not that close anymore. I doubt this will get any better in the future. Look around. Nobody takes care of this infrastructure."

Wang thought about what the village might look like in ten years' time. "More buildings probably," he mused. "I had thought that the volleyball matches would continue no matter what development came here. I never thought things like chess or even just nighttime chatting between villagers would disappear so quickly. And I think in the near future all of the old stone houses will be replaced.

"Times are changing. You see it in other villages, too. Some have more new houses than we do. If we don't build more cement houses, my sons will have difficulty finding girls to marry them. People now are very materialistic, right?"

But Wang couldn't reflect for long. It was time to get back to work. He had two businesses to run.

13

CHASING THE NEXT DREAM

"I still think about the fourteenth and sixteenth holes."

Zhou Xunshu was sitting in the dining room of his Chongqing apartment, five months after his gut-wrenching one-stroke loss at the Handa Fraternity Cup.

"I won't forget it for the rest of my life," Zhou said. "It's not about the difference in prize money for first and second place. What really matters is the honor. If I won the tournament, I think my future as a coach would be more brilliant.

"It's such a pity that I didn't win."

But, over the past several months, Zhou had come to learn that even coming in second had its privileges. First, his top-three finish meant that, in the eyes of the China Golf Association, he was no longer a second-class citizen. Now, he was not just a "professional coach," he was a "professional golfer." It was a distinction lost on 99.9 percent of the Chinese population, but it was an important one to Zhou. It meant he had reached the highest classification possible in his chosen profession.

He was a success. And he was no longer unemployed, as had been the case a year before.

"I never see him resting for one single day," Liu Yan said. "He has such a big family to support."

In fact, Zhou now had two jobs. He was still coaching at Seasons International in Chengdu, earning his eight thousand yuan per month from the club. But these days he was only making the long trip from Chongqing a couple times each month, cramming in as many clients as possible one weekend at a time. Back at home in Chongqing, he had picked up a job as a part-time sales executive for a local golf cart manufacturer. That brought in another three thousand yuan a month, plus a commission for each sale – that is, if he ever managed to make a sale.

"I can't sell anything," Zhou confessed. "They hired me because I am a golfer, and I know people at the management level from different courses. But I don't really like making small talk with people. And I don't like bargaining."

Liu Yan agreed. "In my mind he is inadequate for sales work," she said, before adding with a giggle, "He is good at physical labor – like carrying heavy things."

"They call me every day wanting me to stay in the office," Zhou said. "I am thinking about quitting."

Not long ago, Zhou would've taken just about any job he could find. Now, it seemed, he could afford to pick and choose. After his second-place finish in Beijing, a longtime student – a wealthy aluminum dealer – had convinced the head of Chongqing's first regulation golf course, Sun Kingdom, to sponsor Zhou. He was the best golfer in a city of thirty million, and people were finally starting to pay attention.

It was the kind of arrangement Zhou had dreamed about for years. Sun Kingdom, which had opened back in 2005, was paying him six thousand yuan plus all expenses, just to show up for a tournament. If he met certain performance goals, there were bonuses, too. Zhou was given free rein to use Sun Kingdom's facilities for practice, as well. He could play a round whenever he wanted, free of charge. No questions asked. All he had to do in exchange was wear the Sun Kingdom logo while he played in public.

"Look around," Zhou said, during a cart ride around the club grounds. "This golf course is so in accordance with nature. Basically, this course hardly occupies any arable land. On waste-land like this, the farmers couldn't grow anything. So building a golf course is the best choice."

Sun Kingdom had been built on the site of a very poor village, Zhou said, so poor that "some of the male villagers couldn't even find girls to marry, because of their poverty." The villagers in the area had been relocated to brand-new apartments, and many were now working for the golf course, he believed. Others had received compensation and opened "small-scale" businesses.

It all sounded very good to Zhou. "I welcome developers to go to my hometown and build a golf course." Finally, with Sun Kingdom's backing, Zhou could focus entirely on his game. He didn't have to worry about whether he could afford the airfare or the hotel or his meals. He didn't have to worry if he'd break even at the end of a tournament. It was all taken care of, and a huge weight had been lifted from his broad shoulders. But even with that support, Zhou didn't come close to repeating his performance at the Handa Fraternity Cup for the rest of the season. He placed in the top twenty-five a few times, finishing as high as eleventh at one event. But the magic largely eluded him.

"I played just so-so in the coming tournaments, even though I felt more confident," Zhou said. "I didn't practice very often. It seems I didn't care so much. I felt more comfortable out there, but the result was not the first and foremost. I just golfed without too much stress."

Zhou may have earned the biggest payday in Beijing – 72,000 yuan (about $12,000) after taxes and his mandatory donation to charity – but you wouldn't have been able to tell it from looking around his and Liu Yan's apartment. It was still sparsely decorated, the white walls bare save for a studio portrait of Hanhan dressed as a mouse, his zodiac sign, and a pre-wedding portrait of Zhou and Liu Yan, both dressed entirely in white formal wear, and lounging lovingly like characters in a movie adaptation of a Jane Austen novel, atop a plot of green grass. The display shelves in the dining room, where one might show off fine china or family heirlooms, instead housed a golf trophy, a purple plush toy animal and an odd assortment of liquor bottles and gift boxes Zhou had collected during his various stops around China. Nothing too fancy.

So what had he done with his big prize money?

"You should ask Liu Yan," Zhou said, pointing in his wife's direction.

"I put it in the bank," she said. "Saving most of it for the future."

The family finances were a subject of much good-humored dispute.

"No particular person takes care of the money," Liu Yan insisted. "Anyone who needs to spend money, can spend it."

"Really?" Zhou said skeptically. "Such beautiful words."

"Am I not telling the truth? Did I ever keep you from the money?" his wife replied.

"Zhou bought a pair of shoes with two thousand yuan once," she continued, presenting her evidence. "I've never bought something that expensive. But I know he is working outside, and must wear such things regularly. I'm a housewife. I don't need expensive clothes. It is his first time to buy shoes so expensive. He thinks he needs some prizes for his hard work."

Things had improved for them over the years, Liu Yan said. "When I accompanied him to Kunming for a golf tournament, we didn't check the weather in advance. It cooled down suddenly when the tournament was beginning. Zhou had to pay for a jacket, a very expensive jacket – fifteen hundred yuan. At that time, we even felt buying a jacket was a luxury."

Now, that jacket no longer seemed so expensive – at least, in Zhou's opinion.

"Liu Yan," he said, "do you remember the wool coat we saw at the plaza? The Nautica one? I like it very much. It costs two thousand yuan."

"You already have an expensive coat," she said. "How come you want a new one? Wool is very expensive. If you want one, I want one, too."

"That wool coat is so attractive. If I wore it, I'd look like Chow Yun-fat. I saw it last year, but I didn't have the money. I want to buy it if I see it again. I have that money now."

They were beginning to have the concerns of a typical middle class household. Back in 2005, China's National Bureau of Statistics had stated that members of the country's urban middle class had an annual income between 60,000 and 500,000 yuan. It was the first time "middle class" had been expressed in numbers in China. Zhou felt confident he had risen from being a poor boy from Qixin to become a member of this group. "Yes," he said, without hesitation. "I think I am a middle class."

Liu Yan had different criteria, however. "There are still a lot of things we can't buy now," she said. "Like, I want a car, but I don't have that money. I also want to buy an expensive watch. I know Zhou can afford to buy me a Cartier watch, but we have to think twice before taking the money out. Hanhan has to go to school, and college, so we have to save money for his education."

"I can't afford luxury brands right now," Zhou admitted, agreeing with his wife. "But I can buy some middle-class clothes." And Zhou could catalogue each item of middle-class clothing he'd bought along with its price. There was the 680-yuan sweater, for instance, or the 1,700-yuan suit he picked up in Chengdu. Things he'd never mention to his family back in Qixin – they wouldn't understand – but that wouldn't stop him from spending his money on them. "I would rather spend money on better clothes or meals than on cigarettes and alcohol," Zhou said. "I think these things can change our quality of life."

Still, he wasn't content with his financial situation. "Man should be more aggressive," he explained. "I want to create a better life for my kid. I want to make more money to send Hanhan to study in America. Basically, I want to make more money."

How could he do that with all of his jobs?

"Time is like a sponge," Zhou said. "If you squeeze it, you can find more spare time."

Zhou was sounding more and more like a member of China's new middle class, always striving for more.

For his part, Martin Moore never thought he'd find himself back at Yangzong Lake in southwest China's Yunnan province. Of course, back in 1995, he never thought he'd end up there in the first place, either. Now he was joking about putting a floating office right in the middle of it, because there were times he thought he'd never be able to leave.

His golf course construction management firm had twelve China projects going on simultaneously, and as Martin stood on the banks of the lake, he could see three of them. It was a strange feeling. More than fifteen years earlier, when he was completely new to China, he remembered looking across these mirror-like waters and seeing next to nothing, save for two blights on the landscape – the coal-fired power station to the north and the aluminum factory to the west. Both were scheduled to be shut down, he was assured back then, but both had since tripled in size.

He stood on the red-brown earth of one of his current projects and stared east across the lake at his very first. Spring City Golf Club looked like a bright green layer cake cut into the hillside. Martin knew it intimately. Every green. Every fairway. Every dogleg right or left. The course was the reason he had first come to China, so reluctantly, and it was probably the main reason he was so busy in the country now. Since its completion, Spring City had been consistently rated as one of the top golf courses in Asia. Martin's first China project was still the bar by which the country's new courses were measured.

Reminders of the Spring City job were everywhere. From one of the newer lakeside projects, he could throw a golf ball and hit the dilapidated resort he once called home. While clearing land on another, Martin had discovered some plastic netting that looked familiar – because he had put it there a decade and a half ago. One golf hole he was working on occupied a piece of land that had once served as Spring City's turf nursery. He'd soon be growing grass there again, but for the fairway and green.

"It definitely was weird kicking dirt around on that property," Martin said. "Because I remember I actually spent a few days on the bulldozer myself grading it way back when."

But a lot, too, had changed since his time at Spring City. The previously indestructible golf course market in the United States was gone – golf course closures were consistently outnumbering course openings there. China had made the construction of new golf courses illegal, only to become the only country in the world in the thick of a golf course boom. The colleagues who, early on, had laughed at him for focusing on China – where no one seemed to recognize a golf ball, let alone know how to build a course – were constantly calling him up, knocking on his door.

To those trying to break into the Chinese market, Martin would always say, "Good luck." He'd been working there going on twenty years and had yet to feel he completely understood the vagaries of the place. Cracking China took time and it took patience. Lately, the inexperienced owner on one of his Yangzong Lake projects was making so many bullheaded decisions that Martin questioned whether the course would ever see the light of day. On another, Martin was once again dealing with villager disputes with the local government over land rights and compensation, which was creating havoc with his schedule. He'd seen it all before, of course. They'd find a way around the problems or, if they didn't, he would just move on to another one of his new job leads.

For now, though, Martin was waiting to see how the villager disputes would settle. "Currently they are kind of upset," Martin's Chinese project coordinator said about the villagers living near the construction site. "I think this is the ugly side of China. The owner of the company paid the money for the land to the government, but the government didn't give all the money to the villagers."

Many of the laborers now building the golf course used to grow corn on the land. In fact, corn still grew on what was supposed to be the course's fifth green. According to the project coordinator, this was the last of many disputed sections of the course. What was the exact problem?

"I have no idea," the project coordinator said. "Some government thing. The big boss has been drinking with a lot of people just for that one piece of land."

Indeed, there was lots of determined drinking going on near the golf course projects around Yangzong Lake. While dining at a busy village restaurant near one of his lakeside sites, Martin and a few other members of the project team noticed a colleague – a Chinese man from Kunming – sitting at a large table nearby. He had about twenty men at his table, and an open bottle of *baijiu* sat atop the lazy Susan.

"He works for us," said the owner's representative. "His job is to entertain the farmers, and take care of government issues."

The drinkfest was one of the aspects of working in China that Martin could do without. But such annoyances were unavoidable, and until the industry picked up somewhere else in the world, he was resigned to the fact they were simply part of his reality.

He may have been working in China longer than almost anyone else in the industry, but the place still had a way of surprising him. Sometimes in a good way, sometimes bad, but the country was rarely, if ever, boring. "I still look forward to the times when I get a new lead in some place I haven't been to in China," Martin said. "I like going to a new city. And meeting new people."

Martin doesn't want his sons to get into his line of work. "It's a tough life," he said. He was spending more time on the road than at home in Scottsdale, Arizona. When he was traveling, his schedule was often brutal – red-eye flights broken up by twelve-hour workdays on a construction site. When he wasn't working on a job, he was chasing down new leads.

He was usually up and working by 5 a.m. He liked to say he was a living example of the old US Army motto: "We do more before 9 a.m. than most people do all day." He was averaging less than five hours' sleep a night, by his reckoning, and those handfuls of precious hours were often interrupted by emails and text messages. He maintained three mobile phones – one each for the United States, China and Thailand – and kept all three at the ready on his nightstand.

"I'm addicted," Martin said. "It's almost like I've got one eye open. So if someone sends me an email, it's never one hour old before I read it. If I open my eyes every hour and that thing's got a red light flashing, I'm checking email. And it's not unusual that if it's something that I feel is important, I'll sit there and answer. Throw it down, go back to sleep – or, you know, semi-sleep. This blows some people's minds."

So far, his addictions had paid off. But he knew many aspects of the Chinese market would never be within his control. The China boom, while nowhere close to going bust, was not reverberating quite as loudly as it had in the past. The crackdowns were beginning to have more bite. The numbers were coming back down to earth. Even Mission Hills seemed to be slowing down. "I've never seen them say, 'We're not doing anything,' before," Martin said. It was as good an indication as any that nothing was a sure thing.

Martin was worried he'd put all his eggs in the same Made-in-China basket. He was looking for more leads in Vietnam and

South Korea, so he wouldn't be left with nothing if and when the Chinese market dried up, just like the US market before it.

Martin picked a stone out of the dirt and tossed it in the direction of the lake he couldn't seem to escape.

"It's all weird, man," he said with a sigh. "It makes no sense to me, this moratorium, this golf boom. I sit here every day and wonder about my business. Is it all going to fall apart in a year? Or is it going to go strong for five years? Who knows?"

Now a toddler, little Hanhan was attending preschool. Zhou and Liu Yan were paying five hundred yuan a month, which included eight hours of schooling and lunch five days a week, for their only son to have this early start in his education. With Zhou gone for most of the day, Liu Yan's days had become a bit boring. Lately, a middle-aged woman also from Hunan province, who lived upstairs, would often come down and visit with her. They'd speak in their provincial dialect, watch soap operas and gossip about the neighbors. It wasn't exactly the life she'd dreamed of as a teenager getting ready to leave her village for a job as a caddie at Dragon Lake Golf Club.

That wasn't to say the life she imagined for herself back then was an elaborate one. Ten years before, Liu Yan's dreams had been quite basic, actually. She'd wanted a job, someone to love her, and happiness for her family. Now her dreams were more specific. Looking forward to 2020, she hoped her husband would win many golf tournaments, that her son would grow up happily, and that her parents and Zhou's parents were all at peace.

"I want to live in a villa with lots of pets, children and friends," Liu Yan said. "I want to live in Hunan. Zhou wants to live in Guizhou."

As a young boy in Guizhou province, Zhou, too, had his dreams. Most of all, his desire to get out of Qixin. He did that, and then his dreams got bigger. "Ten years ago, I was a security chief in Guangdong," he said. "I was paid about one thousand yuan a month. I lived in a room with eight people. I didn't have any good clothes. I knew I wanted to marry a girl and have my own family. But my dreams weren't detailed. I just wanted a better life with more money. With hard work, we can only live out our dreams step by step. All I wanted was a stable family with a monthly salary of ten thousand yuan."

So what does a man do when he has already realized all of his dreams before the age of forty?

"It wasn't easy for me," Zhou said, "and now I will pursue more dreams. I want to make more money and attend more tournaments. All I want is to create more conveniences for my son. If I can win a tournament, my life goals will be almost complete."

And that "almost" was at the heart of things. Where the old Zhou's dreams were lacking in detail, some of the new ones were pretty specific. "I want to buy a new house," he said, "with a convenient location and good property management. And I hope I can own a car worth 300,000 or 400,000 yuan." The car bug seemed to be catching in this newly minted middle-class family. While walking past Chongqing's Olympic Stadium, little Hanhan pointed at a sign featuring the famous five-interlocking-rings Olympic logo. "Audi," he said.

Zhou's ambitions for his son were open-ended and expansive. "If he can golf, I hope he can golf. If he can study and go to college, I want him to do that," Zhou said. It seemed there wouldn't be a police academy in Hanhan's future, unless that's what Hanhan wanted.

For Liu Yan, Zhou simply wanted happiness. "I don't know," he said. "How can I plan her life? If she wants to work outside, or just be a housewife, it's all up to her." Asked if there was anything he really wanted to be able to buy for his wife ten years from now, he was sure in his answer. "Yes, I would love to," he said, "but it still depends on if I have that money. If I had the money now, I would buy her anything she wants."

Dinner that evening was at KFC, followed by a stroll through the French superstore Carrefour. Zhou drove his family there in a black Hyundai loaned to him indefinitely by the management at his driving range in Chengdu. "This car costs around 300,000 yuan," Zhou announced dryly during the drive over.

He was wearing a navy Nautica sweater vest over a royal blue golf shirt and a pair of khaki trousers. Liu Yan wore a yellow hoodie and skinny jeans. Walking down the store's aisles, the couple were affectionate and full of laughter. Hanhan, wearing a Uniqlo fleece jacket, stood at the front of the shopping cart as though he were king of the world.

Back in the Hyundai on the drive home, Hanhan sat on his mother's lap in the passenger seat. Zhou quickly turned up the volume on the car stereo.

"Oh, listen," he said excitedly. "It's Hanhan's favorite song!"

First, there was the sound of the Chinese flute. Then, a man sang:

Hair so long
Eyes so brown
Have I seen you somewhere before?
The tundra roses are blossoming on the mountains
And I'd love to pluck one of them just for you
Smiles so innocent
Conversations so coy
Seared into my heart, I won't forget
Butterflies waft over our heads
I just want to say I've fallen for you.

"Sing it, Hanhan!" Zhou urged his son.

Dear girl, I love you
Please let me into your world so I can be with you
Dear girl, I love you
I would do anything for you one lifetime after
another

The little boy sang, and Zhou and his happy family laughed. They were on their way.

EPILOGUE

When this book first came out, in the summer of 2014, I bristled a bit when newspapers wrote of "China's war on golf." It just didn't ring true. Sure, new golf courses were banned, but they were also booming. China's *failed* war on golf seemed more apt.

Little did I know the real war was just getting started.

On March 30, 2015, Chinese authorities announced the closure of sixty-six "illegal" golf courses – roughly 10 percent of all courses in the country – in an apparent attempt to start enforcing the long-ignored ban on golf-related construction. The following day, the Commerce Ministry announced that one of its senior officials was under investigation for "participating in a company's golf event," thus putting him on the wrong side of President Xi Jinping's "eight rules" against extravagance among government officials, part of his expansive and seemingly ceaseless anti-corruption campaign. By the end of the year, reports of golf-related corruption charges would become commonplace. In Guangdong province, the birthplace of golf in modern China, an investigative team was formed to catch officials who took part in any of nine golf-related activities. There was even a public hotline for reporting suspected golf violations.

Later that year, in October, golf in China once again hit the headlines when the Chinese Communist Party updated the discipline rules for its 88 million members to include a ban on owning golf club memberships. No public official should be able to afford such a thing in the first place – but the fact that the new rules lumped golf together with "improper sexual relationships" did nothing to improve the game's already flagging reputation in the country.

China's current laser focus on golf may come as a surprise to those familiar with the blind-eye policy that prevailed for much of the previous decade. There were regular crackdowns during that time, but the number of golf courses continued to rise. This current crackdown feels markedly different, both in seriousness and scope. That's because China is different. This is Xi Jinping's China, and it's clear he's intent on making his mark. Everyone's a potential target in this ongoing crackdown on corruption, and golf is a particularly easy and obvious one – those "illegal" golf courses were still getting built somehow. The majority of Chinese still know golf as "the rich man's game": it's expensive, elitist, and out of reach for most. If you're looking to make a populist move, golf is low-hanging fruit.

In some ways, though, things seem to be China as usual. In advance of golf's return to the Olympics in 2016, the same Chinese government that's been cracking down on cadres for playing golf has been funneling an unprecedented amount of money into its national golf team, entirely in pursuit of those all-important Olympic medals.

So what does the future hold? Every time I am asked that, I am reminded of a new take on an old joke: If you want to make China laugh, tell it about your predictions.

Martin Moore, ironically, did see where things were headed back in early 2014. "It's a shaky market," he said at the time. "I believe the government is being more aggressive now than I've ever seen them." By the end of the year, golf course construction in China had come to a halt. Luckily for Martin, he had been chasing projects in places like Thailand and Vietnam while his competitors were still trying to figure out China. Back in 2012, when Xi Jinping was just rising to power, many were actually optimistic that his government would be "pro golf" – Xi was rumored to have been a golfer himself. Martin was quick to dismiss that theory: "He's totally anti-corruption."

Business was much better for Wang Libo, who built a tiny real estate empire on his triangle of land adjacent to the massive employee dormitories at Mission Hills Haikou. Sales at his restaurant, which now specializes in Hainanese cuisine, have been "very good." So good, in fact, that he added a second level to his building and hired a slew of new employees. Wang began renting out the space once occupied by his convenience store to a Sichuanese restaurant, and he added two new buildings – each three stories tall – which house a mah-jongg parlor, a bar, and rooms for rent. While his income has grown exponentially, Wang's days remain long, and he still worries that the government could take it all away without warning.

Zhou Xunshu didn't compete much after the 2010 season. He participated in six tournaments in 2011, finishing a disappointing fourth in the event held at Sun Kingdom, his home course in Chongqing. In 2012, he played in four of eight domestic tournaments, and in 2013 entered just one. Zhou said his reasons were purely financial. It was becoming harder for players of his generation to do well in tournaments, because increasing numbers of younger, well-off players, with coaches and nothing but time to train, were coming onto the scene. He couldn't support his family from tournament winnings alone, so he couldn't justify the time for practice – time he could spend earning money. Zhou knew stepping back was the right decision, but it still ate him up inside. "I miss competing," he said. "I just enjoy the whole experience, the process of playing the game."

Zhou didn't have much time to stew, working long hours as head pro at a local driving range. Still known as the best golfer in Chongqing, more and more wealthy parents were bringing him their young sons and daughters to mold into Chinese golf stars. These parents paid well. Enough so that, in 2012, Zhou could realize a dream and buy a car – a Volkswagen Sagitar (the Chinese version of the Jetta) – and four years later consider purchasing a BMW 5-Series sedan. He also bought two more apartments, expecting Chongqing's real estate market to continue to grow.

In 2015, Zhou finally made his way to the United States. One of Zhou's promising young students was attending a golf academy in Hilton Head, South Carolina, and the boy's father paid for Zhou and a translator to accompany him for two months. At the end of his trip, Zhou visited New York City. He saw many of the famous sites, but spent more time at one place than any other: the Louis

Vuitton store on 5th Avenue. He dropped $1,500 on one small handbag for his wife.

Was he living the Chinese Dream?

"I've heard of this, but I am not sure exactly what it is," Zhou said. "Something about China achieving this or that. I am not sure how it relates to me, but if the Chinese Dream is successful, then I guess we'll all be successful."

He thought for a bit, then added, "I think I might be living the American Dream. It's the same in China. It doesn't matter where you come from, as long as you work hard and put your heart into your work, you will get rewarded."

ACKNOWLEDGMENTS

I first interviewed Zhou Xunshu at an Omega China Tour stop near Shanghai in late August 2006. I got married a little more than a month later. I bring this up now – I am writing this in late March 2014 – to point out that my dear, dear wife has lived with this project for a long, long time. And she never wavered in her support: even when it was unclear what all this research would amount to; even as I paid for flight after flight to all corners of China out of our own bank account; even after the first attempt to sell the book failed; even after, once the book finally did sell, I missed one deadline, then another, and if we're being honest, probably another after that. Bliss Khaw, thank you for your love and encouragement, your generosity and patience. I love you, and I owe you several years' worth of distractionless vacations.

I will be forever indebted to Zhou Xunshu, Wang Libo and Martin Moore for giving me intimate access to their fascinating lives – in some cases, for several years. This book is as much theirs as it is mine.

The Forbidden Game would not have been possible without the help of the following people, who served as travel companions, translators, transcribers, researchers, advocates, videographers, tech specialists, website caretakers, carpenters and suppliers of writing cabins in the Poconos: Neil Brown, Boruo Chen, Peijin Chen, Elaine Chow, Paul Chung, Bo Feng, Aaron Fleming, Liz Flora, Paul French, Frank Harris, Chris Horton, Shawn Lei, Alice Liu, Kristin Shen, Jay Sheng, Kenneth Tan, Luis Tapia, Sherley Wetherhold and Johnson Zhang.

Many who work in the golf industry in China helped me considerably at various points along the way. I especially want to thank Stewart Beck, Sally Chang, Brian Curley, Michael Dickie, John Higginson, Jim Johnson, Frank Lin, Lu Zhan, Tim Maitland, Richard Mon, David Paul Morris, Patrick Quernemoen, Ray Roessel, Aylwin Tai, Wang Shiwen, Simon Wilson, Xiao Zhijin, Arthur Yeo and Yuan Tian. Due to the off-the-record nature of many of my conversations for this book, the above list is woefully incomplete. Thank you to everyone who helped me try to make sense of things – you know who you are.

For their hospitality and openness, I'd like to thank the good people of Meiqiu, Qixin and Flagstick Golf Course Construction Management; the blue-collar golfers on the Omega China Tour; and the extended families of Zhou Xunshu, Liu Yan and Wang Libo.

Several publications helped me keep my research going as I tried to find a home for the book. For taking an interest in my stories over the years I'd like to express sincere gratitude to Jason Sobel and Kevin Maguire at ESPN.com; Bill Fields and Geoff Russell at *Golf World*; Josh Levin at *Slate*; Andy Davis at *FT Weekend Magazine*; Blake Hounshell and Britt Peterson at *Foreign Policy*; Anders Peter Mejer at *Omega Lifetime*; and Noel Prentice at the *South China Morning Post*.

I'd like to thank Steven Jiang at CNN and Adrienne Mong at NBC for bringing Zhou Xunshu's story to a global audience, and photographer Ryan Pyle for bringing so many of my stories to life.

I owe many a beer to my colleagues at the Asia Society – notably the online team of Megan MacMurray, Tahiat Mahboob, Shreeya Sinha, Geoff Spencer, Bill Swersey and Jeff Tompkins – for being so understanding of my occasional irregular hours and frequent "writing vacations."

Thank you to Oneworld Publications for believing in, and waiting patiently for, this project. Robin Dennis, my wonderful editor at Oneworld, helped turn what was merely a good story into a good book, and meticulously weaved three disparate storylines into one cohesive narrative. You are likely reading this page thanks to the labor of Oneworld's publicity team – Jennifer Abel Kovitz in North America and Henry Jeffreys and Lamorna Elmer in the UK – as well as the hard work of Alex Billington, Alan Bridger, Ruth Deary, Gail Lynch, and Paul Nash.

None of this would have been possible were it not for the tireless efforts of Zoë Pagnamenta, my indefatigable agent, who stuck with me through thick and thin (mostly thin). For my first foray into the mystifying world of book publishing, I couldn't have asked for a better guide.

Finally, to my mother, Sandy Washburn, my father, David Washburn, and my brother, Dave Washburn, thank you for four decades of love, inspiration, and support – and for learning, eventually, to stop asking, "So, how is the book coming along?" It's finished, and it is for you.

INDEX

ABOUT THE AUTHOR

Dan Washburn is an award-winning reporter and managing editor at the Asia Society. His writing has appeared in the *FT Weekend Magazine*, *The Atlantic*, *The Economist*, ESPN.com, *Foreign Policy*, *Golf Digest*, *Golf World*, *Slate*, the *South China Morning Post*, and other publications. Washburn's work has been featured in the anthologies *Unsavory Elements: Stories of Foreigners on the Loose in China* and *Inside the Ropes: Sportswriters Get Their Game On*. He is also the founding editor of Shanghaiist.com, one of the most widely read English-language websites about China. After almost a decade living in China, he now lives in Brooklyn, New York, with his wife Bliss and their dogs Ozzie and Tux. Visit Dan online at danwashburn.com.